PASSIVE SOLAR HOMES

PASSIVE SOLAR HOMES

by the U.S. Department of Housing and Urban Development
in cooperation with the U. S. Department of Energy
Introduction by Martin McPhillips

New York   EVEREST HOUSE   Publishers

Library of Congress Cataloging in Publication Data:

Main entry under title:

Passive solar homes.
    Bibliography: pp. 268-270
    Includes index.

    Originally published: New energy-conserving passive
solar single-family homes. Washington, D.C.: U.S.
Dept. of Housing and Urban Development in cooperation
with the U.S. Dept. of Energy, 1981
    1. Solar houses.   2. Solar energy—Passive systems.
I. United States. Dept. of Housing and Urban Development.
II. United States. Dept. of Energy.
TH7414.N47   1982   728.3   81-22182
ISBN 0-89696-161-3   AACR2

Contents

Preface

The 91 new single-family, energy-conserving passive solar homes described in this report represent construction awards made in the fifth of the series of five demonstration cycles of the HUD Residential Solar Heating and Cooling Demonstration Program. These awards are in addition to 14 construction awards to neighborhood groups for the passive solar retrofit of urban, multi-family, low- to moderate-income housing. A separate report discusses the latter group of awards.

Cycle 5 began with a formal solicitation of homebuilders interested in building and marketing energy-conserving, passive solar homes. From over 550 applications submitted to HUD in 1979, 114 builders were selected to prepare and submit final designs for consideration. HUD provided assistance to these builders through grants of $2,000 each to cover a portion of the cost of completing final project designs. "Kick-off" meetings were held to help participating builders understand the program requirements, and a mid-period design review workshop provided additional technical assistance to each builder. Final designs were submitted in August, with construction awards being announced in September and November 1979.

In addition to describing the single-family homes selected for awards, this report has been designed to use this information to help builders and lenders understand what passive solar is all about, to recognize passive solar buildings, and to provide specific design, construction, and marketing suggestions and details.

The report is presented in three sections. The first section entitled "Passive Solar: What It Is," describes the concept of passive solar energy, explains the various functions which passive solar systems must perform (and by which they can be recognized), and discusses the various types of passive systems found in the Cycle 5 projects.

The second section, "Passive Solar: What It Looks Like," discusses each of the 91 solar home designs and indicates in these descriptions and on the illustrations some of the key points raised in the discussion of passive solar concepts.

The third section of the report, "How To Do It," goes into additional detail on issues of climate requirements and site design concerns, examples of building construction details showing good practice, and suggestions on how to market solar homes.

The appendices address more technical aspects of the design and evaluation of passive solar homes, and provide information on other resources available to the designer, builder, and lender involved in passive solar housing.

Some of the projects in this report may not have been constructed for one reason or another. However, rather than attempt to list only those which are built, HUD has decided to report on all of the designs selected for awards since we believe that the information in these projects will be of great value even if one or more projects are not completed.

Introduction

Has America learned anything over the last decade? I think so, and I think that the lesson can be summed up quite sharply: *watch out for complacency.* When you start napping, that's when a foreign oil producer who's feeding your nasty habit of profligate consumption can start charging you eight times what you used to pay, *and get away with it.*

What I have always liked about solar energy is that it leads back to individual responsibility rather than away from it, bucking a trend that has been getting out of hand for a long time. Someone who owns and lives in a passive solar home, for instance, is reasonably assured that whether it's the sheiks, the ayatollahs, or the oil truck drivers who are going on strike, they will not have to start burning the dining room table to stay warm.

Back in 1976, during the Bicentennial summer, I traveled up and down and across the country as a writer for *Solar Age* magazine. I visited with the pioneers of solar design and building, asking them about their work, their ideas, and their hopes for the future. The more I learned, the more I understood that solar energy was not developing out of the wishful thinking of a bunch of naive idealists, but through the hard work of some incredibly astute, intuitive, and talented folks. These were people of substance who had thrown their energy into solar energy because it was one of the few concepts at the time that was imbued with plain good sense.

Good sense. It's something that has seemed to dwindle in contemporary America: the respect for things that are both simple and practical. The art of killing two or more birds with one stone. The good sense to use the freedom to choose in a wise and wonderful way.

One of the people whom I talked to on that trip summed up what the mass use of passive solar energy would mean. He said it would constitute "a minor complete change in the way the world works." But, as he emphasized at the time, any change for the good would do for now.

Since that time the idea of passive solar homes has come into a kind of maturity. Through the contributions of hundreds of dedicated people, the concepts of passive solar energy have been pretty much ironed out. The techniques for building the various types of passive components have been refined, and builders and designers in every part of the country are learning and using them. It is entirely conceivable that by the middle of this decade passive solar heating will be a standard amenity of most new homes.

And let's hope so, because our energy problem has not gone away; we've just become inured to it. When heating oil reaches two or three dollars a gallon, or when the Arabs start blowing up each other's oil fields again, let us pray that we can read about it calmly in the morning paper as we sip coffee seated in the solar greenhouse attached to our homes.

Much of the credit for bringing passive solar to the attention of the public and of the homebuilding industry must go to the solar program at the Department of Housing and Urban Development. They had originally put their efforts behind *active* solar heating. Large banks of solar collectors were crammed onto roofs, portly storage tanks and bins were crowded into basements, and Murphy's Law reigned supreme. In fact, they subsidized several hundred active solar homes before realizing that they were too complex, too expensive, and didn't really work quite right anyhow.

Fortunately, they turned to passive solar techniques, where the building itself functions as solar collector and storage unit. Worries were calmed concerning corroding collectors, impossible installation details, eternal fine tuning and mechanical tinkering, and outrageous costs that refused to come down. The forest *was* finally seen for the trees.

This book is the summation, as the situation now stands, of HUD's best efforts. It reports on the ninety-one homes that they funded as part of their fifth and final cycle of solar demonstrations. For this fifth cycle they decided to bring passive solar down to earth. Their aim was to show that it was not a twenty-first-century phenomenon, but something that could be adapted to the taste of people who like to live in Colonial, or split-level, or ranch homes. The solar home and the American home would no longer be in opposition to one anther. They would, in fact, seem destined for a wonderful marriage.

But it wasn't necessarily the home buyers who had to be convinced, or the architects; it was the builders. American builders are thought to be an irascible lot, the mavericks of American industry, the first group to take a beating whenever the economy did. They are a collection of mostly independent businesspeople who are justifiably cautious when it comes to new ideas. They know and understand that their products—homes—are pretty sacred to their customers. When it comes to a home, people want what they want. A home says something about who they are and what they've done with their lives. It's where they raise their children and spend most of their free time.

For solar energy to be accepted, it had to be something pretty special and unobtrusive. People had to feel comfortable with it, and it couldn't displace any of the other things that they really wanted in a home. It's to HUD's credit that they were sensitive to the basic sense on which both builders and buyers base their decisions.

Inevitably, however, the idea of the passive solar home must emerge from the confines of HUD's standard claim that it's just another way to heat a house. Of course they would

say that, but it's not really true. A passive solar home with a solar greenhouse becomes something more than an integral heating system. A little bit of the outdoors is brought inside, just enough to let people take a little more pleasure out of their living arrangement. But a solar greenhouse is also a survival strategy. You can grow food in it, and who knows how important that could become under certain kinds of unpleasant circumstances? Heat and food from the same simple greenhouse is much more than you get from a conventional home. And it teaches everyone something about the basics of living. It's not something remote like an oil truck pulling up once a month. There's something substantial to a solar greenhouse it's that kind of all-purpose good sense that we talked about earlier.

Another positive attribute of passive solar homes is that they may well be more attractive investments than conventional homes. There are preliminary indications that solar homes do indeed have an enhanced resale value. Buyers are willing to pay a little more for them. This could mean that passive solar will eventually top the list of what buyers are most interested in seeing in their prospective homes.

One of the truly encouraging aspects about the homes reported on in this book is that they are spread out all over the country. There are some in Maine, some in Georgia and Tennessee, two in Alaska, several in New York, Colorado, and California. Each region of the country demands that a solar home be built a little differently than it would be in another region, but with the across-the-continent emphasis of this book it is made clear that passive solar homes work virtually everywhere in the country. I don't know how many times I've heard someone say, "But solar energy doesn't work here. It's only good for New Mexico and Arizona." I've wondered where they get their information, but I hope

the notion that solar works only in the Southwest can be substantially put to rest.

The homes described in this book also use new construction techniques that are highly energy-conserving. The better a building holds onto its heat, the greater the percentage of the solar contribution, assuming that the solar elements are properly sized and built. These homes were also built with attention to how they were positioned on their building site, and that's probably one of the most important and neglected considerations. A building that takes advantage of the natural assets of its site is quite likely to face less of the extremes of winter. A well-sited home is sheltered from the north wind and open to the summer breezes that blow out of the south. Good siting also means staying away from the high end of the water table. There's nothing like wet soil to draw heat away from a home's foundation.

I know that the effort that went into designing the homes that appear in this book was monumental. The people at HUD put much time and effort into going over these designs with a fine tooth comb, having them reviewed by top solar professionals from around the country, and demanding that essential changes be made before funding was given final approval. I'm not sure that these homes represent the absolute pinnacle of solar and energy-conscious design, but they are certainly up there with the best.

Before handing all the credit to HUD, however, let's go back a few years to the people who really got the ball rolling on passive solar. Most of them started out in New Mexico (probably the origin of the inaccuracy that that is the only place where solar works). There is, first of all, Steve Baer, a free-spirited young inventor who literally inspired a whole generation of solar people in New Mexico. His Zome house, with its famous solar wall built from fifty-five-gallon oil drums was probably the first bold and inventive step taken in solar architecture in this century. It's not the kind of home that most Americans would want to live in, but it proved a point: passive solar works. Baer was followed by a young architect named David Wright, who in a quiet and dedicated way has probably become the single most important designer of solar homes in the world. There is also Benjamin "Buck" Rogers, the Los Alamos Labs scientist who initiated some very important solar research there, and Dr. Douglas Balcomb, who brought that research to maturity. And there is Wayne and Susan Nichols, a husband-and-wife team who were convinced of the commercial viability of passive solar homes and were willing to risk a great deal to prove it.

The present success of passive solar owns a lot to these people and others like them who did what they had to in order to prove a concept. I think the work itself has been its own reward for them, but I hope that some day some kind of history book will give them the credit they deserve, for they were the Edisons and Marconis of passive solar.

It is important that we never forget how far the effort of an individual can take us. From the commitment of a handful of people turned on by a sound and honest idea, less than a decade later the home owners and home buyers across the continent have the option to live in a solar home. They can do something to ease the pressure of staggering fuel costs while adding the power of positive thinking to their everyday environment. They can appreciate that with solar energy there is room for individual style.

What must happen now is for people who have an interest in solar energy to get some of the basic concepts of passive solar design clear in their own minds. Solar energy's biggest problem over the last five years has not been lack of interest but, rather, an unfocused identity. Every time you turned around, there was some new and often completely unworkable scheme turning up in a magazine or at a conference. Consequently, it was seldom that two people could be found who shared the same notion about just what solar energy was.

It is clear now, however, that at least one form has emerged that will stand the test of time and gain ever-widening recognition. That form is the passive solar home. Now it is really up to people to become familiar with the simple principles involved. This book can take anyone wanting to do that quite a long way. In fact, I would guess that unless you have the urge to become a true solar expert, this book can serve quite adequately to help you uphold your end of a conversation on solar energy and passive solar homes.

MARTIN McPHILLIPS
Editor of *The Solar Age Resource Book*
New York City
November 1981

5

In a passive solar home the building itself is designed to accomplish the tasks of heating and cooling. In the winter solar heat is collected through large south-facing glazed areas, and is absorbed and stored in thick masonry walls and floors or water-filled containers. The heat is then distributed via natural convective flow patterns within the building. In the summer the design of the house reduces the incoming flow of sunlight and heat and promotes the ventilation of the living spaces.

A passive solar home can be designed to operate with very little mechanical assistance, although many solar builders and designers prefer to make use of fans, ducts, blowers, and automatic control hardware.

Passive Solar: What It Is

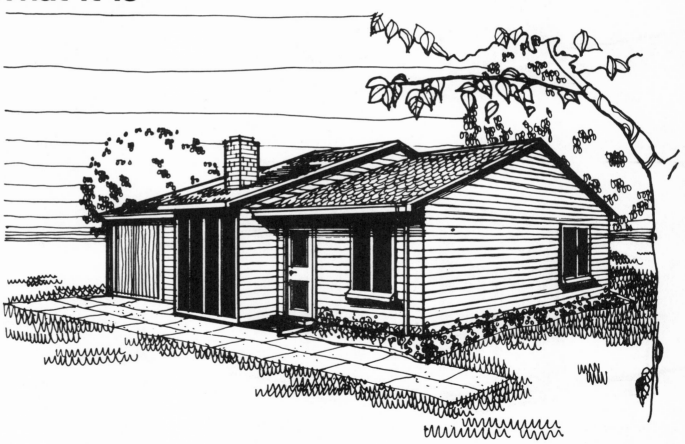

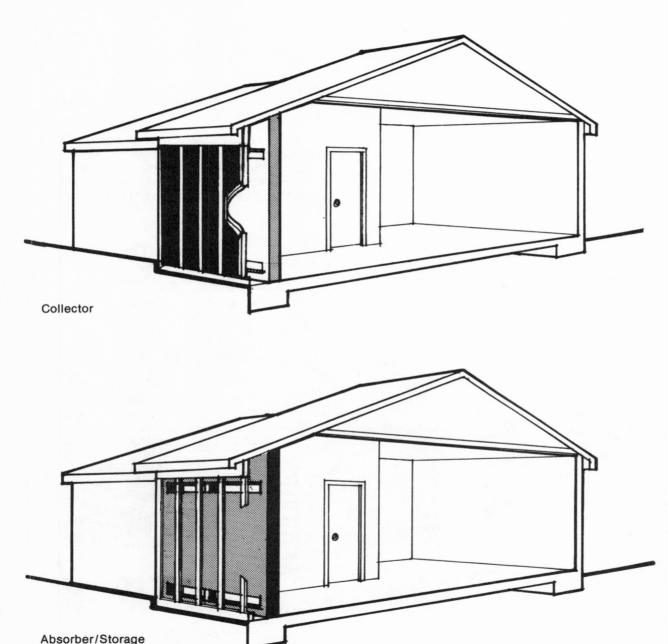

Collector

Absorber/Storage

Passive System Elements

All true passive systems should include and can be recognized by five clearly defined elements. These are: collector, absorber, storage, distribution, and control (or heat regulation device).

Collector refers to the glazing through which solar radiation enters the house. The primary collector(s) should face within 30 degrees of true—not magnetic—south and should not be shaded throughout the heating season during the peak solar collection period between 9 a.m. and 3 p.m. The area of the collector determines how much of the available direct solar radiation the house has the potential to collect. The performance of the collector can be enhanced by directing additional sunlight towards it from a reflective surface.

Absorber refers, in most passive solar systems, to the hard, darkened surface of the storage elements. This surface—which could be that of a masonry wall, floor, or room divider or that of a water container—sits in the direct path of solar radiation. It intercepts the sunlight, which then degrades to heat, which is absorbed by the surface.

Storage refers to the materials used in the construction of the house that are specifically intended to hold the heat produced by sunlight. These materials are sometimes called "thermal mass" and they are usually either masonry (concrete, concrete block, or brick) or water. The difference between the absorber and storage, although they are often the same wall or floor, is that the absorber is an exposed surface whereas storage is the material below or behind that surface.

Distribution refers to the method by which solar heat is circulated from the collection and storage points to different areas of the house. A strictly passive design will use the three natural heat transfer modes—conduction, convection, and radiation—exclusively. This type of distribution requires a house plan that encourages the formation of natural convective flows. The careful layout of interior spaces will allow heat to circulate from the collection and storage points to where it is needed throughout the day and night. It is, however, often desirable to give mechanical assistance to distribution in the form of fans and blowers and to provide ductwork to carry heat from one area of the house to another.

Control or Heat Regulation Device refers to those elements that prevent under- or overheating and heat loss. This includes moveable insulation, which is placed over the inside of the collector area on winter nights to control heat loss. Conversely, moveable insulation can also be used on summer days to control overheating by keeping sunlight out of the house. Control devices may also include: electronic sensing devices such as differential thermostats that signal a fan to turn on; operable vents and dampers that allow or restrict heat flow; roof overhangs or awnings that shade the collector area during summer months.

Throughout the 91 Cycle 5 project descriptions, as well as in the "Passive Solar Construction Details" section found in part three, the five passive elements—also called the recognition factors—are continually stressed. The project descriptions pay special attention to the functional relationship of these five factors.

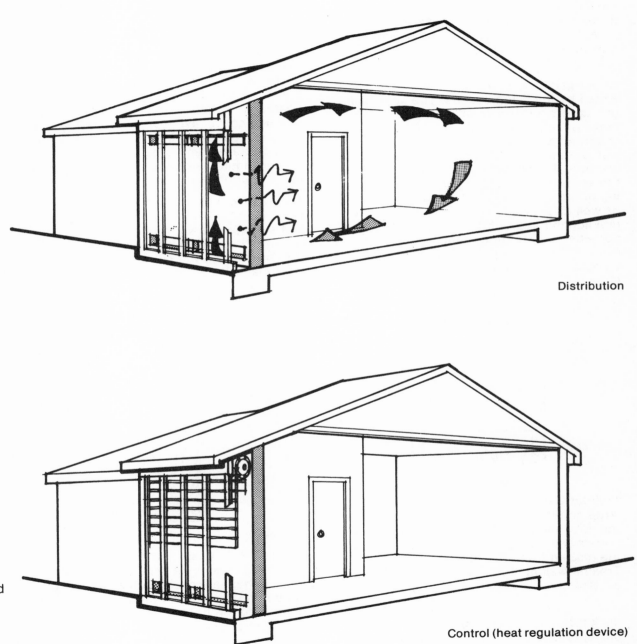

Distribution

Control (heat regulation device)

11

Basic Approaches

Passive solar systems are characterized by three basic approaches. These three approaches are distinguished according to how they "gain" solar heat; they are: Direct Gain, Indirect Gain, and Isolated Gain.

Direct gain occurs where sunlight is collected by the living spaces. The solar radiation enters a room directly through large areas of south-facing glazing. The heat is absorbed and stored by a masonry floor or wall or other materials placed so they are warmed directly by the sun. Direct gain has the advantage of allowing immediate warming of the space when the sun is shining, as well as providing an abundance of natural lighting and outdoor view. It has the potential, on the other hand, of occasionally overheating the living space. Direct gain is a popular and standard passive solar approach.

Direct gain

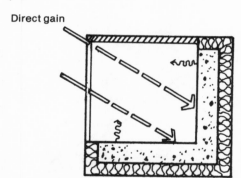

Indirect Gain occurs where, once again, large south-facing glazings are used, but the solar radiation is intercepted by an absorber and storage element that separates the glazing from the living space. The Trombe wall is the best known Indirect Gain system.

In the Trombe wall system, an 8- to 16-inch thick masonry wall (concrete, concrete block, or brick) is built as the south wall of the house. The south-facing surface of the wall is painted black to absorb sunlight, and the entire wall is glazed. A Trombe system can be built to provide heat in two ways. For immediate heating while the sun is shining, the wall can be constructed with two sets of vents: one is located at the ceiling level and the other at the floor level of the living space. As the sun's heat is collected in the cavity between the glazing and the surface of the wall, the tendency of heated air to rise starts what is called a "natural convective loop." Cool air from the room will be drawn into the cavity through the floor level vent to be heated as the already heated air rises and flows into the room through the ceiling level vent.

The second way a Trombe wall system provides heat is by the continuous absorption and storage of solar radiation by the masonry itself. The wall becomes charged with heat that it will discharge to the living space later in the day and after the sun has set. This "time-lag" effect, where heat must travel through the entire thickness of the wall, gives indirect gain systems the advantage of delaying the distribution of heat until it is most needed.

Indirect gain

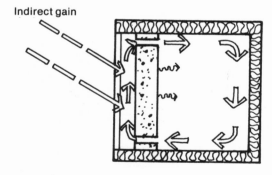

Isolated Gain occurs where the solar radiation is captured by a separate, glazed, normally unheated space such as a greenhouse or atrium. From there the heat is distributed to the house. Isolated Gain also occurs where heat is absorbed by a type of flat-plate collector that uses the natural tendency of heated air to rise as the means of circulating it into the living spaces. (This is called a "thermosiphoning collector.")

When a greenhouse is used as an isolated gain system, it establishes a three-fold advantage. First, the solar heat it collects can be immediately distributed to the living space in a controlled fashion, but heat can also be absorbed by masonry or liquid storage elements within the greenhouse for later use. Second, the greenhouse creates more living space and is an additional, useful amenity of the home. Third, the greenhouse serves as a buffer zone between the main living space and the outdoors, thereby reducing heat loss. The solar greenhouse is also one of the most practical methods for "retrofitting" an existing house with passive solar heating.

A fourth approach, called "sun-tempering," is not a "true" passive system. It uses south-facing glazing, as in a direct gain system, but it has no heat storage capacity. Sun-tempering does not include all five of the "recognition factors." It is most appropriate for severe climates or situations where solar can only offset daytime heating loads.

Isolated gain

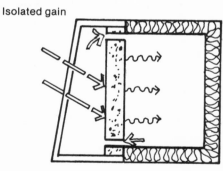

The 91 projects described in this book often include two and sometimes three of these system categories in one house. Sometimes these systems overlap structurally to create a combined effect. This provides a richness which addresses the needs of different spaces and different times of day to satisfy a range of comfort needs.

Passive Cooling

Passive cooling, like passive solar heating, is accomplished through the home's design, layout, and components. In general, passive cooling is a function of how well heat gain is controlled in combination with a variety of schemes for natural and induced ventilation.

Heat can be kept out by shading the solar collection area with vented overhangs, awnings, and vegetation. Moveable insulation can also be closed to deny conductive heat gain through windows.

Natural ventilation is a matter of opening the house to summer breezes and giving that air movement a clear path through the house. Induced ventilation uses the chimney effect, where hot air building up in the house is allowed to rise and vent itself rapidly, thereby creating an updraft. This draw can then be used to pull in cooler air from another source. The source can be as simple as a shaded and planted north yard. A buried earth tube that uses the steady and moderate ground temperature to temper the incoming air is another method, but it is mainly practical in very dry climates where there is little chance that it will support the growth of microorganisms.

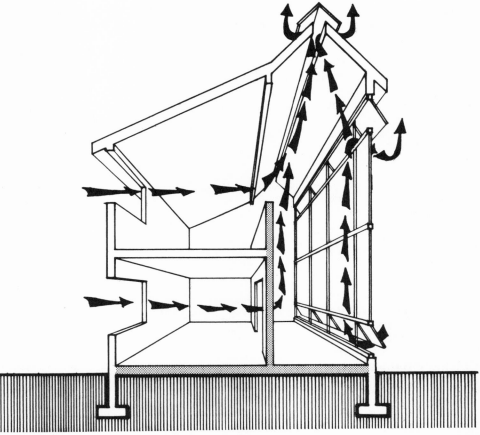

The solar chimney effect (induced ventilation)

The Role of Conservation

The overall performance of a passive solar house depends upon the careful use of energy-conservation measures. These measures include the use of caulking and weatherstripping around windows and at construction joints and the careful insulation of the building envelope. Other measures may include air-lock vestibules around entryways, double- and triple-glazed windows, minimal use of windows on the north, and the placement of unheated spaces so that they will serve as buffer zones along the north wall. A more extensive discussion of energy conservation begins on page 253.

Active Systems

Active solar energy systems make use of hardware—such as rooftop collectors and storage tanks—that is added-on to the structure of a building and requires an outside source of energy (i.e. electricity) to operate. Fluids such as water and air are circulated through active systems by pumps or air-handling equipment.

A passive solar house might also make use of some "active" solar components. The most likely use for active collectors would be to heat water for household use. An active solar water heating system works year-round and can often be depended upon for 60 percent of total need, if it is properly sized.

A thorough discussion of these systems can be found in *Hot Water From the Sun* and also in *Installation Guidelines for Solar DHW Systems*, available from the National Solar Heating and Cooling Information Center.

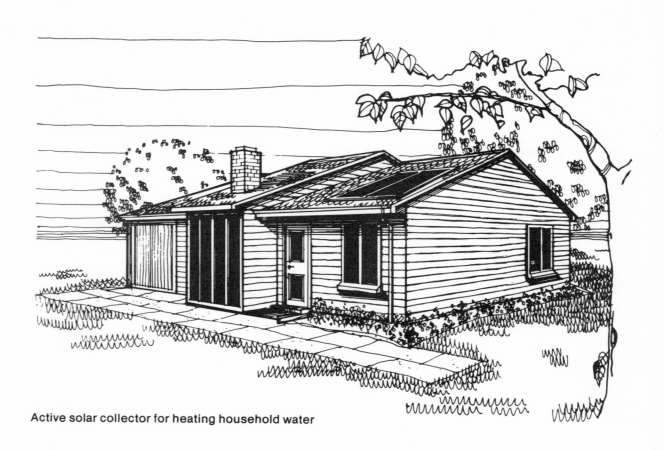

Active solar collector for heating household water

Passive Solar: What It Looks Like

How to Use This Section

This section — Passive Solar: What It Looks Like — includes details, drawings, and written descriptions of the 91 new single-family passive solar homes funded in Cycle 5. These projects are divided among four regions of the country: Northeast, South, Mid-America, and West. Each of these regions is serviced by a Regional Solar Energy Center (RSEC), the name and address of which is given at the beginning of each region.

Each project description cites the location of the passive solar home in the upper left hand corner of the first page. Then, in the left hand column of that page, there is a "data file" that includes the following information:

Builder of the home

Designer of the home

Solar Designer of the passive system

Price — the estimated price of the home

Net Heated Area — the total heated floor area

Heat Load — the predicted annual energy required to heat the home, expressed in millions of BTUs (10^6 BTU). All heat loads for the projects were calculated according to the method described in Appendix 3.

Degree Days — the intensity of the annual heating season for the home's location, expressed as the annual total of degrees Fahrenheit that the daily average outdoor temperature fell below 65°F.

Solar Fraction — the percent of the total calculated heat load that the solar energy system is predicted to be able to supply, calculated as shown in Appendix 3.

Auxiliary Heat — the predicted amount of conventional fuel required to supply the portion of the heat load not supplied by the solar energy system; this amount is expressed as the number of BTUs required per Degree Day per square foot of floor area ($BTU/DD/ft^2$).

Passive Heating Systems — indicates which of the basic approaches to passive solar (direct, indirect, and isolated gain, and sun-tempering) are used in the project. (See page 12 for discussion of these approaches.)

Recognition Factors — the five passive elements — collector, absorber, storage, distribution, and controls (or heat regulation devices) — that are necessary for a complete passive system. (See page 7 for discussion.) **Collector** areas are briefly described and their total square footage given; **Absorber** surfaces are briefly noted; **Storage** elements are noted and their total heat **capacity** expressed in BTUs per degree Fahrenheit; **Distribution** methods are noted; **Control** methods are noted. All five recognition factors are thoroughly described in the text and illustrated in the accompanying drawings.

Active Solar Heating — will appear if the house has active solar equipment, otherwise it will not.

Back-up — describes the type of auxiliary heating system used in the house.

Domestic Hot Water — briefly describes the solar water heating system, if any.

Passive Cooling Type — mentions the passive cooling techniques used, if any.

The written descriptions give a more extensive view of the projects. Details about siting and energy conservation are noted, and the essential relationship between the five recognition factors is carefully laid out. The drawings further illustrate the house and its passive elements, making use of perspectives, floor plans, and sections.

For further information about the projects, builders, and designers, contact the National Solar Heating and Cooling Information Center, P.O. Box 1607, Rockville, MD 20850, or call toll-free: (800) 523-2929 in continental United States, PR, VI; (800) 462-4983 in Pennsylvania; (800) 523-4700 in Alaska and Hawaii.

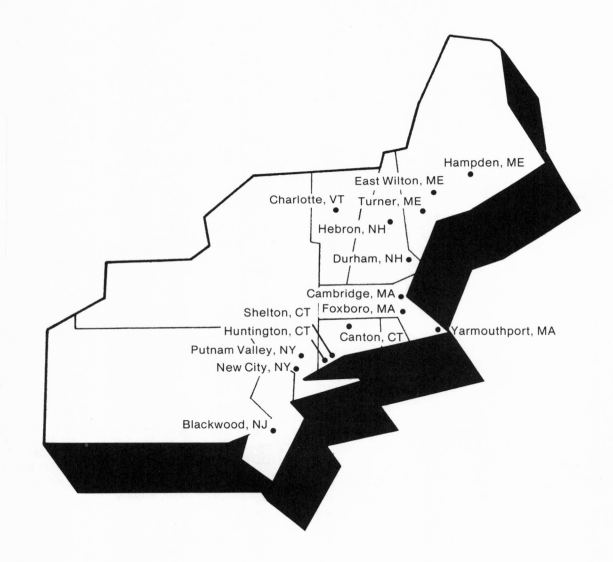

Hampden, ME

East Wilton, ME

Charlotte, VT   Turner, ME

Hebron, NH

Durham, NH

Cambridge, MA

Shelton, CT   Foxboro, MA

Huntington, CT   Canton, CT   Yarmouthport, MA

Putnam Valley, NY

New City, NY

Blackwood, NJ

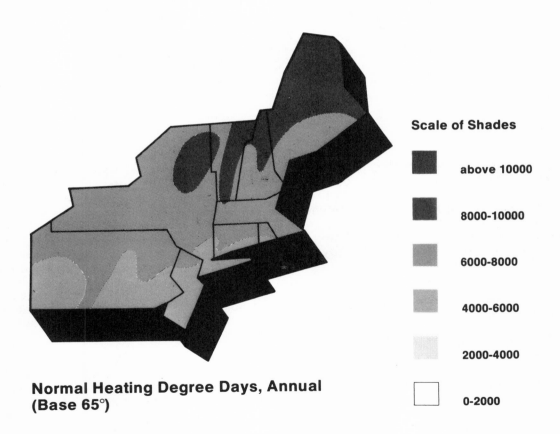

Normal Heating Degree Days, Annual (Base 65°)

Scale of Shades

above 10000

8000-10000

6000-8000

4000-6000

2000-4000

0-2000

The Regional Solar Energy Center for the Northeast is:

Northeast Solar Energy Center
470 Atlantic Ave.
Boston, MA 02110
(617) 292-9250

The states served by it are:

Connecticut
Maine
Massachusetts
New Hampshire
New Jersey
New York
Pennsylvania
Rhode Island
Vermont

Builder: Starbird Lumber Co., Strong, ME

Designer: Sunsystems, Dryden, ME

Solar Designer: Sunsystems

Price: $55,000 to $60,000

Net Heated Area: 1204 ft²

Heat Load: 65.8 x 10⁶ BTU/yr

Degree Days: 8675

Solar Fraction: 71%

Auxiliary Heat: 1.82 BTU/DD/ft²

Passive Heating System(s): Direct gain, indirect gain

Recognition Factors: Collector(s): Triple-glazed windows, double glazing over Trombe wall, 418 ft² **Absorber(s):** Trombe wall surface, concrete floor **Storage:** 8-inch concrete floor slab, concrete Trombe wall—**capacity:** 37,617 BTU/°F **Distribution:** Radiation, convection **Controls:** Vents, shutters; differential thermostat for forced-air system

Back-up: Wood furnace

Passive Cooling Type: Cross-ventilation, solar chimney through Trombe wall, mechanical cooling

This saltbox-style home, updated to make the most of solar energy, is located on a gentle south-southeast slope. A band of tall hardwood trees along the lot's western end protects the home from prevailing winter winds. The rest of the lot is covered with young red pine trees, except where they would shade passive collection.

The compact saltbox layout allows the home to enclose a large amount of interior space with a minimum of exterior wall surface. This is an important part of the overall conservation package. There are 6 inches of fiberglass insulation in the walls and 12 inches in the ceiling. Closets and other low-use areas of the home are located along the north wall; the entryway is sheltered by a recess and by a vestibule.

Except for the south-facing solar collection wall, the entire lower floor of this home is buried. This moderates the inside temperature by exposing the outside surface of the lower-floor walls to the temperature of the earth below the frost line, rather than the subfreezing temperatures of a Maine winter. During the summer, this helps cool the home because ground temperature stays well below summer air temperatures.

This home is heated by two types of passive solar energy **collection**: direct heating through windows and a Trombe wall system.

The direct **collection** relies on a total of 186 square feet of south-facing windows and 26 square feet total of east- and west-facing windows. All windows are triple glazed.

During the day, sunlight passes through the windows and strikes the 4-inch concrete slab floor and the cored concrete block in-

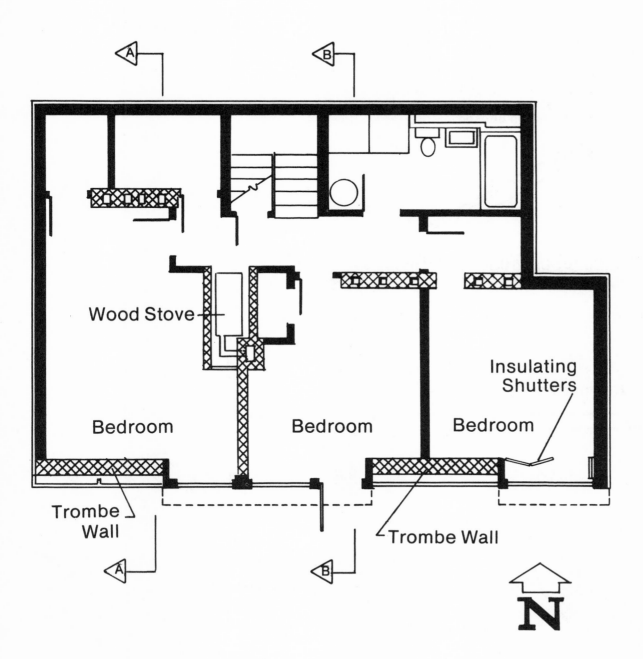

Wood Stove

Insulating Shutters

Bedroom

Bedroom

Bedroom

Trombe Wall

Trombe Wall

N

terior walls. These surfaces function as solar **absorbers**, turning the sunlight into heat. The heat is conducted into the interior mass of the floor and walls, where it is **stored.**

At night, when the air temperature in the living space drops below the temperature of the storage walls and floor, heat from the storage mass is **distributed** to the living space by radiation and convection.

The system has two types of **controls**. The insulating panels are used to cover the windows at night to reduce heat loss to the outside, and they are used on particularly sunny spring and fall days to limit heat gain. White shades are drawn over the windows during summer days to reflect direct sunlight.

If the upper-floor temperature is greater than the lower-floor temperature by a predetermined amount, the second control system is called upon. A differential thermostat turns on a small blower which forces the warmer air through a concrete block interior storage wall, and then out through floor vents on the lower level. This process evens out the temperature of the home by storing some of the upper floor's heat in the block wall, and by circulating the rest of it to the lower floor. The blower can be operated manually as well as automatically.

The Trombe wall consists of a concrete-filled block wall with a black painted exterior surface . A double-glazed window is attached 6 inches in front of the exterior surface. During the day, sunlight is **collected** as it passes through the glazing. It strikes the black surface of the wall, where it is **absorbed** and then **stored** in the solid mass wall. It takes hours for the heat to pass through the wall, finally reaching the living space after sunset. This delay saves the sun's heat for **distribution** as radiant and convective heat from the wall at night.

If additional heat is needed during the day, vents at the top and the bottom of the concrete wall are opened. Heated air between the glazing and the mass wall rises and enters the living space through the top vent. As it does so, cold air from the floor is drawn through the lower vent into the space in front of the Trombe wall, where it is heated. Daytime heating is **controlled** to some extent by opening and closing these vents.

Back-up heating is provided by a woodburning furnace. An insulated hatch on the north wall allows access to stored wood. An air duct system from the stove is integrated with the internal wall/blower system to provide heat **distribution** to the entire living space.

Water pipes are wrapped with electrical resistance heating strips to prevent freeze damage when the home is unoccupied and the woodburner is unused.

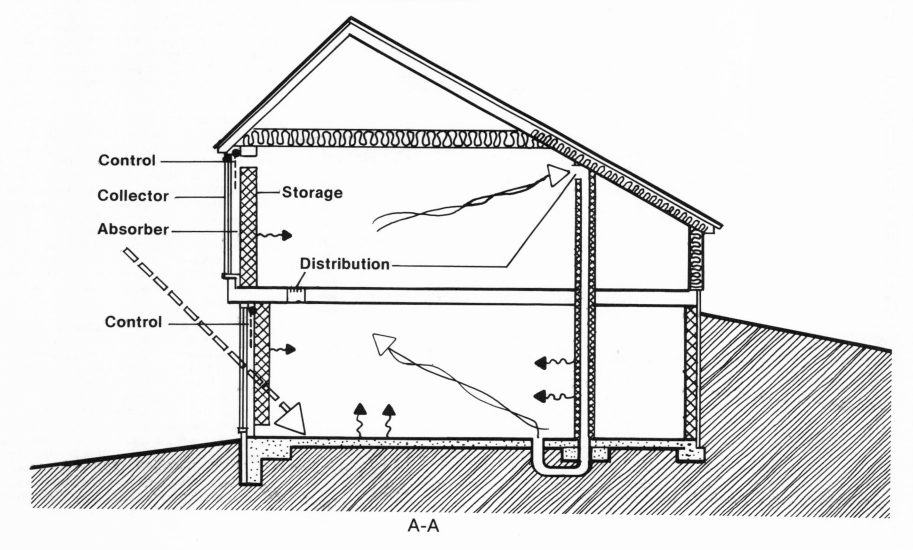

Control

Collector

Absorber

Storage

Distribution

Control

A-A

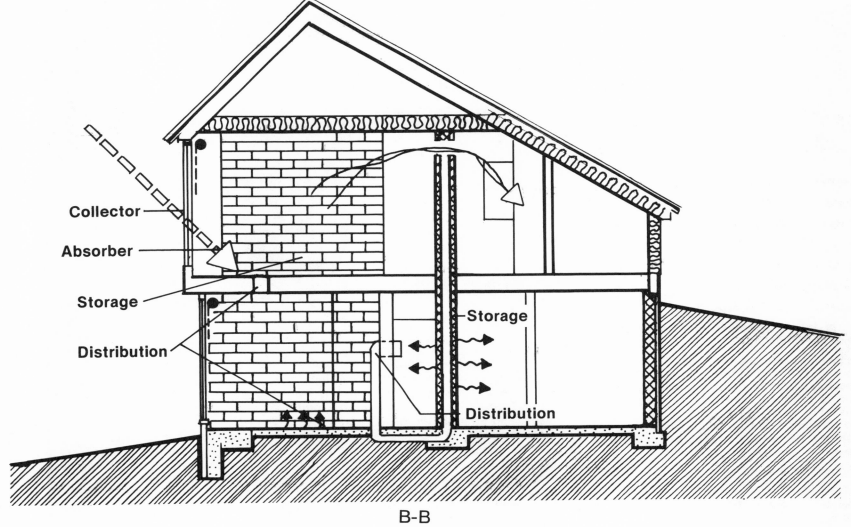

Collector

Absorber

Storage

Distribution

Storage

Distribution

B-B

21

Yarmouthport, MA

Builder: Worthington Associates, West Dennis, MA

Designer: Derek Romely, Architect, South Dennis, MA

Solar Designer: Derek Romely

Price: $45,000 to $50,000

Net Heated Area: 1959 ft²

Heat Load: 70.9 x 10⁶ BTU/yr

Degree Days: 5621

Solar Fraction: 56%

Auxiliary Heat: 2.78 BTU/DD/ft²

Passive Heating System(s): Direct gain, indirect gain, sun-tempering

Recognition Factors: Collector(s): South-facing glass over Trombe wall, skylight, 611 ft² **Absorber(s):** Ceramic tile over concrete floor, surface of Trombe wall **Storage:** Concrete floor, masonry Trombe wall—**capacity:** n/a **Distribution:** Radiation, natural convection **Controls:** Manual window vents in Trombe walls, moveable insulation

Back-up: Central wood stove, electric resistance baseboard heaters

Domestic Hot Water: 67 ft² flat-plate collectors, 80-gallon storage

This design reflects an effort to include passive solar features without sacrificing the appeal of traditional style. Extensive south-facing glass, 1½-story high Trombe walls, and an attached greenhouse are incorporated into the familiar New England saltbox design. The compact, multilevel house has a steep, wood shingle roof and clapboard siding. It is to be built in the Old King's Highway Historic District, which is dedicated to the preservation of the historic character of the area. All of the other sub-

division homes are based on such traditional designs as the Cape Cod, the saltbox, and the yankee barn. These homes have rustic settings on large wooded lots.

To conserve energy, the solar saltbox is partially bermed on the east and west. The north side of the building is sheltered from winter winds by the garage. The effects of winter winds are also minimized by a stand of evergreens to the north. Further protection against winter heat loss is provided by

N

Wood Stove

Living/Family

Masonry Wall

Dining

an air-lock entry. The house is carefully caulked and weatherstripped; walls and roof are insulated with fiberglass batting (R-23, 30).

On the north, east, and west, windows are triple glazed. The glass on the south side of the house is double and there are operable skylights above the bath, landing, and entry. All windows are fitted with insulating shades and operable exterior canvas awnings. The lower-level interior living space is open to permit unobstructed heat flow, and high-activity areas are located on the south side of the building where they will receive direct heat. The attached 2-story greenhouse is one of the two passive solar heating systems. Solar heat is **collected** through its south-facing sliding glass doors and windows, and through fixed glass panels on the east and west. The floor of the greenhouse and adjacent living space is ceramic tile on a 6-inch concrete slab. Incoming heat is **absorbed** by the tile and **stored** in the massive floor.

Heat **distribution** is facilitated by an open well above the living/family area. Heat stored in the mass floor is radiated upward and moved by convection to the second floor where it collects at the ridge of the cathedral ceiling. A ceiling fan pushes this heated air into the second-story hall and bedrooms and then down the stairwell to be reheated by the warm floor.

Control of the greenhouse system relies on manually closing quilted insulating drapes over the greenhouse glazing to prevent nighttime heat loss.

The Trombe walls on either side of the greenhouse provide heat to the adjacent living room, dining room, and bedrooms. Heat **collection** for the Trombe walls takes place through exterior sliding glass doors on both upper and lower levels. These doors can be opened for maintenance and summer cooling. The Trombe walls are 12-inch filled concrete block, painted black; they **absorb** and **store** heat collected through the glass.

At night, the Trombe walls **distribute** radiant heat directly into the living and dining areas on the first story, and into both bedrooms on the upper level. Excess heat that is absorbed by the Trombe walls on the lower level may spill into the airwell and contribute to whole-house circulation, but the main function of the walls is to heat the adjacent living and sleeping spaces.
Control of heat from the Trombe wall system is accomplished by manually opening the vents in the walls during the day to permit the air that is heated between the wall and exterior glass to circulate into the living spaces. At night, these vents are closed to prevent a reverse flow.

When cooling is required during the summer, ventilation is induced by opening the skylights, the greenhouse glazing, and the access door to the attic. The resulting convective circulation pulls heat upstairs through the airwell and out of the house through the skylights and attic. The greenhouse is vented directly through the upper-level sliding glass windows. Moveable exterior canvas awnings are opened out over the greenhouse and Trombe wall glazing at the beginning of the summer. These shade those areas from direct sunlight to prevent them from absorbing heat. The design includes a Solafern™ domestic water preheat system. Two flat-plate collectors with a net collection area of 60 square feet are located on the roof above the greenhouse. An air-to-water fin-coil heat exchanger is located in the 80-gallon domestic hot water storage tank.

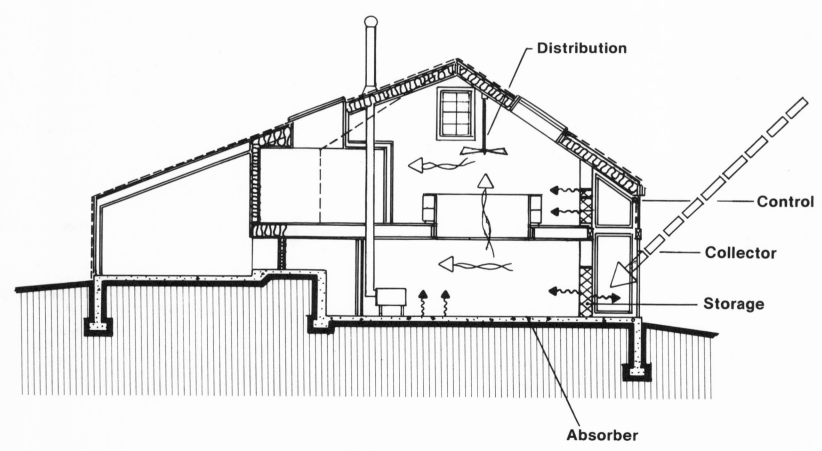

Distribution

Control

Collector

Storage

Absorber

A-A

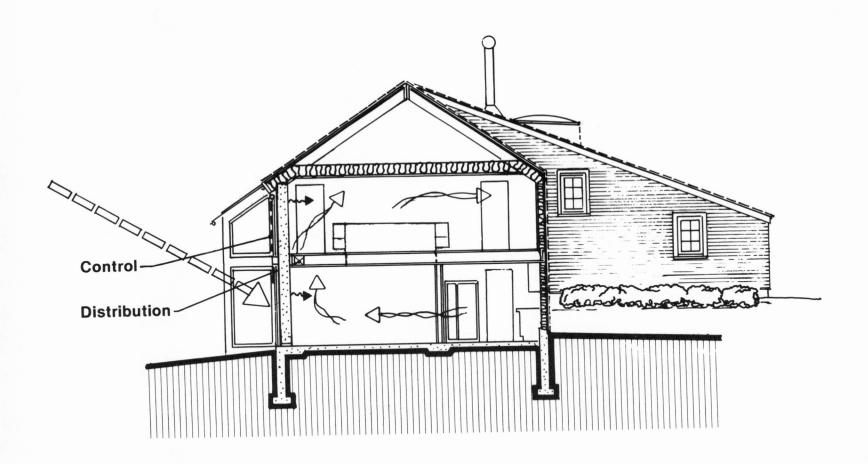

Control

Distribution

B-B

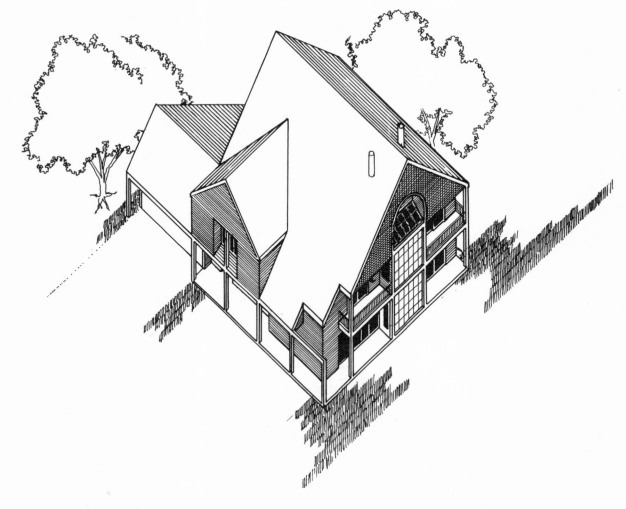

Foxboro, MA

Builder: Orlando Homes, Inc., Foxboro, MA

Designer: The Ehrenkrantz Group, New York, NY

Solar Designer: The Ehrenkrantz Group

Price: $130,000

Net Heated Area: 2443 ft²

Heat Load: 80.4 x 10⁶ BTU / yr

Degree Days: 4788

Solar Fraction: 46%

Auxiliary Heat: 3.7 BTU / DD / ft²

Passive Heating System(s): Direct gain, isolated gain, sun-tempering

Recognition Factors: Collector(s): South-facing glazing, sliding glass doors, 331 ft² **Absorber(s):** Floor tiles over concrete slab floor, brick wall **Storage:** Concrete floor, brick wall—**capacity:** 8009 BTU / °F **Distribution:** Natural and forced convection, radiation **Controls:** Moveable insulation (pull-down shade), overhangs, sun screens, vents, thermostat

Back-up: Electric resistance heater, air-to-water heat pump (44,000 BTU / H)

Domestic Hot Water: 36 ft² liquid flat-plate collectors, 100-gallon storage

This design illustrates a well-integrated blend of passive solar heating features and traditional styling. The 2-story, 4-bedroom house with cedar shingle exterior will be a part of a 25-lot development in which 19 homes have already been built and sold. The major passive design element is a 2-story attached greenhouse set into an arched recess and flanked on either side by second-story balconies and porches. The garage and utility room are located along the north wall to protect against winter heat loss. Glazing on non-south walls has been minimized, and all windows and corners are

caulked. Operable insulated shades protect all windows from winter heat losses and excessive heat gain in the summer. In addition, the glazing in the greenhouse can be covered with an operable slatted sunshade in the summer.

Direct solar radiation provides passive heating to rooms on both levels of the house. On the first floor, solar heat is **collected** directly through the recessed glass sliding doors on both sides of the greenhouse. On the western side of the house, sun shines into the living and dining rooms directly through double-hung windows. The family room, breakfast room, and kitchen **collect** heat and light from similar windows on the east side.

In the living and family rooms, solar heat is **absorbed** and **stored** in a floor that consists of a 5-inch concrete slab overlaid with a 2-inch quarry tile. The floor in the kitchen, breakfast, and dining rooms is hardwood with relatively low storage capability.

Each of the bedrooms on the second story also **collects** solar heat directly through glazing on the south, east, and west walls. The south-facing master bedroom and first bedroom each open onto recessed balconies through glass sliding doors that are directly above those on the lower level, and are identical in size. The second and third bedrooms open onto west-facing recessed balconies through glass doors; double-hung windows permit additional penetration of heat and light into the master bedroom from the east. All windows and doors that function as passive solar collectors are double glazed. On the second story there is nominal storage for solar heat in the bedroom floors which have 2-inch quarry tile on top of a plywood subfloor.

At night, the heat that is stored in the mass floors of the living room, family room, and bedrooms is **distributed** to these spaces by radiation.

The 2-story, attached, greenhouse has fixed double-glazed **collection** windows on the front; its glass doors open onto porches on each side. Two of the interior greenhouse walls are made of 12-inch common brick. On the first story, the third wall is a glass sliding door leading to the living room. On the second story, the third wall of the greenhouse is brick with a door opening into the first bedroom.

Like the rest of the lower-level south-facing rooms, the greenhouse has a floor of quarry tile on top of the concrete slab. These masonry floors and walls **absorb**

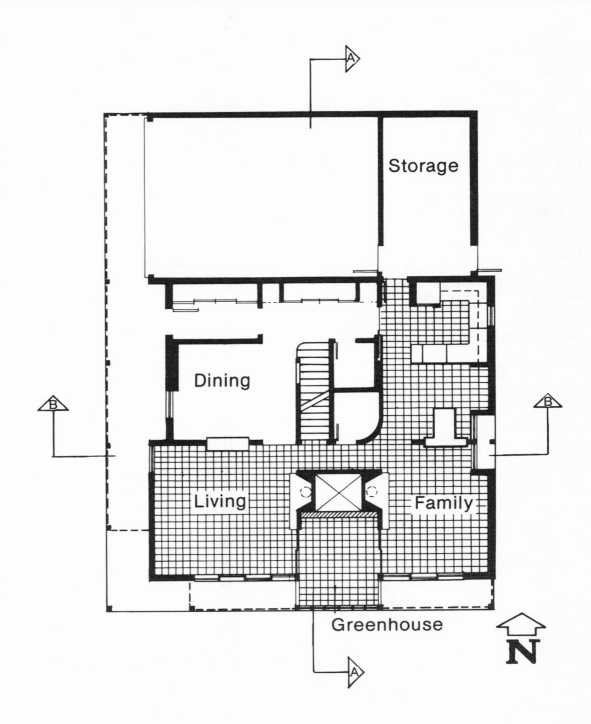

solar heat during the day and **store** it until temperatures drop in the evening. When interior temperatures are lower than the temperatures of the walls and floor, stored heat is radiantly **distributed** into the living and sleeping spaces. Additional heat **storage** is provided by the brick chimney mass and hearth located behind the greenhouse wall on the lower level. Undesirable winter heat loss is **controlled** by manually closing insulation shades over windows.

In the winter, transfer of passive solar heat is integrated with the **distribution** of heat provided by the back-up air-to-air heat pump in the basement. The ducting system associated with the heat pump ties the greenhouse into the forced-heat distribution system through a 2-story riser and two return ducts that open into the greenhouse floor. This hybrid distribution system is **controlled** by a dual-stage thermostat that senses both house and greenhouse temperatures.

When the house temperature falls to 72°F, the fan in the heat pump unit is activated. If the greenhouse temperature is greater than 75°F, a by-pass damper in the basement blower unit opens, allowing heated greenhouse air to circulate into dining and sleeping spaces through grilles under exterior windows. Cold air is returned to the blower through a central duct and then circulated to the greenhouse for reheating. If the temperature in the greenhouse is below 75°F,

and the house temperature is above 70°F, the by-pass damper closes, isolating the greenhouse from the house. Air is then circulated only within the conditioned living spaces, distributing residual heat. When the temperature in the house falls to 70°F, heat from the auxiliary heat pump will be distributed to living space via the duct system. The heat pump will work in conjunction with the greenhouse as long as the greenhouse can provide useful heat. If the

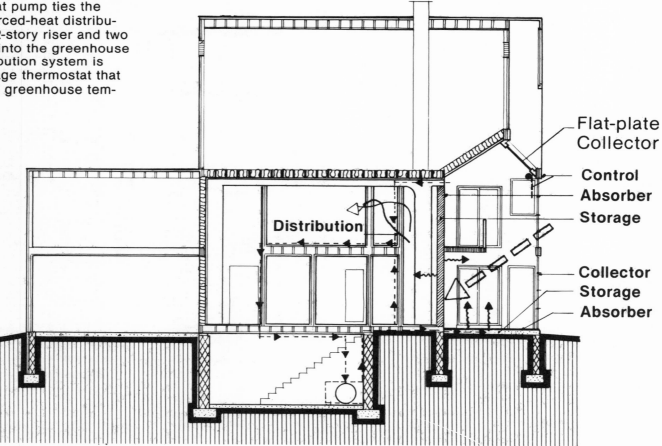

Flat-plate Collector

Control

Absorber

Storage

Distribution

Collector

Storage

Absorber

A-A

house temperature is above 72°F, the heat pump will shut off, but the fan will continue to circulate air until the house temperature reaches 74°F, at which point the blower will also shut off.

In addition to summer cooling provided by the heat pump, opening ground-level greenhouse doors and the attic vent will induce ventilation of the greenhouse. Cross-ventilation of the rest of the house is ac-complished by opening north, south, east, and west windows and bedroom doors. An interior sunscreen can be manually closed across greenhouse glazing to reduce admission of direct sunlight.

A prepackaged active solar domestic water heating system has been included in the design. A Grumman collector with 36 square feet of exposed area is mounted inside the greenhouse, just beneath the glazed ceiling at an angle of 45 degrees from the horizontal. Installing the collector inside the greenhouse reduces heat loss to outside air. The heat transfer medium is a 40 percent solution of propylene glycol that also contains rust inhibitors. The stone-lined, 100-gallon steel water storage tank is fiberglass insulated, and located in the first-story utility room.

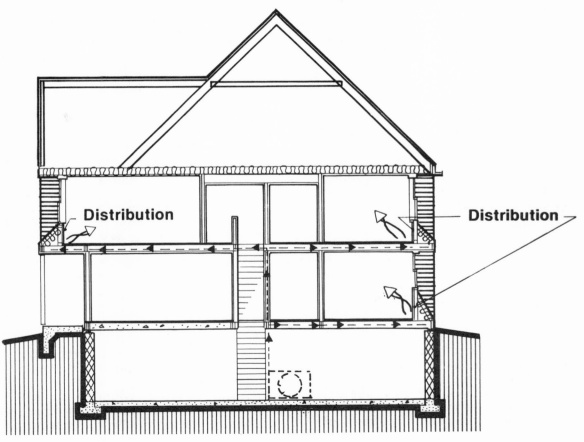

Distribution

Distribution

B-B

Builder: Urban Development and Investment Corporation, Cambridge, MA

Designer: Brook/Elton Partnership, Cambridge, MA

Solar Designer: Brook/Elton Partnership

Price: $65,000

Net Heated Area: 1498 ft²

Heat Load: 55.6 x 10⁶ BTU/yr

Degree Days: 5634

Solar Fraction: 66%

Auxiliary Heat: 2.16 BTU/DD/ft²

Passive Heating System(s): Direct gain, indirect gain, isolated gain, sun-tempering

Recognition Factors: Collector(s): South-facing windows, greenhouse glazing, 416 ft² **Absorber(s):** Concrete block wall, concrete floor slab **Storage:** Concrete block wall, concrete floor slab—**capacity:**10,844 BTU/°F **Distribution:** Radiation, natural and forced convection **Controls:** Vents, dampers, thermostats, jalousie

Back-up: Water-to-air heat exchanger, wood stove

Located near Boston, a city known for its elegant townhouses, this and other homes in its development take the idea of the townhouse and update it for the solar future.

Tall pine trees covered the 14 acres of land that is now the site of the development. Except where they have been cleared to prevent shading of solar collectors or to allow the construction, the trees were retained.

The townhouse design evolved in an era when saving building heat was important. Homes that share a common wall are intrinsically energy conserving because they have less surface area exposed to the elements. This townhouse also benefits from modern insulation technology: the north wall has a value of R-19 and the roof, R-35. All windows are triple- or quadruple-glazed.

The large pines shield the house from cold winter winds. Both the north and south entrances have vestibules to limit the volume of heated air lost to the outside when a door is opened. The north wall of the home is bermed with earth to reduce the difference in the temperatures between the two sides of the wall. Summertime cooling is achieved by cross-ventilation through the open layout of the home and by the shade provided by the pines.

This home uses solar heat in three ways. The first occurs when sunlight is admitted through the house's 35 square feet of south-facing windows. When the sunlight strikes the interior of the home, it turns into heat, which "tempers" the inside temperature. This method is an incomplete solar energy system because there is no way to

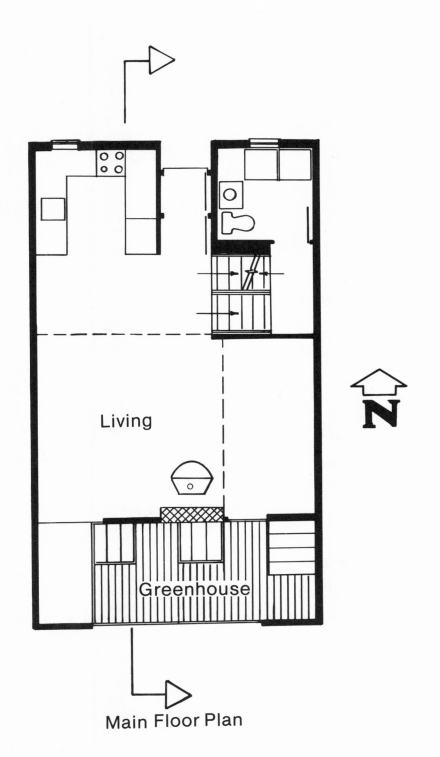

N

Main Floor Plan

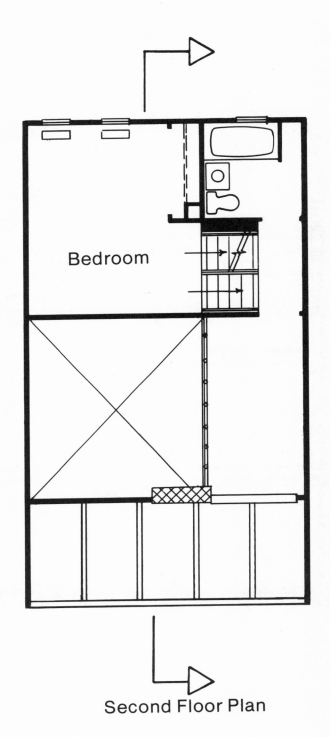

Second Floor Plan

31

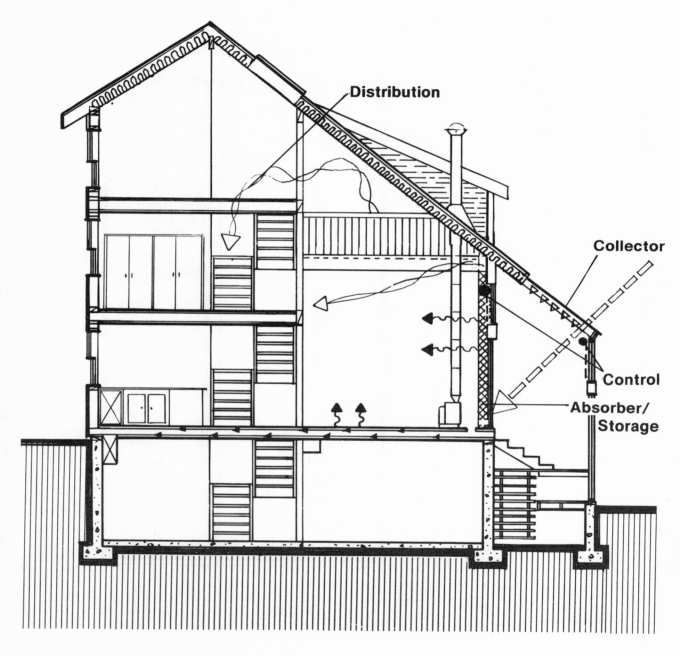

Distribution

Collector

Control

Absorber/ Storage

control the heat gain or to store it. However, by providing some daytime heating, it allows the other two systems to store a larger amount of heat for nighttime use.

The second system **collects** sunlight through the glazing of the greenhouse. Some of the sunlight which passes through the glazing strikes a dark-colored concrete block wall where it is **absorbed** and turned into heat. Much of this heat passes into the concrete block wall where it is **stored**. At night, when the air temperature in the house falls below the **storage** wall temperature, heat is **distributed** from the wall by radiation and convection.

Not all the heat from the absorber surface of the wall is stored in the wall directly. Some of this heat warms the air in the greenhouse. This warm air may be carried by convection through vents in the concrete wall into the living space.

When the living space becomes hot enough, an automatic **control** opens a damper to a fan-driven duct system which pulls the greenhouse air through cavities in the concrete block wall into the living room, and then through the hollow Flexicore™ concrete floor slab. There the air heats the concrete. At night, the heat is **distributed** as it radiates from the wall and floor into the living space.

The blower system is also used to even out the temperatures in the home. It does this by drawing hot air from the ridge of the home and distributing it throughout the living space.

This entire system is **controlled** by a differential thermostat that monitors greenhouse temperatures and operates the motorized damper. Conventional thermostats control the fan and back-up system.

The designers chose to include little heat storage in the greenhouse itself. Although this design tradeoff allows the nighttime greenhouse temperatures to drop to near the outside temperature, it also allows more of the daytime greenhouse heat to be stored for use in the home's living space. At night, the greenhouse functions as a buffer zone by cutting down convection and radiation losses from the living space.

The home's third solar system also makes use of the greenhouse. Solar energy is **collected** through the roof of the greenhouse, and then through triple-glazed windows between the greenhouse and the living space. It is **absorbed** by the surface of the Flexicore™ concrete floor. The heat is **stored** in the floor until the living space cools down; the heat is **distributed** as it radiates into the room. This system is **controlled** by a jalousie on the roof of the greenhouse that provides summertime shading.

In an effort to eliminate the infiltration associated with combustion, the designers specified an electric back-up system. When the thermal storage mass falls below a specified temperature, water from a standard 85-gallon electric domestic hot water tank is circulated through a heat exchanger placed in front of the air circulation fan. The forced air in the duct system picks up heat from the heat exchanger and carries it to the living space.

This townhouse is also equipped with a Franklin stove to supplement the electric back-up system.

Putnam Valley, NY

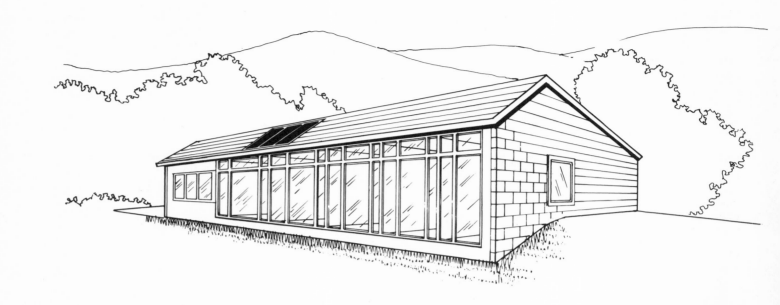

Builder: Robert Brown Butler, Katonah, NY

Designer: Robert Brown Butler

Price: $60,000 (plus land)

Net Heated Area: 1473 ft²

Heat Load: 42.0 x 10⁶ BTU/yr

Degree Days: 5732

Solar Fraction: 90%

Auxiliary Heat: 0.54 BTU/DD/ft²

Passive Heating System(s): Direct gain

Recognition Factors: Collector(s): South-facing glazing, clerestory windows, 368 ft² **Absorber(s):** Ceramic tile floors, masonry walls and floors **Storage:** Ceramic tile floors, masonry walls and floor—**capacity:** 24,583 BTU/°F **Distribution:** Natural and forced convection **Controls:** Garage-type thermal shutters, overhang, thermostats

Back-up: Woodburning stove, electric resistance heaters

Domestic Hot Water: Three-panel active DHW system (84 ft²)

Scattered deciduous trees surround this small rectangular ranch house on a 1-acre lot in an old orchard under development in Putnam Valley, New York. The house sits on a slight slope facing south and fits naturally into the protective 4-foot berming on the east, west, and north sides. Low shrubs planted on these three sides provide additional protection from the wind.

Although it is one of the few single-story houses in the neighborhood, this passive solar house conforms to the larger, more conservative houses by reason of its conventional cedar siding and window size and arrangement.

Ceiling to floor thermopane™ glass takes up the entire south wall and acts as a **collector** for the passive solar heating system. Narrow panels divided into upper and lower casement windows alternate with

wide panels of fixed glass giving uninterrupted southern exposure to the south-facing living room, four bedrooms, and playroom.

Heat is **absorbed** and **stored** in the masonry and ceramic tile floors of all these rooms which range in a uniform pattern with rear doors opening onto a long, narrow hallway. This hallway separates the southern rooms from those on the north.

Additional solar heat is **absorbed** and **stored** in 7-foot, 4-inch high, 10-inch thick masonry walls in all rooms. Clerestory windows top these walls and have been planned to allow natural light to pass through to the north side of the house.

All north rooms receive heat **distributed** by natural convection made possible by opening doors from the south rooms to allow

34

heat to be drawn to the cooler north side. East and west ends of the house have as their only glazing two bubble windows that collect heat in the morning and afternoon. On the building's north face, where dressing room, bathrooms with skylights, entrance, closets, kitchen, and dining room are located, there are few windows.

The innovative feature of this house, designed to **control** heat loss, is a series of overhead garage-door-type thermal shutters. Standard commercial garage door hardware has been used to install these shutters inside the glass of each room on the south side. Each shutter has five 20-inch panels filled with 6-inch thick translu-

cent insulation. Operation is by individual room switches.

The shutters function to keep heat in on cloudy winter days and winter nights. In summer they drop behind the glass facade to keep heat out. At that time the casement windows, every 10 to 12 feet along the

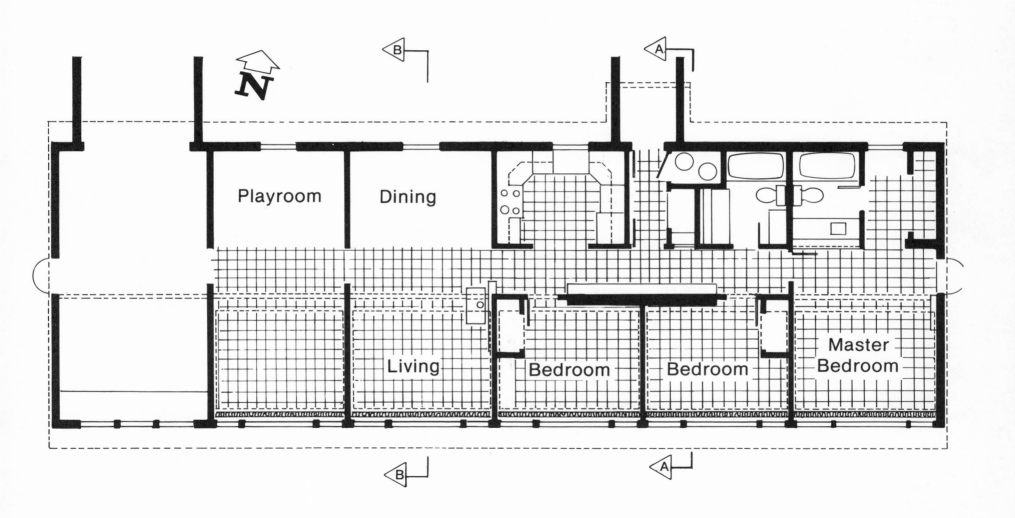

south side, are opened to expel heat which may have accumulated between windows and shutters. An overhang along the south side partially shades the collector during summer and permits upper awning windows to remain open in rainy weather.

From spring to autumn, removeable screens are placed over the windows to help reduce incident radiation. Berming around the house helps lower temperature extremes at the base of the exposed sections. Further cooling in summer comes from the 6-inch concrete slab on polyethylene vapor barrier base that lies under the entire house.

The roof (R-33) and exterior walls (R-26) are heavily insulated. During extremely hot weather, perforated ducting, with vent fans at each end under the ridge of the roof, removes excess heat. The small north windows are caulked at the seams and fitted snugly with translucent thermal interior shutters letting natural light in even when closed. Bathroom skylights are filled with 10-inch translucent insulation.

The builder expects an average of 6 inches of snow coverage from December to March to provide extra insulation on the roof and around the base of the house, with a high percentage of the radiation striking the snow being reflected into the house.

Back-up heat is supplied by a thermostatically controlled, cast-iron woodburning stove set between kitchen and playroom in a central part of the house fairly equidistant from all rooms.

Electric resistance heaters, controlled by thermostats, are mounted on the hall side of the interior masonry walls. Combined with the stove these provide the back-up heating system for the whole house.

Domestic hot water is provided by a roof-mounted, three-panel active solar collector (84 square feet).

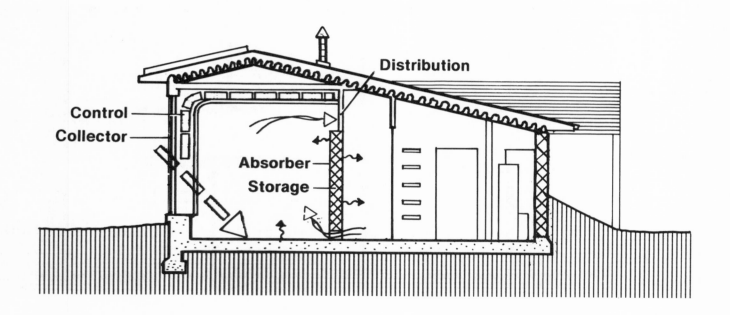

A-A

The passive solar system in this house is expected to satisfy a large part of the annual heating demands. Consequently, use of mechanical equipment has been kept to a minimum. The designer/builder believes such equipment not only raises initial construction costs and requires constant maintenance but also decreases the owner's appreciation of the climate control inherent in the design.

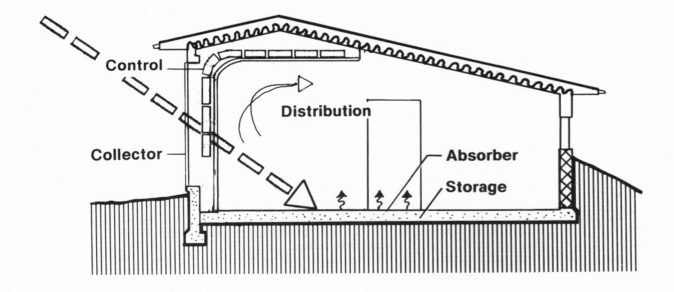

B-B

Shelton, CT

Builder: Building Co-ordinators, Shelton, CT

Designer: Sunspace, Inc., Shelton, CT

Solar Designer: Vic Reno, Walpole, NH

Price: $85,000

Net Heated Area: 1900 ft²

Heat Load: 61.9 x 10⁶ BTU/yr

Degree Days: 5617

Solar Fraction: 49%

Auxiliary Heat: 2.96 BTU/DD/ft²

Passive Heating System(s): Direct gain

Recognition Factors: Collector(s): South-facing double glazing, greenhouse windows and sliding glass doors, 225 ft² **Absorber(s):**Concrete floor **Storage:** Concrete floor—**capacity:** 16,677 BTU/°F **Distribution:** Radiation, natural and forced convection **Controls:**Overhang, vents, insulated shutters

Active Solar Heating: Air flat-plate collectors (160 ft²), 700 ft³ rock storage

Back-up: Electric resistance heaters

38

This 2-story contemporary Cape Code style design in Fairfield, Connecticut, combines energy-conservation features with active and passive solar space heating systems. The gambrel roof deflects winter winds, and the siting of the house provides protection from infiltration as well as access to summer breezes. The garage and low-activity spaces located to the north further reduce winter heat loss. Fiberglass insulation has an R-value of 32 in the roof, and 21 in the walls and floors. The air-lock vestibule is located on the east, away from prevailing winds. The single north window is triple-glazed; all other windows are double glazed.

The major passive heating system is a 2-story, south-facing greenhouse which includes a "fair weather" breakfast area. In the greenhouse, solar heat is **collected** through fixed windows and sliding glass doors. The masonry floor **absorbs** and **stores** the heat, which is later re-radiated into the greenhouse. Passive solar heat from the greenhouse is **distributed** through whole-house circulation if the bedroom doors and the door and windows between the greenhouse and interior rooms are opened.

When these doors and windows are closed, greenhouse-heated air is supplied to the flat-plate collectors mounted on the greenhouse roof, where the temperature of warmed air from the ridge of the greenhouse is boosted. When the house thermostat calls for heat, air that has been heated in the active collectors is **distributed** directly to the house through the air handling and ducting systems connected with the back-up electric resistance furnace. When the interior temperatures are adequate, the air handling system transfers air from the active collectors directly to a remote rock storage bin in the basement for later distribution and use.

During winter nights, the greenhouse is isolated from the rest of the house and insulating shades are drawn across all greenhouse windows to **control** heat loss.

Summer cooling results from shading windows, inducing natural cross-ventilation, and reversing the active distribution system to store cool air at night and transfer it to the house during the day.

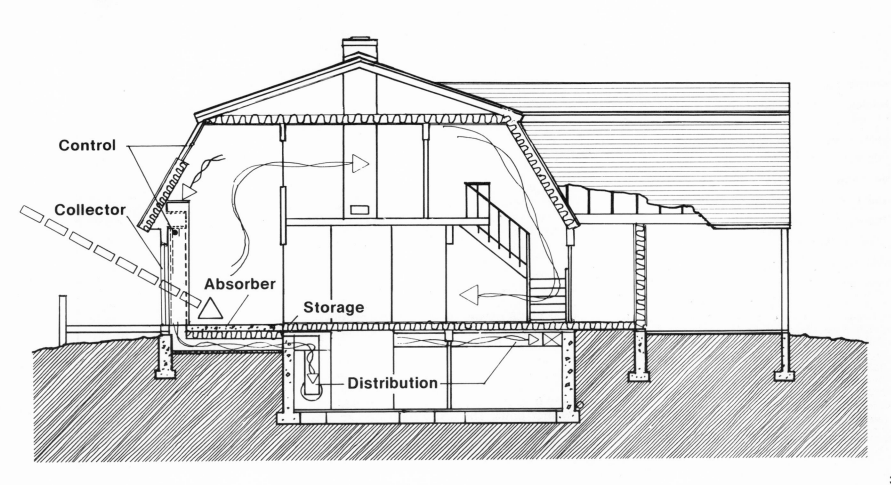

Control

Collector

Absorber

Storage

Distribution

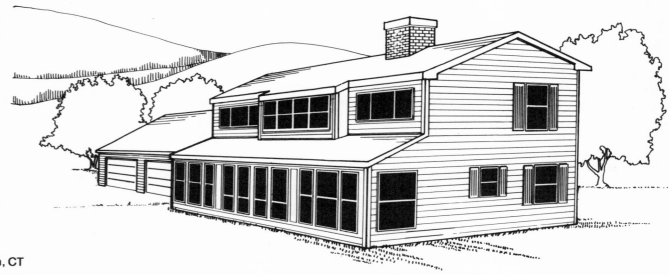

Builder: Suncatcher Construction, Shelton, CT

Designer: Wormser Scientific Corporation, Stamford, CT

Solar Designer: Wormser Scientific Corporation

Price: $115,000

Net Heated Area: 2178 ft²

Heat Load: 64.7 BTU/yr

Degree Days: 5897

Solar Fraction: 58%

Auxiliary Heat: 2.05 BTU/DD/ft²

Passive Heating System(s): Isolated gain, sun-tempering

Recognition Factors: Collector(s): Greenhouse glazing, second-floor glazing, 349 ft² **Absorber(s):** Slate floor in greenhouse, black chrome coating on ends of 55-gallon steel drums **Storage:** 110 gallons of water by wood stove, 1540 gallons of water in water wall—**capacity:**38,200 BTU/°F **Distribution:** Radiation **Controls:** Sliding glass doors, venetian blinds, insulating shades, fan, overhang

Back-up: Electric air-to-air heat pump (19,500 BTU/H)

40

All of the south-facing windows on the first floor of this house and most of those on the second floor are part of a greenhouse that spans the length of the house. There is one set of sliding glass doors between the greenhouse and the living room as well as another set in the family room. The balance of the wall is covered with water-filled 55-gallon drums stacked two high and lying on their sides perpendicular to the greenhouse. This water storage system is topped by a layer of 3½ inch fiberglass batts and a plywood shelf for plants on the greenhouse side and books on the living room side. Above the shelf, the two rooms are separated by a conventional 2- x 4-inch wall with 3½-inch batts. The water wall opening into **the greenhouse is glazed while the opening on the living room side is covered by polished aluminum venetian blinds.**

While the greenhouse is a 2-story space, the center portion of the upper level is occupied by the center bedroom, which extends to the exterior wall. The central bedroom does have an opening on each side into the greenhouse, and each bedroom to either side of the central bedroom has two sets of sliding windows opening into the greenhouse space.

The system **collects** heat in winter through all the greenhouse glazing, and the heat is **absorbed** and **stored** by the dark slate floor and the steel drums, whose ends are covered with a selective coated copper foil for improved **absorption**. Direct sunlight is also **collected** in the center bedroom upstairs. When heat is needed in the house, the venetian blinds allow heat to be **distributed** into the rooms by radiation from the water wall storage. When the sliding glass doors are opened, heat is **distributed** by convection from the warmer greenhouse into the house. Similarly, windows in the side and center bedrooms open into the upper greenhouse space to receive the warm air flow.

To control heat loss at night, insulating shades are pulled down over the windows and glass doors (combined value R-15). If necessary, the wood stove in the family room is used. Two 55-gallon water-filled drums are located next to the stove to absorb and store heat. A door in the family room opens to expose more surface area of

these drums, allowing stored heat from the wood stove to heat the room after the fire has burned out.

These passive features are augmented by good conservation measures. The garage is located to the north and west of the house to block winter winds. There is a double air-lock entry between the garage, the rear entry, and the house, while the front entrance to the house is through the greenhouse. All walls are insulated with 3½-inch fiberglass batts and 2-inch polystyrene sheathing (R-24), and 12-inch batts (R-40) are installed in the ceiling joists.

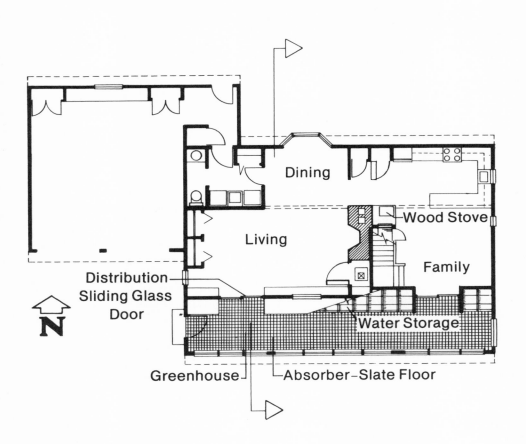

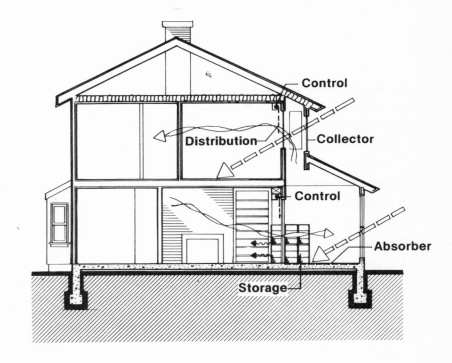

Hampden, ME

Builder: Campbell Construction Co., Bangor, ME

Designer: William R. Sepe, Camden, ME

Solar Designer: Richard Hill, University of Maine, Orono, ME

Price: $109,250

Net Heated Area: 1585 ft²

Heat Load: 66.1 x 10⁶ BTU/yr

Degree Days: 7784

Solar Fraction: 61%

Auxiliary Heat: 2.06 BTU/DD/ft²

Passive Heating System(s): Direct gain, isolated gain

Recognition Factors: Collector(s): South-facing windows and skylight, 498 ft² **Absorber(s):** Concrete mass floors, stone chimney mass **Storage:** Concrete mass floors, stone chimney mass—**capacity:** 11,314 BTU/°F **Distribution:** Radiation, forced convection **Controls:** Thermostat, damper, insulating curtain, shades

Back-up: Gas wall furnaces (12,600 BTU/H), electric baseboard heaters (12,750 BTU/H)

This 2-story, 3-bedroom home in a rural Maine subdivision is intended for middle- and upper-income families. The styling acknowledges traditional building forms, with a neutral-colored board and batten exterior and a conventional roof tilt.

In the winter heating mode, a ground-level greenhouse with operable skylight and windows provides a passive solar **collection** area for convective and radiant heating of the first-story living and dining rooms. Each room also receives limited amounts of direct sunlight, as do the upper-level bedrooms, which are sun-tempered spaces.

Heat is **absorbed** and **stored** for nighttime use in the mass floors of the greenhouse and first-story living areas, as well as in the stone chimney mass in the center of the house.

Fan-assisted **distribution** of solar-heated air begins when the greenhouse temperature reaches 85°F. A thermostat activates a fan in a foot-level vent between the greenhouse and the crawl space beneath the living area, and a motorized damper automatically opens. Heated air is pulled through the plenum and into the dining room through floor vents against the rear dining room wall. Cool air circulates back into the greenhouse when double-hung windows in the greenhouse/living area wall are partially opened.

Nighttime heat losses are controlled by closing quilted insulating curtains on all windows and by closing windows and doors between the greenhouse and adjacent rooms.

For summer cooling, windows and skylights are opened to permit natural cross-ventilation. Shades are closed during the day, reducing heat gain, and opened at night to allow heat to radiate from the house to the cooler night air.

Energy-conservation features include triple glazing and air-lock entry. Low-use rooms form a buffer zone along the north side of the house.

The builder offers an optional "Suntap™" passive thermosiphon domestic water heater that uses Freon 114™ as the heat transfer medium.

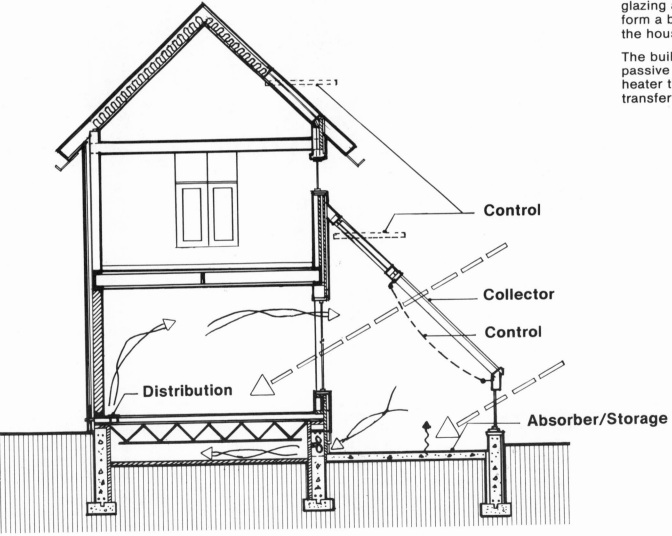

Control

Collector

Control

Distribution

Absorber/Storage

Turner, ME

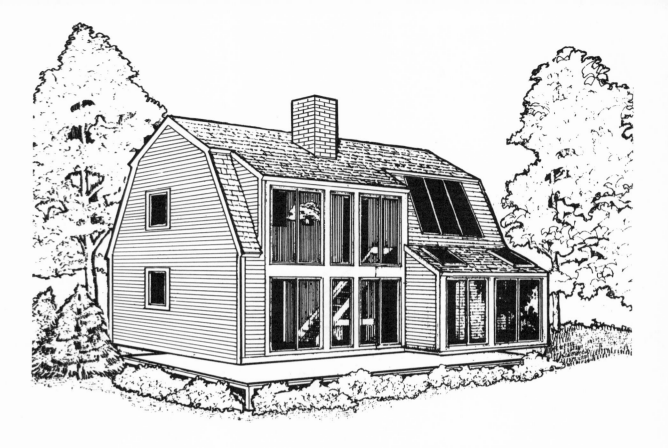

Builder: Heritage Builders, Turner, ME

Designer: Traditional Living, Inc., Hartland, VT

Solar Designer: Traditional Living, Inc.

Price: $85,000

Net Heated Area: 1320 ft²

Heat Load: 68.7 x 10⁶ BTU / yr

Degree Days: 7511

Solar Fraction: 45%

Auxiliary Heat: 3.77 BTU / DD / ft²

Passive Heating System(s): Sun-tempering, direct gain, isolated gain

Recognition Factors: Collector(s): Greenhouse glazing, skylights, glass doors and windows, 279 ft² **Absorber(s):** Greenhouse floor, brick pavers on concrete slab, greenhouse mass wall **Storage:** Rock storage bed, mass floor and wall—**capacity:** 7489 BTU / °F **Distribution:** Radiation, natural and forced convection **Controls:** Moveable quilt insulating shades, exterior bamboo roll shades, room thermostats, and sensor in rock bed

Back-up: Central airtight wood stove, electric resistance heater

Domestic Hot Water: Flat-plate collector, double-walled heat exchanger

44

This modified 2-story gambrel Cape design specifies pre-cut post and beam construction. The site is part of a 95-acre, 20-lot development; the house is priced for young professionals. A 2-story greenhouse and a small attached single-story greenhouse are prominent design features. The extensive south-facing glass, however, is oriented away from the street, preserving the traditional appearance of the house.

Three passive systems are combined with a back-up wood furnace unit to meet winter heating needs. First, in the single-story greenhouse, solar heat is **collected** through double-glazed sliding doors and two sky-

lights. Heat is **absorbed** and **stored** in the concrete floor and in the mass wall divider between the greenhouse and living area. During winter nights, greenhouse heat is **distributed** from the mass wall divider into interior living spaces. If additional heating of the first story is desired during the day, French doors between the greenhouse and living area may be opened. Operable doors, windows, and quilted insulating shades over south-facing glass **control** heat gain.

Second, besides using heat produced by the small greenhouse, the living area attached to it **collects** direct radiation as well through the French doors.

Lastly, the 2-story greenhouse **collects** solar heat through double-glazed fixed panels and sliding doors. Because there is no thermal mass in the greenhouse itself, the heat accumulates and rises through the floor to the peak of the upper level of the greenhouse.

When the air temperature at the peak reaches 90°F, a fan is activated by a thermostat and pulls heated air through a duct into a rock **storage** bin located beneath the smaller greenhouse. Cool air from the rock bed is returned to this greenhouse through ducts.

The **distribution** system for solar heat from this rock bed is integrated with the back-up wood stove. The duct system is equipped with an air-handler that features a reversible fan and motorized damper. This draws heat out of the rock bed for distribution to living and sleeping space.

Nighttime heat losses are **controlled** by interior greenhouse doors, creating a buffer zone across the south glazed wall.

Because summer temperatures in New England are moderate, cooling can be accomplished easily through shading and cross-ventilation. The high angle of incident summer sunlight prevents significant heat absorption by the mass wall or interior floors, and opening the skylight, glass sliding doors, and interior doors permits cross-ventilation through the upper and lower levels. The large greenhouse can also be used as a porch with shading provided by a stairway, the second-floor deck and operable exterior bamboo shades.

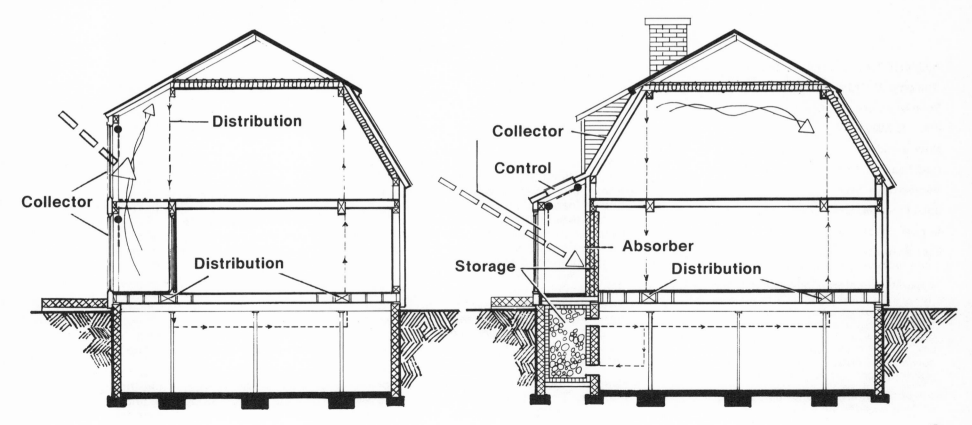

Hebron, NH

Builder: EVOG Associates, Inc., Hebron, NH

Designer: EVOG Associates, Inc.

Solar Designer: EVOG Associates, Inc.

Price: $59,000

Net Heated Area: 1348 ft²

Heat Load: 70.3 x 10⁶ BTU / yr

Degree Days: 8177

Solar Fraction: 59%

Auxiliary Heat: 2.66 BTU / DD / ft²

Passive Heating System(s): Direct gain, indirect gain, isolated gain, sun-tempering

Recognition Factors: Collector(s): South-facing fiberglass glazed panels, 336 ft² **Absorber(s):** Masonry Trombe wall, water walls, concrete mass floor surface **Storage:** Masonry Trombe wall, water walls, concrete mass floor—**capacity:** 6493 BTU / °F **Distribution:** Radiation, natural convection **Controls:** Manually operable Trombe wall vents, dampers and vents, interior doors

Back-up: Electric resistance heater (27,600 BTU / H), woodburning stove

Designed for young professionals or two-income families who are buying their first home, this 1,500 square foot, split-entry house features contemporary styling. The lower level of the compact building is bermed on the windy north side, and a buffer zone consisting of an air-lock entry, utility room, and storage space provides further protection against heat loss. Low-use rooms are concentrated on the lower level; activity spaces, which need to be warmer, are located on the second floor. Glazing on the east and west sides of the house is minimal, and there are no north-facing windows.

Passive heating is provided by a 2-story masonry Trombe wall and two lower-level water walls. One water wall is located in an enclosed space in front of the utility room. Solar radiation is **collected** through fixed fiberglass windows and is **absorbed** and **stored** in the water wall. At night, the stored heat rises to the ceiling by convection, and a vent allows hot air to be distributed into the master bedroom above the water wall whenever the vent is opened. The second water wall is separated from another lower-level bedroom by folding doors. Incoming solar radiation is absorbed and stored in the water-filled tubes. When the folding doors are open, the bedroom is heated by radiation from the tubes.

The vented 2-story thermosiphoning Trombe wall **collects** heat through south-facing fiberglass panels, and then **absorbs** and **stores** it in mass masonry. During the

46

day, when the door to a third bedroom is open, heated air is drawn through an open vent in the Trombe wall and into the upper-level kitchen, living room, and dining room and then back through this third bedroom on the lower level.

The second-story rooms also receive direct radiation, which is stored in concrete floors. At night, heat from the water walls, Trombe wall, and mass floors is **distributed** by being radiated back into living and sleeping spaces. Vents in the Trombe wall are manually closed to prevent reverse thermosiphoning.

In the summer, cross-ventilation induced by opening windows, cools the house. Overhangs on both levels provide shade and minimize heat gain.

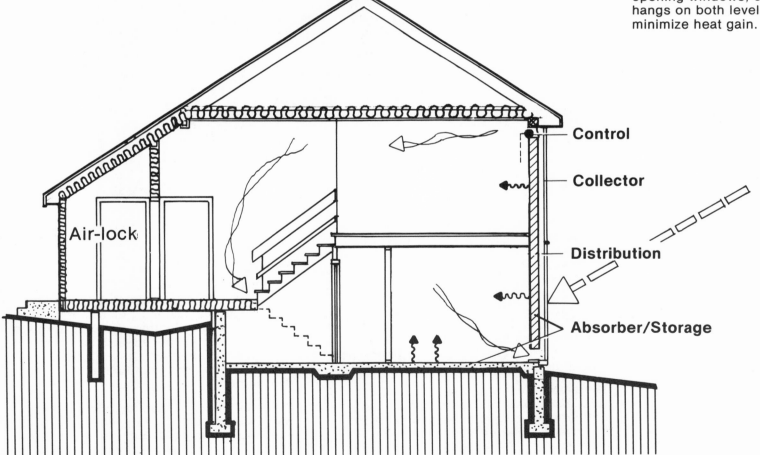

Air-lock

Control

Collector

Distribution

Absorber/Storage

Durham, NH

Builder: Walter W. Cheney, Inc., New Market, NH

Designer: Walter W. Cheney

Solar Designer: Walter W. Cheney

Price: $89,900

Net Heated Area: 1472 ft²

Heat Load: 72.0 x 10⁶ BTU / yr

Degree Days: 7383

Solar Fraction: 63%

Auxiliary Heat: 2.99 BTU / DD / ft²

Passive Heating System(s): Direct gain, isolated gain, sun-tempering

Recognition Factors: Collector(s): South-facing glazing, 429 ft² **Absorber(s):** 55-gallon steel drum surfaces, stone surface of concrete slab **Storage:** Water in steel drums, concrete slab, stone mass wall—**capacity:** 15,434 BTU / °F **Distribution:** Radiation, natural and forced convection **Controls:** Roof overhang, vents, insulated window quilts, sliding doors

Back-up: Electric baseboard heat (34,000 BTU / H), wood stove (35,000 BTU / H)

48

Located on a 3½-acre site in a cold climate, this house is part of a proposed 12-unit, all passive solar development. A pine and hardwood forest on the north end of the lot shields the house from the northwest wind. The traditional saltbox roof also deflects winds, and the garage, located on the north side of the house, acts as a buffer zone.

There are a few windows on the east and west elevations and none at all on the north, but glazing is extensive along the south wall. Solar energy is **collected** through second-floor windows, directly warming two bedrooms during the day.

Through other second-floor windows, the sun is **absorbed** and **stored** by six 55-gallon drums located in alcoves off of the bedrooms. On the first floor, there are 120 square feet of **collecting** windows, through which the sun strikes a 9-inch concrete floor slab, finished with natural stone, that **absorbs** and **stores** heat for later **distribution**.

A 12-inch thick x 7-foot long stone mass wall that is located 3 feet inside the south wall also stores heat. Both the wood stove and the stairs to the second floor are located behind the mass wall. Finally,

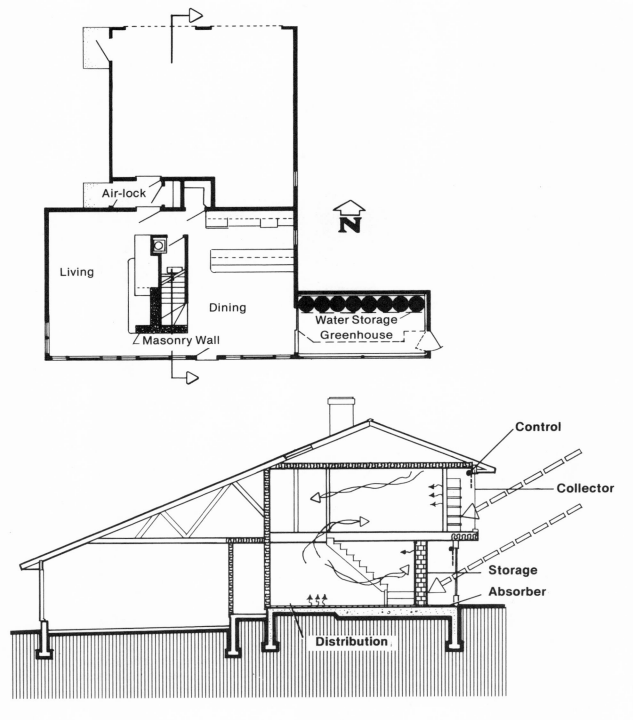

Air-lock

Living

Dining

Masonry Wall

Water Storage
Greenhouse

N

Control

Collector

Storage

Absorber

Distribution

there is a first-floor greenhouse—adjacent to the dining room—with 120 square feet of south wall glazing. The greenhouse has 16 water-filled 55-gallon drums inside its berm-protected north wall. All of these systems contribute to heating and cooling the house.

During a winter day, the sun charges the first-floor slab and the water drums. Due to the open plan, heat is easily distributed from the south wall via circulation to all other parts of the house. If necessary, the sliding doors between the greenhouse and dining room can be opened, allowing heat to pass into the house. At night, insulating blankets are pulled down over the double-glazed house and greenhouse windows to **control** heat loss (combined R-5). The concrete floor slab and stone mass wall radiate heat on the first floor while heat radiates from the drums on the second floor. A register in the living room ceiling allows heat to be **distributed** by convection up to the second floor. Warm air also flows through vents from the greenhouse into the master bedroom.

The roof overhangs the second floor, which in turn overhangs the first floor, so that all southern windows are shaded from May to August. Most windows are kept open to allow ventilation, but insulating shades are pulled down over the windows in front of the second-floor water drums. The drums are allowed to absorb heat from the bed-rooms, just as the concrete slab and stone wall absorb heat from the first-floor spaces. At night, the insulating shades are raised, and heat from the mass wall, the slab, and the water drums radiates to the cool night air. The operable skylight is also opened to allow heat to escape by convection. The various passive features are aided by well-insulated walls (6-inch batts, total R-20) and roof (12-inch batts, total R-38).

Builder: Pierre Realty, Charlotte, VT

Designer: Aukerman Associates, Burlington, VT

Solar Designer: Harris Hyman and Aukerman Associates, Lamoine, ME

Price: $67,500

Net Heated Area: 1724 ft²

Heat Load: 97.3 x 10⁶ BTU/yr

Degree Days: 7876

Solar Fraction: 54%

Auxiliary Heat: 3.07 BTU/DD/ft²

Passive Heating System(s): Direct gain, indirect gain, sun-tempering

Recognition Factors: Collector(s): Double-glazed south wall, 443 ft² **Absorber(s):** Concrete mass and Trombe walls, greenhouse mass floor, living area mass floor **Storage:** Concrete mass and Trombe walls, greenhouse mass floor, living area mass floor—**capacity:** 35,711 BTU/°F **Distribution:** Radiation, natural convection **Controls:** Manually operable doors, windows, Trombe and mass wall vents, insulating shades, ceiling vents

Back-up: Two woodburning stoves, electric resistance heaters

Domestic Hot Water: Passive preheat piping set into floor slab

This Cape Cod style, single-story, 3-bedroom home is located on a level, treeless lot in a 13-unit subdivision. Its energy-conserving features include: automatically operated insulating shades for the double-glazed, south-facing windows; the separation of living spaces from the north wall by a continuous hallway; the location of a buffer zone along the north wall; and wind protection provided by the garage.

The entire south wall of the house is in effect a double-glazed collector that includes a sliding door that opens into the living room. Living spaces are arranged along the east-west axis of the house, and, except for the living room, are separated from south-facing fixed windows by mass storage walls. A narrow greenhouse occupies the space between the mass wall and glazing in front of the kitchen and dining room. The Trombe wall in front of the bedroom is separated from the glazing by a narrow maintenance space.

During winter days, solar radiation is **absorbed** and **stored** by the Trombe and mass storage walls and concrete floors; when bedroom doors and manually operated upper Trombe wall vents are opened, convective circulation **distributes** heat to the living spaces. At night, the mass walls and floors radiate stored heat into the interior. Closing shades, hall doors, and wall vents **controls** both radiant and convective heat losses.

Summer convective cooling is maximized by opening north windows, hall doors, ceiling vents above the Trombe and mass walls, and the floor-level return register at the base of the walls. The induced cross-ventilation pulls cool air in through north windows and vents hot air out through the continuous ridge vent.

A passive domestic water preheat system is set into the concrete floor in the living room. The pipes rest in a bed of very fine granite chips between bricks just below the surface of the slab. The pipe system is covered with slate, and is expected to provide about 50 percent of the annual domestic hot water load.

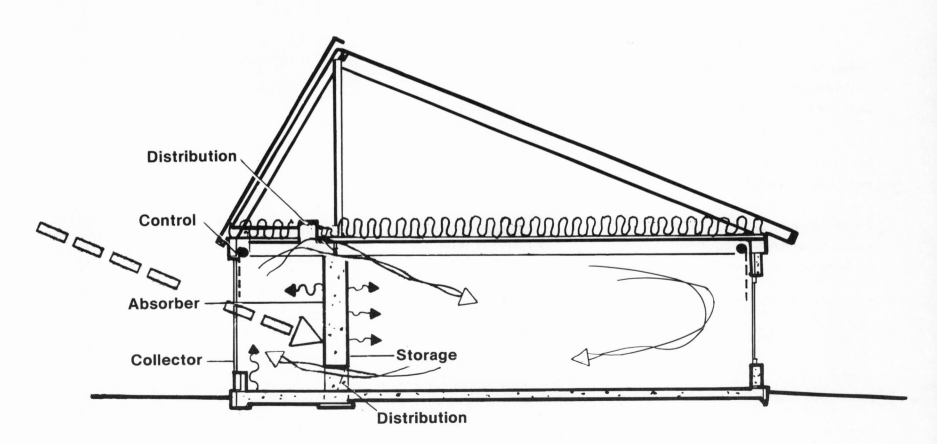

Distribution

Control

Absorber

Collector

Storage

Distribution

Builder: Hartford-West, Inc., West Simsbury, CT

Designer: Richard Reinhart, Farmington, CT

Solar Designer: Energy Research Group, Farmington, CT

Price: $150,000

Net Heated Area: 2200 ft²

Heat Load: 99.9 x 10⁶ BTU/yr

Degree Days: 6350

Solar Fraction: 35%

Auxiliary Heat: 4.69 BTU/DD/ft²

Passive Heating System(s): Direct gain, sun-tempering

Recognition Factors: Collector(s): South-facing glass, 396 ft² **Absorber(s):** Concrete wall and floor, tile floor **Storage:** Concrete wall and floor—**capacity:** 17,349 BTU/°F **Distribution:** Radiation, natural and forced convection **Controls:** Vents, shutters, damper, operable shades, insulated panels

Back-up: Air-to-air heat pump (35,000 BTU/H), electric resistance heaters

Domestic Hot Water: Flat-plate collectors (74 ft²), 120-gallon storage

52

This contemporary Connecticut design reflects styling that has had wide market acceptance in the suburban Hartford area. The house is set into a south-facing slope which provides earth-berming for the lower level on the east, west, and north; this siting enhances exposure to summer breezes while reducing exposure to winter winds. Winter heat loss is further limited by the garage on the north side and the air-lock vestibule on the east; by fiberglass insulation with R-values of 21 in the walls, and 34 in the ceiling and roof; by a buffer zone of low-use spaces on the north; and by insulating shades or shutters on all glazing.

During winter days, solar heat is **collected** through double-glazed east-, west-, and south-facing windows. On the lower level,

heat is **absorbed** and **stored** in the concrete walls, and in concrete and tile floors of the bedrooms. Additional storage is provided by the masonry walls of the 3-story stairwell. Stored heat is later **distributed** as it radiates back into the stairwell, living room, and sleeping spaces when interior temperatures drop. When interior windows between the stairwell and upper-level bedrooms are open, solar-heated air will be **distributed** to these bedrooms by convection. Excess solar heat from the lower-level bedrooms is **distributed** to upper levels when bedroom doors are open.

Solar heat can also be distributed throughout the house by the air handling unit in the heat pump back-up system. Every year in the fall, a damper in the ceiling-level return air vent is manually opened. The fan in the air handler pulls solar-heated air from the top of the stairwell through the return duct and **distributes** it to living and sleeping spaces via the duct system. During winter nights, heat loss is **controlled** by manually closing exterior insulating shades on stairwell glazing and interior insulating shades on all other windows.

To reduce solar heat gain during the summer, the shades can be closed during the day and then opened at night to re-radiate house heat outside. At the beginning of the cooling season, a panel of rigid insulation is removed from the attic vent in the stairwell ceiling, and the damper is opened. If the exterior windows in the stairwell are opened and the upper windows are closed, then cool air is pulled up through the stairwell, and hot air is exhausted through continuous ridge vents in the attic. Whole-house cross-ventilation is induced by opening other windows and skylights. If the floor level return vent in the upper hall is opened, the air handler can distribute cool air pulled into the stairwell from outside.

A Sunworks™ active solar system heats domestic water with four collectors mounted on the roof.

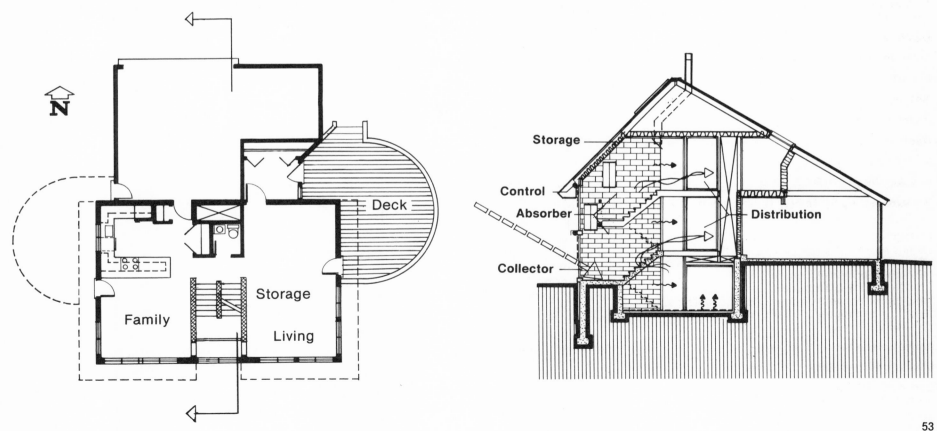

New City, NY

Builder: Bonnerville Construction Corporation, Monsey, NY

Designer: Perillo Associates, Hawthorne, NY

Solar Designer: Perillo Associates

Price: $125,000

Net Heated Area: 2550 ft²

Heat Load: 146.0 x 10⁶ BTU/yr

Degree Days: 4862

Solar Fraction: 38%

Auxiliary Heat: 7.34 BTU/DD/ft²

Passive Heating System(s): Direct gain, isolated gain, sun-tempering

Recognition Factors: Collector(s): South-facing windows, greenhouse glazing, 466 ft² **Absorber(s):** Block wall, concrete floor surface **Storage:** Block wall, concrete floor—**capacity:** 12,230 BTU/°F **Distribution:** Radiation, natural and forced convection **Controls:** Moveable insulation in greenhouse, shutters, registers, vents, trellis

Active Solar Heating: See DHW

Back-up: Furnace (88,000 BTU/H)

Domestic Hot Water: Liquid flat-plate collectors (105 ft²)

Rockland County, New York, has unusually high utility and fuel rates, second only to the nation's highest in New York City. This fact was a major consideration for the builder when he planned this center hall, contemporary passive solar house. As a result, he has kept to a minimum the energy consumption of the house's simple auxiliary heating system.

The house is currently the only passive solar house in a growing subdivision where market demand has been for large residences with clearly designated living areas. However, its design is sufficiently inconspicuous to let it blend in with more traditional homes in the neighborhood.

Two greenhouses flanking the front approach on the south side act as passive solar **collectors** for heating the dining room and living room. In addition, five clerestory windows over the 2-story living room and three pairs of windows in the two south-facing bedrooms upstairs act as **collectors**.

Each greenhouse has a 6-inch concrete slab floor covering a total of 466 square feet. The radiation is **absorbed** and **stored** in a solid 12-inch concrete block wall with black painted textured surfaces facing south. A 6-foot sliding glass door is located in each storage wall in the greenhouses, allowing the sun to directly enter the house, and in the case of the living room

54

on the west side, strike the 4-inch solid concrete slab floor for additional heat storage.

Heat is **distributed** into the living and dining rooms from the two greenhouses by radiation and then natural convection conveys the heated air through high registers into upstairs bedrooms. A two-zone fan system moves the air through a central duct system and this mechanically assisted convective loop continues to circulate stored heat at night.

Control features include a window quilt that can be lowered inside the sloping and vertical glass of the greenhouses. Translucent window shutters fit inside all windows and can be closed at night to prevent heat loss.

Along the south front is a trellis with removeable wooden slats which are taken down in winter and reinstalled in summer.

Two layers of ¾-inch polystyrene perimeter insulation wrap the entire house at the foundation wall. All windows are double glazed and have 1½-inch thick wood-framed polystyrene shutters (R-6). Exterior walls have 6-inch fiberglass (R-19) insulation. Attic, roof, and exposed overhang have 9-inch fiberglass batt insulation (R-30).

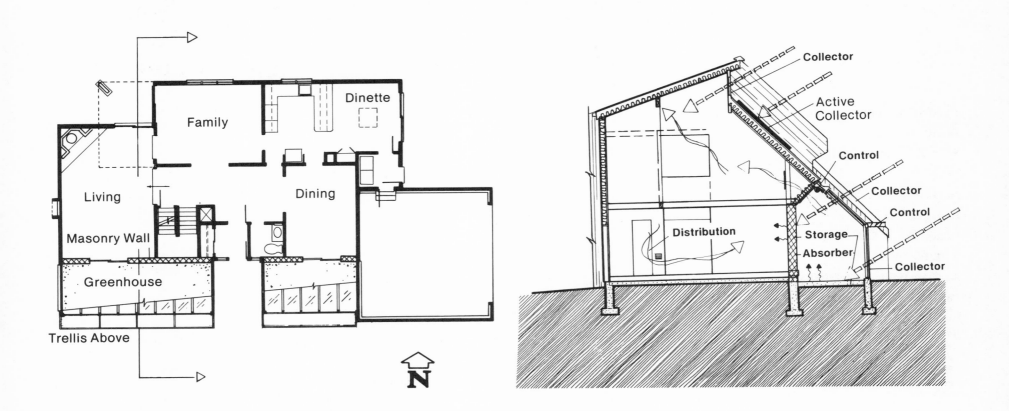

Blackwood, NJ

Builder: Diamond Crest, Inc., Blackwood, NJ

Designer: Princeton Energy Group, Princeton, NJ

Solar Designer: Princeton Energy Group

Price: n/a

Net Heated Area: 1691 ft²

Heat Load: 43.2 x 10⁶ BTU/yr

Degree Days: 4812

Solar Fraction: 72%

Auxiliary Heat: 1.56 BTU/DD/ft²

Passive Heating System(s): Indirect gain, sun-tempering

Recognition Factors: Collector(s): Double-glazed windows, acrylic panels, 296 ft² **Absorber(s):** Water wall surface **Storage:** Water wall—**capacity:** 8075 BTU/°F **Distribution:** Radiation, forced convection **Controls:** Moveable insulation, awnings

Back-up: Gas furnace (50,000 BTU/H)

Domestic Hot Water: Liquid flat-plate collectors (84 ft²), 80-gallon storage

This contemporary ranch design in the New Jersey Pine Barrens is a passive solar modification of a best-selling model. The basic "energy-efficient" building package includes R-25 insulation in the walls, R-45 insulation in the ceiling, foundation and ductwork insulation, air-lock entries, insulating glass windows, and operable insulating shades. Low-activity areas are located along the north wall to create a buffer zone. The passive solar features added to the building design include increased south-facing glazing, three water walls, solar control awnings, and an active solar domestic water heating system.

In the family room, living room, and master bedroom, solar heat is **collected** through south-facing fixed windows. The heat is **absorbed** and **stored** in water-filled polyethylene drums. **Distribution** occurs as these water walls radiate solar heat to the interior of the house. Each of these rooms also receives solar radiation through south-facing sliding glass doors, but there is no storage mass for these collection areas. Solar heat can be **distributed** by the blower in the back-up gas-fired, forced-air heating system. If air temperature in the solar-heated rooms is adequate, the blower circulates the air throughout the house. If

56

temperatures fall below a preset point on the thermostat, the furnace is automatically activated and boosts the temperature to the desired level.

Insulating shades are lowered on the living side of all windows at night to **control** heat loss, and they are raised again each morning to permit solar collection.

Canvas roll-down awnings are adjusted at the beginning of the cooling season to protect storage walls from solar gain. Insulating shades may be lowered during the day, and then raised at night to permit radiation of house heat to the outdoors by opening doors and windows to induce natural cross-ventilation.

A Sunworks™ solar domestic water heating system with single-glazed flat-plate collectors is included in the design.

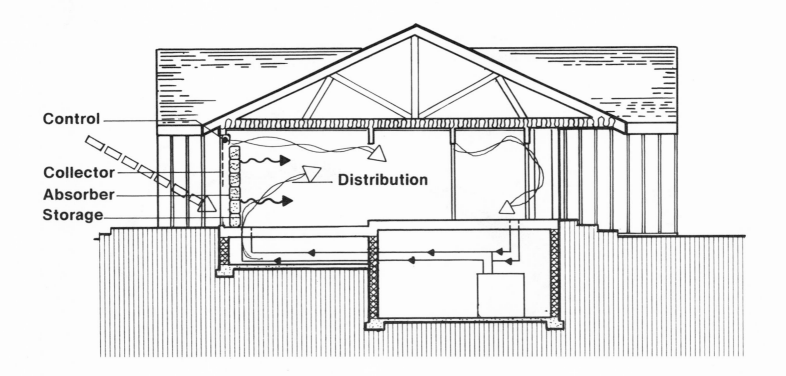

Control

Collector

Absorber

Storage

Distribution

South

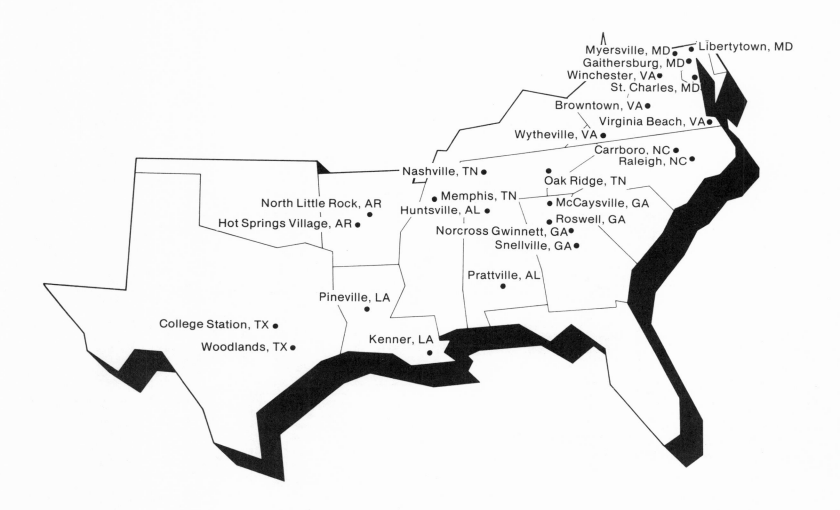

Myersville, MD ●
● Libertytown, MD
Gaithersburg, MD ●
Winchester, VA ●
St. Charles, MD ●
Browntown, VA ●
● Virginia Beach, VA
Wytheville, VA ●
Carrboro, NC ●
Raleigh, NC ●
Nashville, TN ●
● Oak Ridge, TN
North Little Rock, AR ●
● Memphis, TN
Huntsville, AL ●
● McCaysville, GA
Hot Springs Village, AR ●
● Roswell, GA
Norcross Gwinnett, GA ●
Snellville, GA ●
Prattville, AL ●
Pineville, LA ●
College Station, TX ●
Kenner, LA ●
Woodlands, TX ●

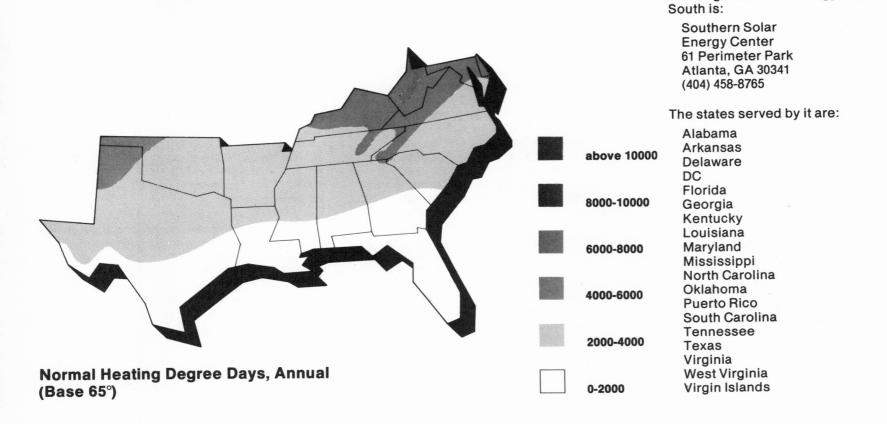

Normal Heating Degree Days, Annual
(Base 65°)

above 10000

8000-10000

6000-8000

4000-6000

2000-4000

0-2000

The Regional Solar Energy Center for the South is:

Southern Solar
Energy Center
61 Perimeter Park
Atlanta, GA 30341
(404) 458-8765

The states served by it are:

Alabama
Arkansas
Delaware
DC
Florida
Georgia
Kentucky
Louisiana
Maryland
Mississippi
North Carolina
Oklahoma
Puerto Rico
South Carolina
Tennessee
Texas
Virginia
West Virginia
Virgin Islands

Gaithersburg, MD

Builder: Trellis and Watkins, Inc., Columbia, MD

Designer: Trellis and Watkins, Inc., Columbia, MD

Solar Designer: Trellis and Watkins, Inc.

Price: $190,000

Net Heated Area: 2737 ft²

Heat Load: 91.2 x 10⁶ BTU/yr

Degree Days: 4224

Solar Fraction: 27%

Auxiliary Heat: 5.72 BTU/DD/ft²

Passive Heating System(s): Direct gain, sun-tempering

Recognition Factors: Collector(s): South-facing glazing, atrium skylights, 449 ft² **Absorber(s):** Ceramic tile-covered concrete floor, masonry fireplace/planter **Storage:** Ceramic tile-covered concrete floor, masonry fireplace/planter— **capacity:** 9,518 BTU/°F **Distribution:** Radiation, natural and forced convection **Controls:** Registers, ducts, overhangs, shades

Back-up: Air-to-air heat pump (35,000 BTU/H)

Passive Cooling Type: Natural and induced ventilation

A partially wooded lot that stretches along a north-south axis is the site for this custom house. The house is located at the north end of the site. From there, the land drops gradually to the south, bottoms out across a creek, and rises again on the opposite side. This location allows good exposure on the south side for maximum sunlight and summer breezes, as well as protection from winter winds which prevail from the north-west. The compact form of the house reduces exterior surface area, with the garage on the north side and the roof of the house providing one continuous surface that deflects the wind. Additional buffer spaces, such as closets, bathrooms, laundry, and stairs are located on the north side. There is also an enclosed, unheated air-lock entry connecting the house with the garage and the covered front porch. There are minimal windows on the north, east, and west elevations.

The house's centerpiece is a 2-story combination family room/atrium that opens onto all the other spaces. The kitchen and breakfast room are located to the east to receive morning sun while the living room is oriented for late afternoon sun on the west. On the second floor of the atrium, there is a balcony onto which all the bedrooms open.

The low, winter sun is **collected** through all the south windows and through three skylights in the roof of the atrium. Some of the solar energy heats the south-facing spaces directly, and the remainder is **absorbed** and **stored** by the ceramic tile-covered concrete floor and a masonry fireplace/planter. At night, heat **distribution** is by radiation back to the living spaces from the floor and planter. The warm floor also induces a convective flow that **distributes** heat to the second-floor spaces. The windows are triple

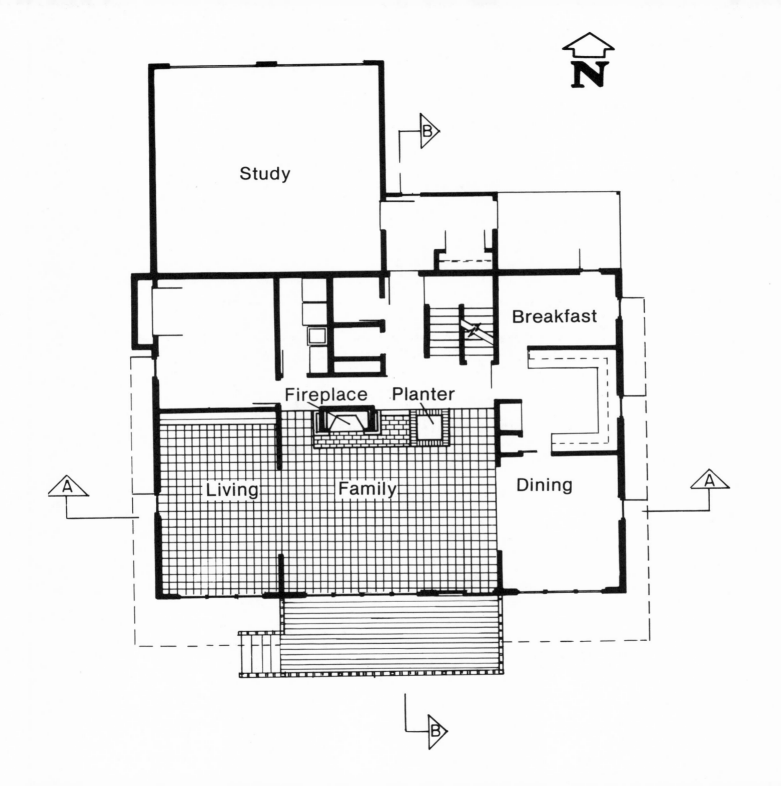

Study

N

B

Breakfast

Fireplace   Planter

Living   Family   Dining

A   A

B

glazed to **control** heat loss at night, and drapery space has been provided that will allow the homeowner an extra degree of protection. On very cold days, when the back-up heating system is in operation, the heat pump draws its return air from the top of the atrium space, thereby using and recycling the warm air that has stratified there.

A 4-foot wide deck, running the full length of the second floor, shades the first-floor glazing from midday sun between April and August. The second-floor glazing is shaded by a 2-foot overhang. In addition, these windows are protected by split bamboo drop shades that are manually controlled from the deck. The three skylights provide the only direct sunlight to the atrium space for a substantial portion of the summer. Because there are operable windows on all sides of the house, natural cross-ventilation will reduce the need for heat pump air conditioning on all but the hottest, most humid days of the year.

The building is well insulated for this climate; walls are 2- x 6-inch wood studs with full fiberglass batt insulation for a total insulating value, with sheathing and cedar siding, of R-23. Ceiling construction above the second floor includes 10 inches of fiberglass batts in the joists; the total roof value is R-31. Attic spaces are well ventilated with soffit and ridge vents. Where there are overhanging exterior soffits, as at the window recesses, 5½-inch batts are installed in the construction for a total value of R-24.

The floor over the unheated basement includes 3½-inch batts for a value of R-14.

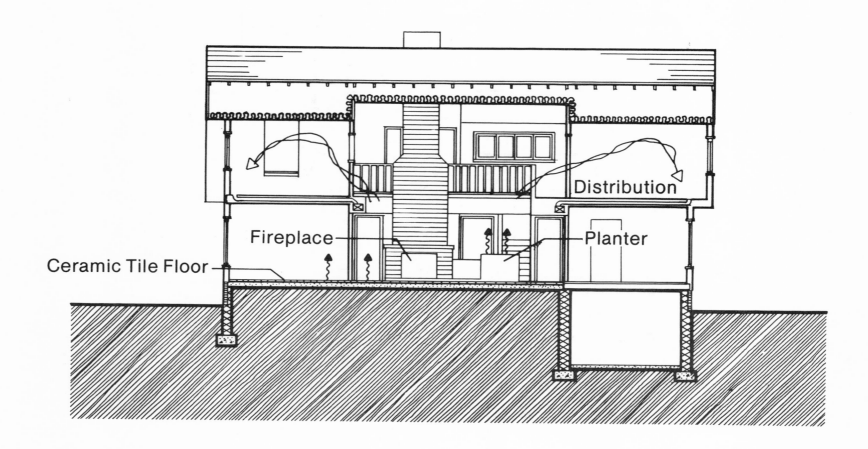

A-A

Along the house perimeter, a 1-inch foam-board (R-5) is installed across the face of the first-floor slab and turns under the slab for 2 feet. Finally, all cracks around windows, doors, and exterior corners are hand-chinked prior to insulation to minimize air infiltration into the building envelope.

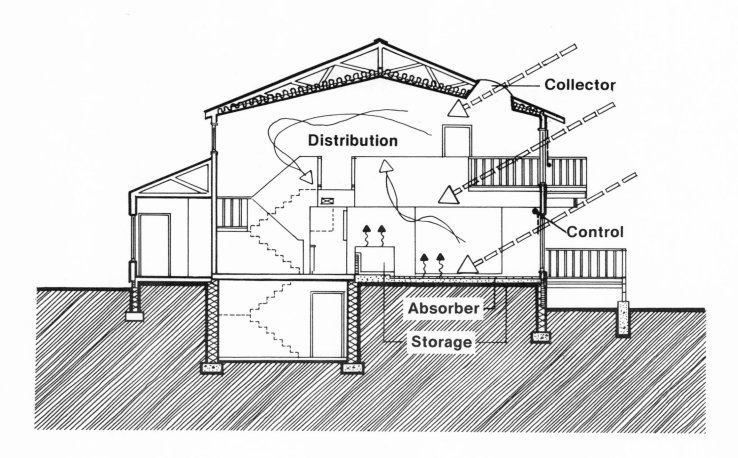

Collector

Distribution

Control

Absorber

Storage

B-B

Myersville, MD

Builder: M.S. Milliner Construction, Inc., Myersville, MD

Designer: Malcolm B. Wells, A.I.A., Brewster, MA

Solar Designer: Solar Energy Systems and Products, Inc., Emmitsburg, MD

Price: $120,000

Net Heated Area: 2036 ft²

Heat Load: 46.1 x 10⁶ BTU / yr

Degree Days: 5087

Solar Fraction: 63%

Auxiliary Heat: 1.63 BTU / DD / ft²

Passive Heating System(s): Direct gain, sun-tempering, isolated gain

Recognition Factors: Collector(s): South-facing clerestory windows and glazing, 248 ft² **Absorber(s):** Concrete floors and wall **Storage:** Concrete floors and wall—**capacity:** 18,100 BTU/°F **Distribution:** Radiation, natural and forced convection **Controls:** Roll-down aluminum shades, overhangs

Back-up: Air-to-air heat pump (16,000 BTU/H), woodburning stove, electric strip heaters

Passive Cooling Type: Earth-cooled air from underground tubes, natural and forced ventilation

64

This house was built "underground," using the earth for shelter from the elements, and it also uses passive solar features to provide much of its heating requirement.

The site is well suited for an earth-sheltered, passive solar house. Located in a custom home subdivision, the 4-acre site is on the south side of a 10 percent grade that also slopes off to both east and west for good drainage. A stand of pine trees,

along with a higher hill to the northwest, affords protection from the prevailing northwest winter winds.

To augment the **collection** of solar energy, the house is built on two levels, with the north half higher than the south half. This division permits a row of south-facing clerestory windows for the northern rooms. Sunlight is **collected** through these and a double band of south windows and through

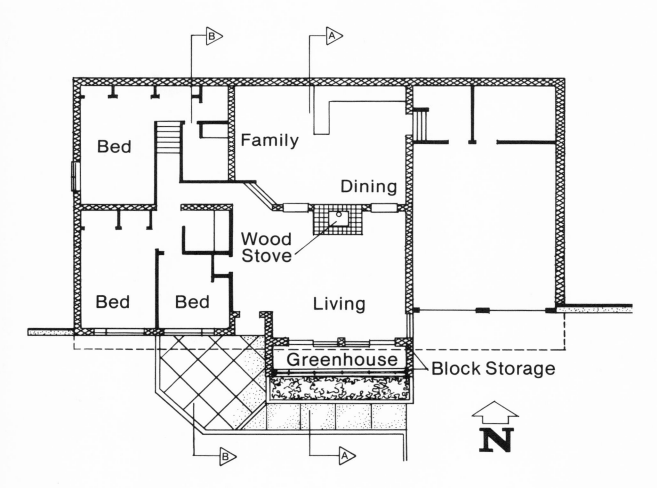

Wood Stove

Bed

Bed

Bed

Family

Dining

Living

Greenhouse

Block Storage

N

the greenhouse, which is on the lower level and in front of the living room. While part of the solar energy warms all of the rooms directly, much of it is **absorbed** and **stored** in the house's internal masonry. The interior north walls of all rooms are stuccoed 12-inch cored concrete block. The roof is stuccoed 8-inch to 12-inch precast concrete with additional 2-inch concrete topping. This **absorbs** solar heat that collects in the rooms by day and is able to **store** most of it because it is underground, not exposed to the elements. The exposed concrete floor slab of the greenhouse also **absorbs** and **stores** solar energy. Heat is distributed from the greenhouse into the living room by convection when the sliding door is opened. There is also a continuous register in the greenhouse ceiling that opens into the hollow cores of the concrete plank roof. Since the cores of the plank run toward a continuous vent on the north rooms (about 4 feet above floor level), heat also flows directly from the greenhouse to these rooms.

At night, heat is **distributed** as it radiates out from the walls and ceiling to warm the rooms. While the greenhouse register and sliding door are closed to isolate it from the house, radiant heat from its floor and walls keeps it warm enough to act as a buffer for the living room. Additional radiant heat can be provided by the centrally located wood stove.

Windows, as well as the sliding glass door at the greenhouse, are double glazed and heat loss through them at night is **controlled** by roll-down interior insulating shades (R-15). The louvers at the clerestory can also be covered at night with moveable insulating panels to **control** heat loss. Glazing for the greenhouse consists of two layers of Teflon® film sandwiched between two layers of crystal glass (R-4). Both entrances are separated from living spaces by air-lock vestibules.

The two roofs overhang the south-facing glazing at both levels to shade the windows

65

from summer sun. Vines are planted at the overhangs and a vine-covered trellis is located at the main entrance in front of the windows. These vines extend the window shading into late summer and early fall to prevent overheating. As solar heating is required, they are trimmed back.

An aluminum slat shade is extended over the greenhouse in summer while ventilation is induced by opening the vents located in the east and west walls; the ventilation is aided by a thermostatically controlled fan. In the main part of the house, a 6-inch diameter buried tube that tempers combustion air for the wood stove in winter also provides low-humidity, earth-cooled air in the summer to both levels of the house. Warm air in the house is absorbed in the thermal mass walls and roofs from where it is absorbed by the earth, which has a nearly constant temperature for natural cooling. Also, any excess warm air is exhausted through fixed louvers in the clerestory by the effects of natural heat rise.

The passive features of the house are augmented by the conservation features of the earth-sheltered design. With 80 percent of the roof and wall surfaces covered with earth, insulation value is inherent. In addition, effects of prolonged cold or warm spells are delayed up to a week, by which time conditions should moderate.

The concrete roof planks with interior stucco and exterior 2-inch concrete are topped by 5 inches of polystyrene insulation, 4 inches of stone, and a minimum of 14 inches of earth for a total average thermal value of R-31. The earth is planted with crown vetch to provide a thick protective ground cover

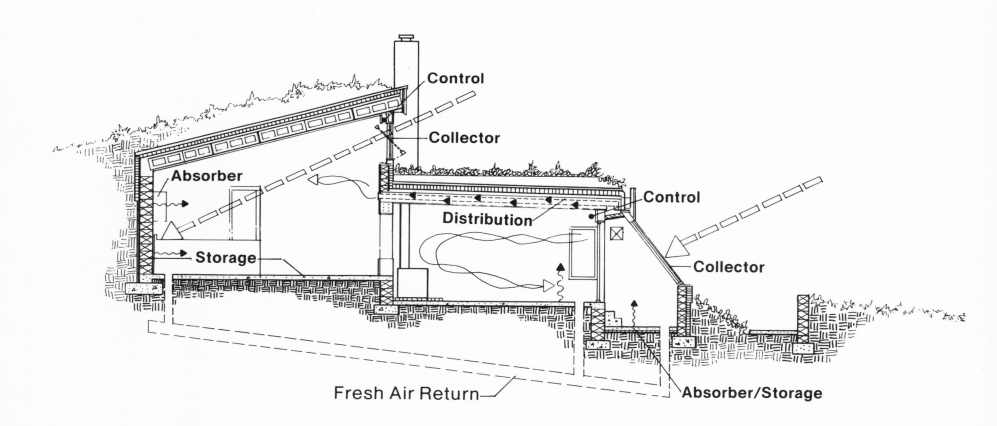

A-A

which will shade the earth and provide evaporative cooling in the summer. Wall construction is solid concrete block with varying widths of polystyrene insulation applied to the outside of the wall. There is 5-inch insulation down to 8 feet; below that there is 1 inch of insulation. The insulation is covered by a special cement waterproofing. The average wall thermal value is R-23. The exposed south wall has 4-inch polystyrene over block, with stucco finish on both sides (R-23). At the clerestory level, construction is 2- x 6-inch wood frame with full fiberglass batts (R-22). Floors are left uninsulated, except within 3 feet of the south face of the house, to permit the earth mass in contact with it to reach room temperature and serve as a storage area to hold excess heat and moderate the room temperature.

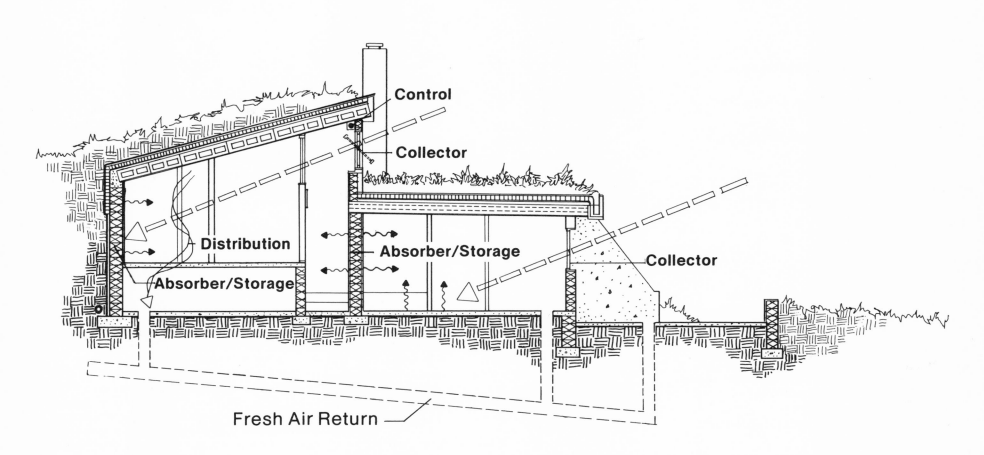

B-B

Wytheville, VA

Builder: Bradco Construction Company, Inc., Wytheville, VA

Designer: Chris Umberger, Architect Inc., Wytheville, VA

Solar Designer: Bob Livingstone and Chris Umberger

Price: $75,000

Net Heated Area: 1694 ft²

Heat Load: 77.3 x 10⁶ BTU/yr

Degree Days: 4907

Solar Fraction: 60%

Auxiliary Heat: 3.80 BTU/DD/ft²

Passive Heating System(s): Direct gain

Recognition Factors: Collector(s): South-facing clerestory windows, double-glazed windows, and sliding glass doors, 355 ft² **Absorber(s):** Quarry tile over concrete floor, masonry wall, brick wall **Storage:** Concrete slab floor, masonry wall— **capacity:** 26,286 BTU/°F **Distribution:** Radiation, natural and forced convection **Controls:** Window shutters, canvas awning

Back-up: Air-to-air heat pump (20,000 BTU/H), wood stove

Domestic Hot Water: Liquid flat-plate collectors (49 ft²), 80-gallon storage tank

This contemporary home is located on the south side of a gradual slope. Earth has been bermed on the north and east sides of the house so that the floor level is about 4 feet below grade, giving the house a low profile on those elevations. On the west side, there is a large air-lock vestibule entry, and a storage room that opens only to the outside.

The house is split in two along a central east-west axis. The southern half contains the living areas (living room, dining room, and kitchen) which receive copious solar exposure. The roof over this area slopes up to the north at a 3 in 12 pitch. The sleeping level in the north half of the house is 16 inches higher than the south. All three bedrooms and both bathrooms are located on this side of the house, which has a steep 7 in 12 pitch roof. The different roof slopes enable a string of south-facing clerestory windows to be located above the spine of the house, letting the sun into the bedrooms. Along the north elevation, each bedroom has one small window, while there is but one win-

68

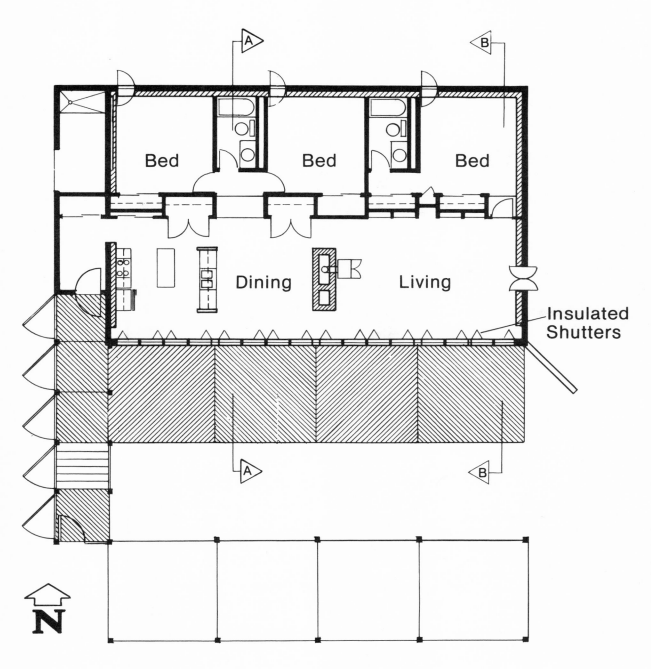

Bed

Bed

Bed

Dining

Living

Insulated Shutters

N

dow on the east elevation. There are no windows on the west to prevent overheating of the interior on late summer afternoons. All glazing is double.

The extensive glazing on the south elevation and the smaller clerestories provide the bulk of the house's natural lighting and heating. Through the array of south-facing glazing, the sun is **collected** during the day to warm the living spaces directly. Much of this solar energy is **absorbed** by the quarry tile and **stored** in the concrete slab floor. Sun shining through the clerestory windows strikes the masonry wall along the north side of the bedrooms and is **absorbed** and **stored**. As the sun progresses from east to west, it also strikes the brick walls on the interior of the kitchen and living room. Heat stored in the slab and the walls is **distributed** as it radiates to the rooms throughout the evening. The warmth of the slab also induces convection currents to **distribute** heat throughout the house, easing temperature variations between different rooms. Through vents located high on the north wall of the kitchen, dining room, and living room, heated air is drawn and moved to hollow walls between the bedrooms and bathrooms.

Nighttime heat loss through each window is controlled by an interior shutter that consists of a 1-inch thick piece of polystyrene encased in wood. When closed, the shutter gives the window opening a thermal value of R-7.

In the summer, a canvas awning is extended to shade the south windows, but not the clerestories, from the sun. All windows are opened to let in breezes, which come from the southwest. The clerestory window shutters can be closed 80 percent during the summer to reflect most of the heat while still permitting ventilation through the open window. As cooler air enters the house from outside, the heat rises and exhausts through the clerestories.

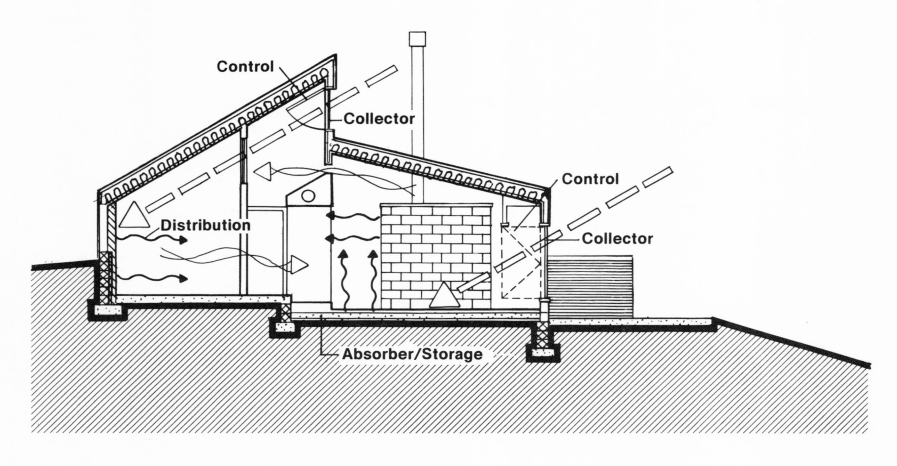

Control

Collector

Control

Distribution

Collector

Absorber/Storage

A-A

To preheat incoming city water for household use, there are two liquid flat-plate solar collectors. These are ground mounted on a frame at a 45 degree slope and attached to a concrete pad.

The house construction is very effective for this climate. Ten-inch fiberglass batts are installed in the roof framing for a value of R-33. The wall construction consists of a 6-inch wood frame wall, filled with fiberglass-batts and finished with wood sheathing and plywood siding. Inside the framing is an 8-

inch thick solid brick wall along the north, east, and west elevations. The thermal value of this combination is R-24. Below grade, wall construction changes to an 8-inch block with concrete-filled cores, 2-inch polystyrene insulation, and 4-inch solid brick (R-11). The floor is a 4-inch concrete slab with a 1-inch polystyrene thermal break between it and the foundation wall. There is also a layer of 1½-inch polystyrene insulation below slab within 2 feet of the foundation.

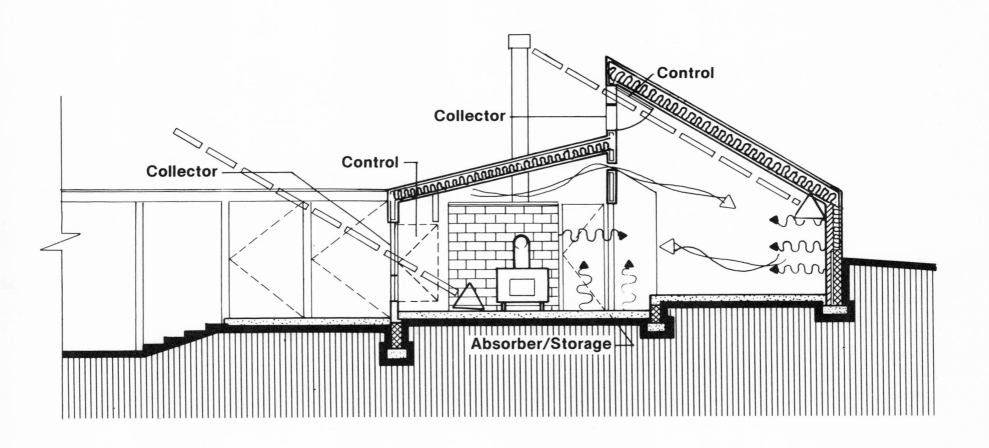

Control

Collector

Control

Collector

Absorber/Storage

B-B

Carrboro, NC

Builder: Capricorn Building Company, Carrboro, NC

Designer: Designworks, Carrboro, NC

Solar Designer: Aircomfort, Inc., Raleigh, NC

Price: $70,000

Net Heated Area: 1304 ft²

Heat Load: 39.1 x 10⁶ BTU/yr

Degree Days: 3514

Solar Fraction: 41%

Auxiliary Heat: 4.65 BTU/DD/ft²

Passive Heating System(s): Direct gain, indirect gain

Recognition Factors: Collector(s): Double-glazed sliding glass doors, skylights, south-facing panels, 269 ft² **Absorber(s):** Water tubes, brick pavers **Storage:** Water tubes, brick pavers— **capacity:** 6781 BTU/°F **Distribution:** Radiation, natural and forced convection **Controls:** Vents, awnings, thermostat

Back-up: Air-to-air heat pump (23,500 BTU/H), woodburning stove

Domestic Hot Water: Liquid flat-plate collectors (46 ft²), 42-gallon storage

72

This contemporary house has been designed to compete in a very active speculative home market; the approach has been, therefore, to work largely within existing construction methods and materials to arrive at a design that is both energy efficient and economical. The lot on which this 2-story, wood-frame home is built slopes from north to south, affording it maximum exposure to the sun's path across the southern sky. Tall deciduous trees to the southwest have been left standing to deflect winter winds.

Collection of solar heat by the greenhouse at the southeast corner of the house occurs through four double-glazed sliding doors, and through a pair of Kalwall™ skylights (also double glazed) on the pitched roof. A vertical Kalwall™ **collector** is used to heat water tubes just west of the front entrance. Another pair of sliding glass doors **collects** direct solar radiation for storage in the lower-level master bedroom. Roof-mounted, active flat-plate collectors are used to preheat domestic water.

Solar radiation is **absorbed** and **stored** in the greenhouse by eight Kalwall™ water tubes, and the 1⅝-inch brick pavers of the floor.

Separating the lower greenhouse from the living and dining room behind it is a pair of sliding glass doors that allow solar heat into these areas. Water tubes are also used to **absorb** and **store** heat in the "solar battery™" within the central staircase. Three more water tubes **absorb** and **store** heat in the master bedroom.

Distribution of heat is accomplished by radiation from storage masses as well as natural and forced convection. Heat that

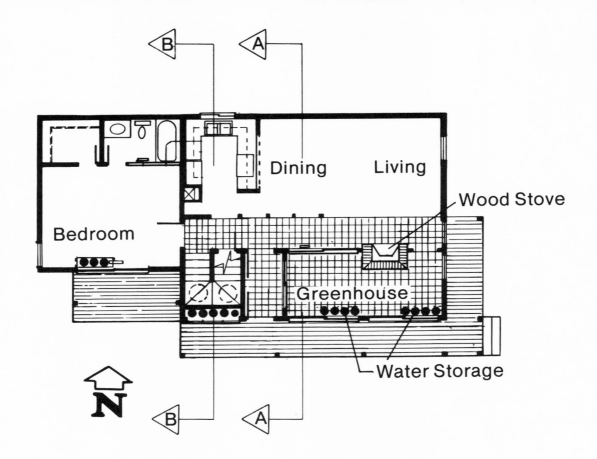

Dining   Living

Wood Stove

Bedroom

Greenhouse

Water Storage

N

gathers near the greenhouse ceiling can either flow into upper-level living areas through a window and vents, or be drawn in by a thermostatically **controlled** through-wall fan. Heat from the water wall on the other side of the front entrance is distributed by a convective loop that pulls cool floor air into the water wall through vents, so that it can be heated and rise through hinged damper grilles at the top of the stairwell. From there it rises to the upper level. Another natural convective loop is set up when bedroom doors are left open so that the heated air can pass through north wall floor vents as it cools and loses buoyancy. At night when storage masses

are supplying heat, a fan draws warm air that has risen to the ceiling of the utility area at the top of the stairs through a vent to the heat pump air handler. From there it is distributed to all rooms through ducts and floor registers. The master bedroom, too, is included in this network. When heat from storage masses is insufficient to meet the demands of the thermostat, the heat pump will turn on to make up the difference. The woodburning stove can be fired up to restrict use of the heat pump.

During summer, the storage masses are shaded by retractable awnings over all southern apertures. Heat that does gather

in the greenhouses can be vented by opening ducts that connect to three 14-inch turbine fans on the roof. The turbines can be used to vent the entire house by opening the doors and windows to the greenhouse. Cross-ventilation is set up by opening east and north bedroom windows. A central air conditioning system also uses the central duct system.

Extensive caulking and weatherstripping, and a 6-mil vapor barrier throughout the entire energy envelope help to reduce infiltration. Floor insulation over the crawl space is rated at R-19, walls are R-11, and the roof is R-30.

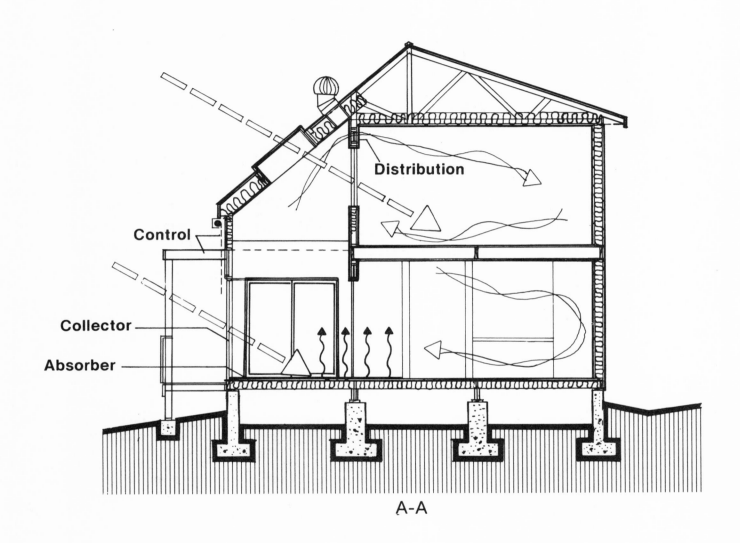

Distribution

Control

Collector

Absorber

A-A

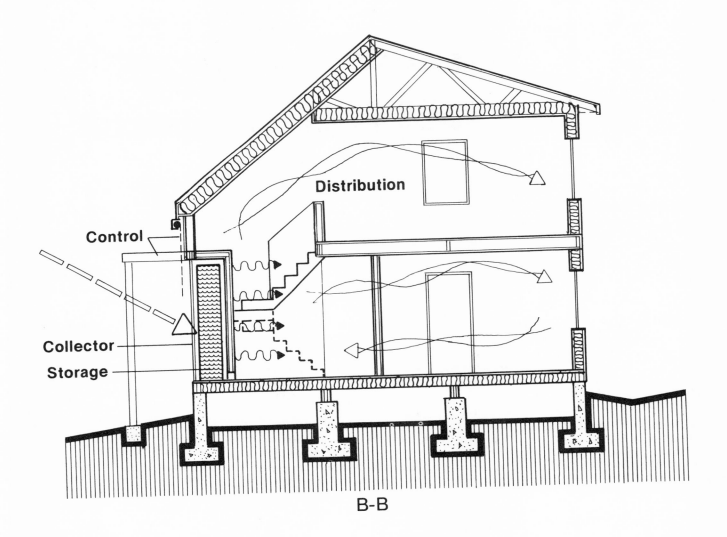

Control

Distribution

Collector

Storage

B-B

Roswell, GA

Builder: Charles Siler Builder, Inc., Marietta, GA

Designer: Richard M. Sibly, Atlanta, GA

Solar Designer: Richard M. Sibly

Price: $72,500

Net Heated Area: 1823 ft²

Heat Load: 44.2 x 10⁶ BTU / yr

Degree Days: 2961

Solar Fraction: 76%

Auxiliary Heat: 2.22 BTU / DD / ft²

Passive Heating System(s): Direct gain, indirect gain (Trombe wall), isolated gain

Recognition Factors: Collector(s): Double glazing, single glazing, 607 ft² **Absorber(s):** Concrete walls, black metal plates **Storage:** Concrete slab floor, Trombe wall, rock storage area—**capacity:** 44,012 BTU / °F **Distribution:** Radiation, natural and forced convection **Controls:** Overhangs, shades, damper, vent

Back-up: Gas forced-air furnace (48,000 BTU / H), woodburning fireplace

Domestic Hot Water: DHW preheat 40-gallon tank located at peak of solar chimney

Passive Cooling Type: Radiant cooling to night sky, natural and induced ventilation, stack effect

The site of this project is a portion of vacant pasture on a gentle south-facing slope. The architect, recognizing the energy-conservation potential in landscaping, has combined plantings and earth berming to protect this rustic contemporary home from winter winds. The 5-foot high earth berms, located on the west, east, and north walls, also provide a thermal lag for reducing temperatures during the hot Georgia summer. The evergreens planted to the northwest side deflect and diffuse the coldest of winter winds. Together, the earth berms and plantings create a pleasing entrance from the street side and a private rear yard.

The style, floor plan, and siting of this house place strong emphasis on market appeal and demonstrate that tradition can mix well with passive design. The 2-story floor plan is one that has had great success in

the area. The overall design follows a line that has been well accepted by Atlanta area home buyers.

This house is notable for the innovative passive heating approaches that provide a major part of its energy needs. Three passive **collection** types are used: (1) over 100 square feet of south-facing double glass collects heat for all of the major living and sleeping spaces except the kitchen; (2) nearly 300 square feet of double-glazed Trombe wall fill the entire balance of this south wall, providing long-term storage; (3) an isolated system is formed by approximately 200 square feet of single glazing that covers a portion of the south-sloping roof.

Absorbers include three major surface areas, two of which are black-painted con-

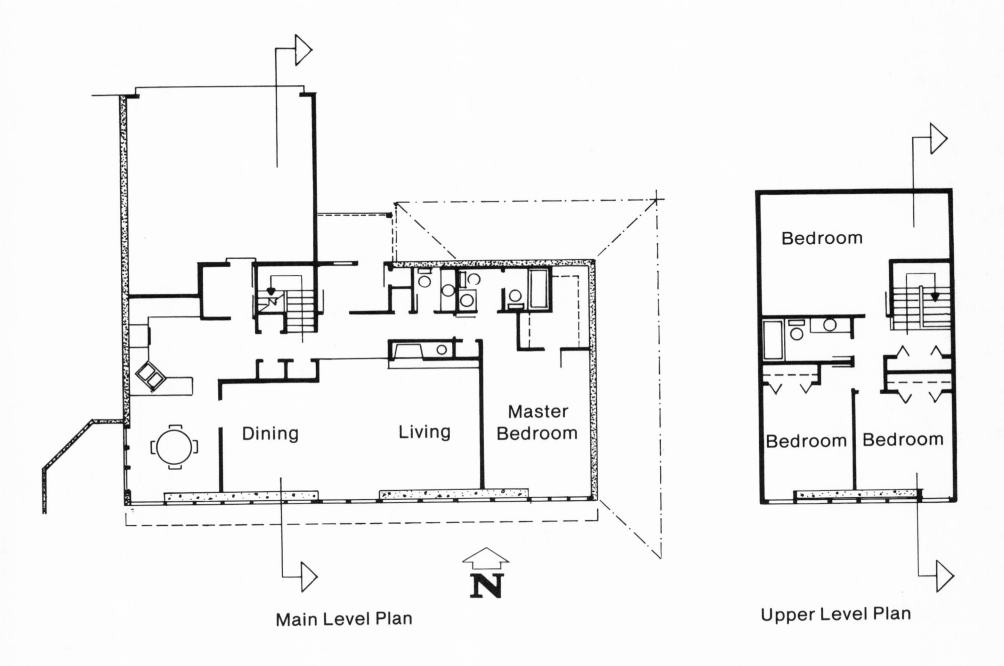

Dining

Living

Master
Bedroom

N

Main Level Plan

Bedroom

Bedroom   Bedroom

Upper Level Plan

crete walls. The other is blackened metal plates installed below the glazed part of the south roof.

Storage for the direct radiation is a massive concrete slab floor, as well as 8-inch concrete block perimeter walls with exterior insulation. The Trombe wall uses 12-inch concrete-filled blocks to store heat for later use. Heat from the roof collector is stored in a 500-cubic foot rock storage area below the living room and master bedroom floors.

Radiation and natural convection **distribute** heat throughout the living spaces. The rock storage bin also radiates heat, but these flows are delayed and continue for many hours after sunset. They provide heat for the living spaces during cloudy and night-time periods. Natural convection occurs both within rooms and throughout the whole house.

A strong convection loop is established in the winter when the Trombe wall is being

charged with solar energy. The air in this partially closed loop leaves the bottom of the rock storage, is heated and as it rises, passes between the glass cover and blackened masonry of the Trombe wall. It is then further heated as it turns and rises up the face of the site-built roof collector. This air is then ducted past a domestic water preheat tank to a high point in the roof where a fan draws it down into the rock storage area below the living and bedroom

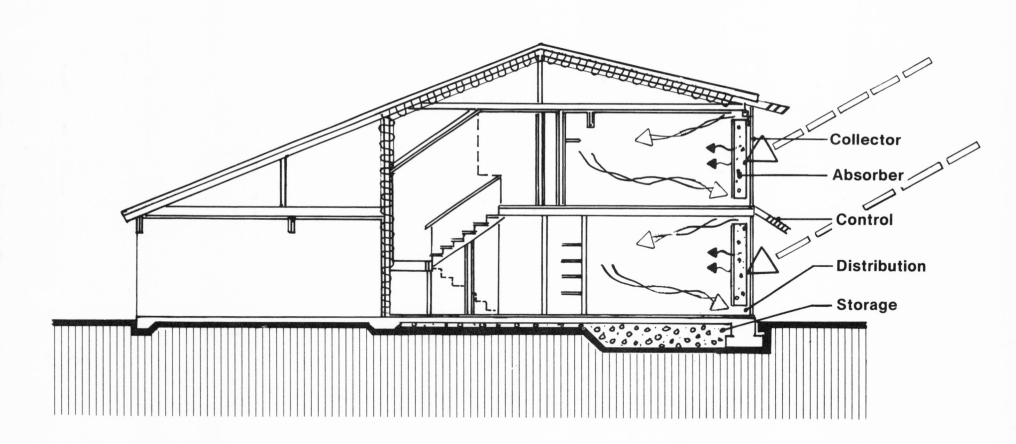

Collector

Absorber

Control

Distribution

Storage

floors. From there it directly heats the room above.

This house makes use of a number of **control** features that respond to outside climatic fluctuations in order to maintain inside comfort. The roof overhang and fixed louvers shade the southern glass and Trombe walls from April until September. Polyethylene-faced backdraft dampers automatically prevent reverse thermo-siphoning of the Trombe walls, and the solar roof permits these devices to be vented to assist interior air circulation during periods when heating is unnecessary. A decorative living room fan helps to eliminate air stratification by forcing warm air at the ceiling back down into the room.

Back-up heating is provided by a fireplace and a small gas-fired forced-air system activated by a clock thermostat. A conventional cooling system sharing the heating unit's fan and duct system provides back-up air conditioning. A gas-fired water heater tank supplies the balance of the domestic hot water needs. All back-up systems, including the fireplace, water heater, and furnace, receive their combustion air directly from the outside, rather than waste already heated inside air.

Walls not shielded by earth berms have 6-inch studs sheathed with 1-inch rigid insulation. The roof is insulated with 12-inch fiberglass batts. The floor slab is poured on 1 inch of rigid insulation. The building is carefully zoned with garage, service, and storage areas on the north side. The entrance is a well-planned, naturally lit air-lock vestibule.

This Roswell, Georgia, house effectively combines outstanding passive design with a popular style to achieve both energy efficiency and great marketability.

St. Charles, MD

Builder: St. Charles Homes, St. Charles, MD

Designer: Princeton Energy Group, Princeton, NJ

Solar Designer: Princeton Energy Group

Price: $80,000

Net Heated Area: 2098 ft²

Heat Load: 46.1 x 10⁶ BTU/yr

Degree Days: 4224

Solar Fraction: 71%

Auxiliary Heat: 0.95 BTU/DD/ft²

Passive Heating System(s): Direct gain

Recognition Factors: Collector(s): South-facing windows, south-facing skylight, 260 ft² **Absorber(s):** Quarry tile floor **Storage:** Concrete floor slab—**capacity:** 7830 BTU/°F **Distribution:** Radiation, natural and forced convection **Controls:** Insulating curtains, roll-down awnings, operable skylight shutter

Back-up: 26,500 BTU/H electric air-to-air heat pump

Domestic Hot Water: Active 75 ft² liquid collectors, 80-gallon steel storage tank

Passive Cooling Type: Earth tubes, induced ventilation

St. Charles is a new planned community in southern Maryland. In order to enhance market acceptance of passive houses, the builder chose the best selling model home design for modification with passive solar heating and cooling features. Also included are active solar panels to heat domestic water. The rectangular house has been located so that its long dimension runs from east to west. Its basic wall construction is 2- x 6-inch wood studs with full fiberglass batt insulation, ½-inch insulating sheathing, and aluminum siding (R-22). In the roof trusses, 6-inch batts are installed with an additional 6 inches of cellulose blown in over them (R-43).

All windows are double glazed and are complemented by roll-down insulating curtains (R-15) to further cut heat loss at night.

Few of the windows are on the east or west elevations, and the amount of south-facing glazing was increased to 260 square feet. This glazing includes five sliding doors, one each to the kitchen and dining room and three to the family room, and a sun garden window in the kitchen. All south windows have exterior roll-down awnings to block the rays of high altitude summer sun.

With all awnings and south-facing insulating shades raised, solar energy is **collected** through the south-facing windows for daytime heating on cold weather days. Some of the energy warms the rooms immediately, while the rest is **absorbed** by the tile flooring for **storage** in the floor slab that is 6 inches thick for the entire southern half of the house. A skylight of double-layer acrylic located over the stairwell also **collects** solar

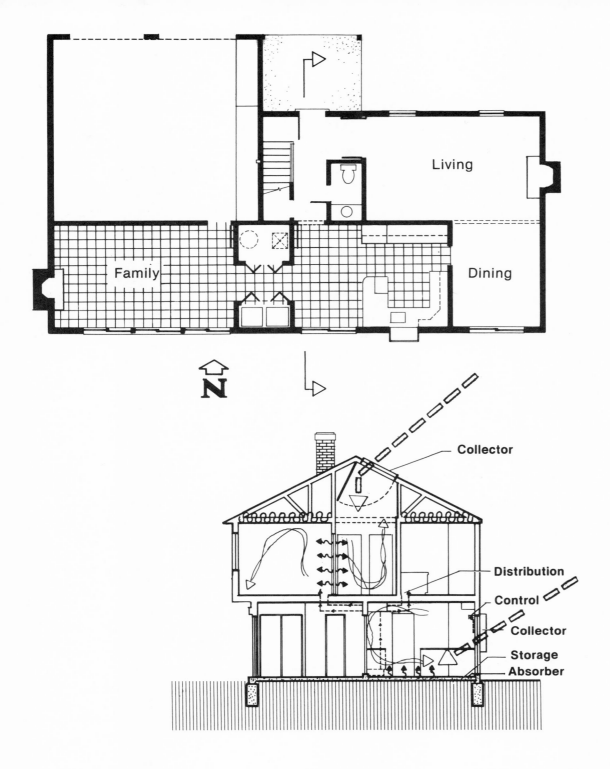

Living

Family

Dining

N

Collector

Distribution

Control

Collector

Storage

Absorber

heat for the stairwell and the upstairs gallery.

Convection induced by the heated rooms **distributes** warmth to spaces without direct access to sunlight. In addition, heated air from the kitchen, dining room, and family room on the first floor is **distributed** to the balance of the house through the ducts of the back-up heating system by a blower that pulls air in from those rooms. At night, with all shades drawn, heat radiates from the thickened floor slab, inducing convection to further heat the spaces. The insulating curtains on all windows **control** the loss of heat at night. The skylight is equipped with a moveable shutter (R-6) that also helps to **control** heat loss.

Awnings are extended in summer to reduce heat gain, and the skylight is opened to provide natural exhaust for hot air. The cooling system consists of eight 50-foot sections of drainage pipe located 4 feet below grade with a common inlet on the south side of the house which receives prevailing summer breezes. Air entering the system is cooled by the earth before it enters the house and, along with natural ventilation, keeps the house comfortable.

Libertytown, MD

Builder: Hartman Briddell Watkins, Rockville, MD

Designer: Landon M. Proffitt, Frederick, MD

Solar Designer: Solar Energy Scientific and Technical Services, Frederick, MD

Price: $75,000

Net Heated Area: 1675 ft²

Heat Load: 81.4 x 10⁶ BTU/yr

Degree Days: 5060

Solar Fraction: 47%

Auxiliary Heat: 5.13 BTU/DD/ft²

Passive Heating System(s): Direct gain, indirect gain (Trombe wall), isolated gain

Recognition Factors: Collector(s): South-facing glazing, mass wall glazing, greenhouse glazing, 301 ft² **Absorber(s):** Concrete slab, block mass wall **Storage:** Concrete slab, block mass wall—**capacity:** 4950 BTU/°F **Distribution:** Radiation, convection **Controls:** Operable vents and winds, moveable insulation, sunshades

Back-up: 19,500 BTU/H electric air-to-air heat pump, wood stove

This compact, 2-story house combines three methods of solar **collection** for heating: direct radiation, Trombe wall, glazing, and a greenhouse. At the upper level, direct solar radiation is **absorbed** and **stored** in a 12-inch deep by 30-inch wide concrete ledge located at windowsill height and running the length of the living/dining room. The block wall on the lower floor serves as the **absorber** and **storage** element for both the Trombe wall system and the adjacent greenhouse. Heat rises through the floor vents from the Trombe wall and greenhouse for **distribution** to the living/dining area on the upper level. Cooler air flows down through floor vents along the north side of the house to the basement, where it re-enters the greenhouse or Trombe wall through intake vents near the floor. Through-vents are located in the second bedroom on the house's south side to the first bedroom on the north. At night heat radiates from the mass slab, Trombe wall, and greenhouse wall to the interior spaces.

Overnight, the greenhouse is shut off, and, to control heat loss through all windows and vents, they are closed with curtains. Summer overheating is controlled by overhangs and additional fold-down panels above the Trombe wall. Both the greenhouse and Trombe wall have separate exterior vents for exhaust cooling in the summer.

As a conservation measure, earth is bermed to a 7-foot depth at the north side of the house; insulation values are R-18 and R-33 in the walls and ceilings.

82

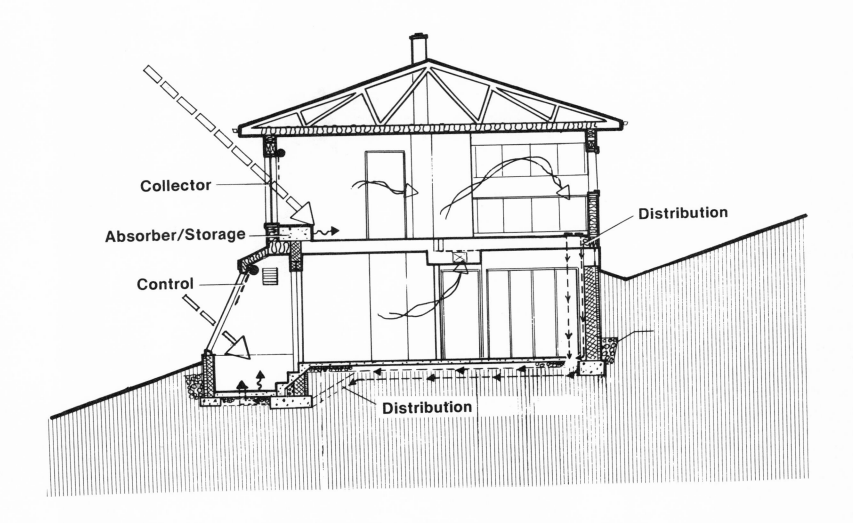

Collector

Absorber/Storage

Control

Distribution

Distribution

83

Virginia Beach, VA

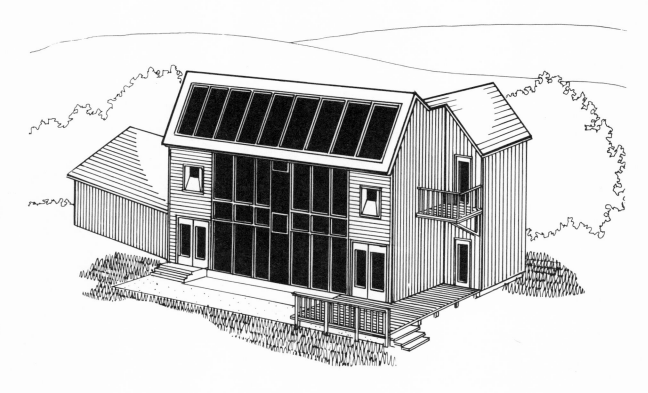

Builder: Warren L. Smith, Inc., Virginia Beach, VA

Designer: The Design Collaborative, Virginia Beach, VA

Solar Designer: Atlantic Solar Center, Inc., Virginia Beach, VA

Price: $125,000

Net Heated Area: 2512 ft²

Heat Load: 52.9 x 10⁶ BTU/yr

Degree Days: 3479

Solar Fraction: 55%

Auxiliary Heat: 2.58 BTU/DD/ft²

Passive Heating System(s): Indirect gain

Recognition Factors: Collector(s): South-facing insulated glass, south-facing Trombe wall glass 551 ft² **Absorber(s):** Solid brick wall **Storage:** Solid brick wall—**capacity:** 1511 BTU/°F **Distribution:** Radiation convection **Controls:** Canvas Trombe wall shades **Active Solar Heating:** 297 ft² liquid flat-plate collectors, 1000-gallon steel storage tank, hydronic distribution to back-up air system

Back-up: Electric air/air heat pump (63,000 BTU/H)

Domestic Hot Water: Active (see above) 80-gallon stone-lined storage tank

For energy conservation, this house has been designed with air-lock entries, a garage located on the northwest to block winter winds, and insulation values of R-24 in the walls and the crawl space floor and R-39 in the second floor ceiling.

This house features a solar mass wall system located on the south side of the house for the full height of both floors. To admit natural light to the south-facing rooms, the wall is in two parts with standard windows located between the two sections as well as on the left and right. The wall is 12-inch thick solid brick; a layer of glazing is in-

stalled in front of the brick, separated from it by 4 inches.

In winter, the sun's heat is **collected** through the glazing and is **absorbed** and **stored** in the wall. Gradually through the day and into the night, the wall **distributes** heat directly to the rooms by radiation. The mass of the wall makes this effect more pronounced in the evening. Also, the wall induces convection currents which **distribute** warm air through the house to the rooms on the north side. In the summer, heat gain by the Trombe wall is **controlled** by a canvas shade.

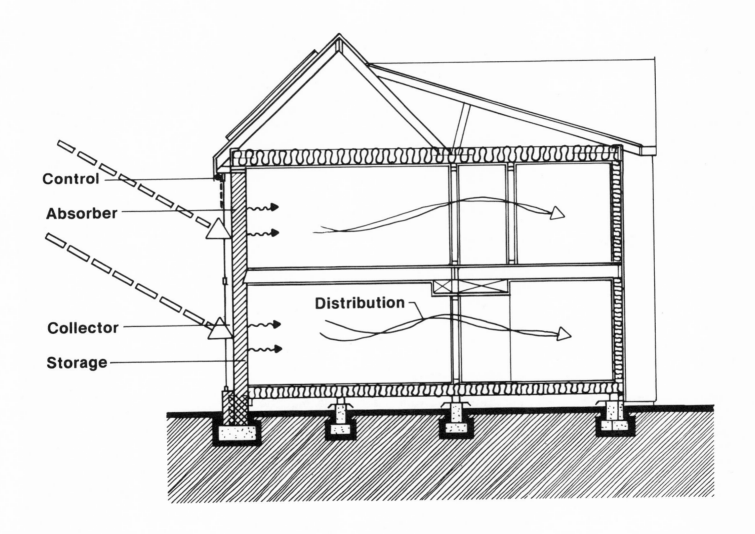

Control

Absorber

Collector

Storage

Distribution

Builder: Solar Design Studio & Assoc., Winchester, VA

Designer: New England Log Homes, Inc., Hamden, CT

Solar Designer: Solar Design Studio & Assoc., Winchester, VA

Price: $97,000

Net Heated Area: 1920 ft²

Heat Load: 55.9 x 10⁶ BTU / yr

Degree Days: 4305

Solar Fraction: 68%

Auxiliary Heat: 2.25 BTU / DD / ft²

Passive Heating System(s): Isolated gain, sun-tempering

Recognition Factors: Collector(s): South-facing dormer windows, double glazed acrylic panels, 369 ft² **Absorber(s):** Concrete slab floor, fiberglass water tanks **Storage:** Concrete slab floor, water in fiberglass tanks—**capacity:** 14,510 BTU/°F **Distribution:** Radiation, natural and forced convection **Controls:** Vents, ducts, dampers, insulated shades

Back-up: Air-to-air heat exchanger, electric resistance baseboard heaters, woodburning stove

Domestic Hot Water: Liquid flat-plate collector (63 ft²) used for DHW and hot-tub heating

This updated log house combines the traditional qualities of a log cabin—snug in winter, cool in summer—with passive solar components to meet the demands of climate in Virginia's northern Shenandoah Valley. The compact farmhouse design is in keeping with other rustic but high-priced houses on 5-acre lots in a rural development north of Winchester.

In the case of this house, the south-facing back porch has been transformed into a solar **collector** by enclosing all three of its sides in double-walled acrylic glazing. The south glazing is fixed except for a center sliding door; the east and west sides can be dismantled in summer to provide cross-ventilation.

Energy is **absorbed** and **stored** in the 6-inch concrete slab floor of the porch and in eight fiberglass water tanks, each 2 feet by 8 feet by 12½ inches, set along the south log wall of the house.

The second-floor southern exposure has a row of seven conventional dormer windows under a 1-foot-wide overhang.

Heat stored in the water tanks is **distributed** by natural convection, rising through a row of warm air vents at the top of the porch wall into the upstairs bedrooms. Excess heat is returned through a vent at the peak of the roof and pulled down a chimney duct by a destratification fan. The forced-air return duct continues under the living area slab floor and returns to the greenhouse/porch. At the base of the south wall of the house is a row of return air vents with backdraft dampers that allow a natural convecting flow to occur through the greenhouse. A dual directional damper at floor level at the base of the chimney duct diverts warm air from the second-floor ridge directly to the first-floor living areas at times when no heat is stored in the greenhouse.

Window quilts on all inside windows (R-5) and adjustable insulating shades (R-8) on the greenhouse glazing **control** heat loss in winter and heat buildup in summer. Roof insulation is R-36. Between all logs, two layers of rope caulk, two layers of foam gasket, and a hardboard spline minimize infiltration.

Back-up heat comes from electric base-board heaters and a woodburning kitchen range that sits back to back with a fireplace with adjustable outside air intake, glass doors, and an air-to-air firebox heat exchanger.

An active solar collector on the south roof of the carport heats domestic hot water and is also used for a hot tub on the porch.

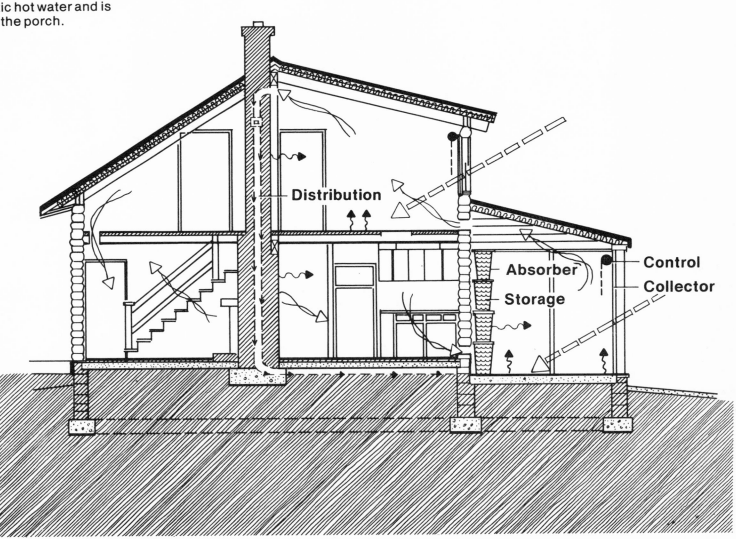

Distribution

Absorber

Storage

Control

Collector

Winchester, VA

Builder: Hinman Homes, Inc., Stephens City, VA

Designer: Crawford Hinman, Stephens City, VA

Solar Designer: One Design, Inc., Winchester, VA

Price: $130,000

Net Heated Area: 2035 ft²

Heat Load: 45.3 x 10⁶ BTU / yr

Degree Days: 4224

Solar Fraction: 76%

Auxiliary Heat: 1.29 BTU / DD / ft²

Passive Heating System(s): Direct gain, indirect gain

Recognition Factors: Collector(s): South-facing windows, acrylic panels, 402 ft² **Absorber(s):** Surface of fiberglass water tanks, brick wall **Storage:** Brick wall, water in fiberglass tanks—**capacity:** 18,835 BTU / °F **Distribution:** Radiation, natural convection **Controls:** Moveable insulating shades, window quilts, overhang, vents

Back-up: Air-to-air heat pump, woodburning stove

Domestic Hot Water: DHW preheat system

Passive Cooling Type: Natural and night ventilation

This passive solar house is a contemporary adaptation of a New England saltbox. Its innovative southern elevation of glass does not face the street. From the north with its prim center hall entrance, the house looks completely traditional with typical carriage lamps, small paned windows with shutters, and lintel moulding. The house is on a ridge of a heavily wooded, 2-acre lot outside of Winchester, Virginia, in a development where traditional homes are popular and tastes are conservative.

Garage, breezeway, evergreens, and heavy woods to the northwest protect against winter winds. The advantage of the ridge site, however, is its exposure to summer breezes and good drainage to cut down problems of indoor humidity.

The primary solar **collectors** are five floor-to-ceiling acrylic panels on the south side,

three upstairs and two down. Two French doors on the ground floor and double-hung windows on both floors, all double glazed, also act as **collectors**. All of these windows are standard "six-over-six," small pane sash structure that match the conventional windows on the east, west, and lower north sides. On these three elevations windows are triple glazed.

Owing to the deep saltbox dip of the roof, there are no upstairs windows to the north. Under these eaves, there are closets, bathrooms, and storage areas that act as buffers for the rest of the rooms.

Much of the collected solar energy is **absorbed** by modular fiberglass water tanks snapped together in five stacks of four tanks each. They stand behind the acrylic glazing at a distance of about 6 inches. Each tank has a capacity of 14.7 cubic feet and measures 94 x 12 x 22.5 inches.

Direct solar radiation to the living space, however, is **absorbed** and **stored** in a dark brick wall that forms the central core of the ground floor plan. Its "S" shape frames the woodburning kitchen range and the fireplace and chimney in the living room.

Distribution of heat is by radiation and natural convection. The water walls provide radiant heat at night when bifolding doors, closed in the daytime primarily to conceal the tanks, are opened to allow heat to radiate into the living room and three upstairs bedrooms. Heat from the water wall behind the kitchen is circulated via the toe space and cabinet soffit.

Heat loss is **controlled** by moveable insulating shades on the water wall glazing and window quilts (R-3) on all windows and doors. These shades and quilts are raised and lowered according to the time of day and the fluctuations of weather.

Cooling during the summer is by natural ventilation. Contributing to the efficiency of the system is an overhang, 1 foot 8 inches deep, which surrounds the house and shades all windows from summer sun. Continuous ridge and soffit vents will release attic heat.

The builder has paid close attention to energy-conserving features, with an emphasis on sealing and caulking. Front and side entrances have insulated air-lock vestibules. Waste heat from the refrigerator is used to preheat the domestic hot water.

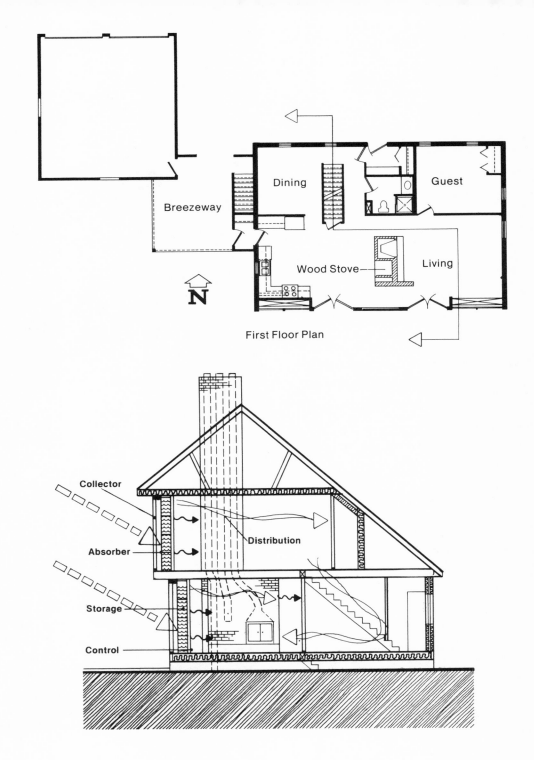

First Floor Plan

Browntown, VA

Builder: W. Allen Nicholls, Inc., Front Royal, VA

Designer: Design Konstruction, Bentonville, VA

Solar Designer: Design Konstruction

Price: $56,500

Net Heated Area: 1232 ft²

Heat Load: 56.3 x 10⁶ BTU/yr

Degree Days: 4350

Solar Fraction: 64%

Auxiliary Heat: 3.73 BTU/DD/ft²

Passive Heating System(s): Direct gain

Recognition Factors: Collector(s): South-facing windows and doors, clerestory windows, 308 ft² **Absorber(s):** Concrete slab floors, mass walls, surface of plastic containers **Storage:** Concrete slab floors, mass walls, water in plastic containers—**capacity:** 30,170 BTU/°F **Distribution:** Radiation, natural and forced convection **Controls:** Operable window quilts, thermostat

Back-up: Heat pump with an electric resistance coil wood stove

Passive Cooling Type: Natural and induced ventilation

The east, north, and west sides of this small rectangular house are three solid concrete block walls that are backed into the south-sloping side of a hill. The south-facing side of the house features two levels of glass. The site is on five acres of relatively uncleared land in a rural subdivision on a ridge of the Shenandoah Valley in Warren County, Virginia.

Collectors for the passive solar system are panels of double glass in the ground floor where the living room, flanked on each side by a bedroom, is located. On the upper floor, where a central family room looks down into the living room, a den to the west, and the kitchen/dining area to the east, a row of clerestory windows collects sunlight.

Concrete slab floors and the 12-inch solid walls **absorb** and **store** the direct solar heat. In addition, a specially insulated storage room, virtually underground at the center rear of the house, holds 1,152 1-gallon plastic containers for supplemental storage.

Heat is radiantly **distributed** from the storage walls and floor, and to avoid waste, a damper and fan system draw stratified air from the top of the clerestory area into the remote water storage closet. During periods of overheating, air can also be drawn through floor ducts beneath the concrete slab and discharged into the storage room. The storage closet can discharge through a series of **distribution** ducts to provide nighttime heating through the baseboard upstairs and from the ceiling of the ground floor.

All windows are fitted with hand-operated window quilts to **control** nighttime heat loss. A wood stove and a heat pump with an electric resistance coil provide back-up heat. When temperature in the storage area and the rest of the house is below the required level, auxiliary heat comes on and is distributed through slab vents and ducts.

In the summer, excess heat is released from the house through a vent stack whose fan pulls air through the hollow floor slab and exhausts it via a roof ventilator. Lower sections of the upstairs glass open for summer ventilation.

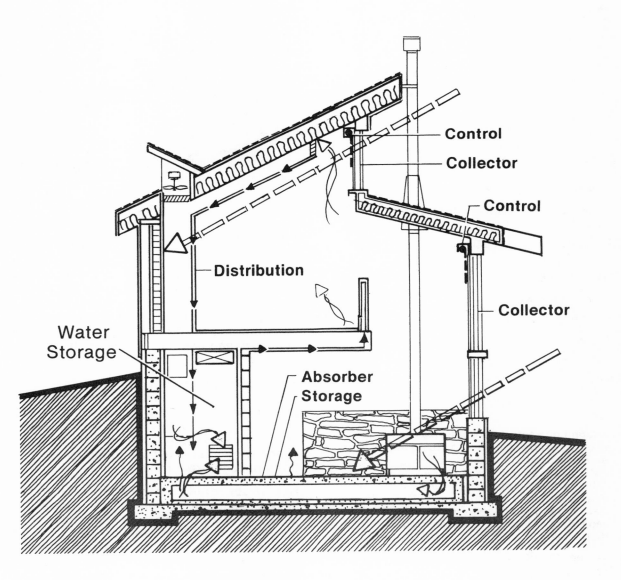

Builder: Wood Builders, Inc.

Designer: Donald Barnes, AIA, Architect, Raleigh, NC

Solar Designer: Donald Barnes, AIA, Architect, Raleigh, NC

Price: $85,000

Net Heated Area: 1700 ft²

Heat Load: 36.5 x 10⁶ BTU / yr

Degree Days: 3393

Solar Fraction: 59%

Auxiliary Heat: 2.66 BTU / DD / ft²

Passive Heating System(s): Isolated gain, direct gain

Recognition Factors: Collector(s): Glass and plastic glazed panels, south-facing windows, double-glazed sliding doors, clerestory windows, 354 ft² **Absorber(s):** Quarry tile pavers, concrete tribution, natural and forced convection **Controls:** Fixed overhangs, roll-down insulating quilts, slab floor **Storage:** Concrete mass slab floor— **capacity:** 15,444 BTU / °F **Distribution:** Radiant distribution, natural and forced convection **Controls:** Fixed overhangs, roll-down insulating quilts, slab floor **Storage:** Concrete mass slab floor— **capacity:** 15,444 BTU / °F **Distribution:** Radiant distribution, thermostat

Back-up: Woodburning stove and electric resistance heaters

Passive Cooling Type: Natural and induced ventilation

This traditional ranch-style home has its north side facing the street, which makes its appearance similar to other homes in the subdivision. The site slopes gently to the south and has no significant obstruction of its solar access.

Solar **collection** occurs on the south side of the building through two pairs of sliding glass doors and the clerestory windows of an atrium, and at eleven glass and plastic glazed panels divided (six and five) between two **collection** walls in the master bedroom and great room.

Heat is **absorbed** in the atrium and the hallway behind it by ½-inch quarry tile pavers, and **stored** by the 4-inch concrete slab beneath. In the collection wall **absorption** occurs in the black-enameled corrugated aluminum set within the space between the glazing and the interior wall. Heated air from this space is **distributed** in the following manner: as it rises to the top

of the wall, it is pulled through a duct by a fan to the bottom portion of a double plenum. This plenum runs along the bottom of the wall; from here the heated air is fed into every other core of double-core block positioned to form a concrete duct all the way back to the north wall. The hot air travels down one core of the block to the north wall, where a distribution duct directs its flow back down the other core, where it flows back into the collection space of the wall to be reheated and redistributed in the same manner. The fan is thermostatically set to cut out if the temperature of the absorber wall drops below a set point.

Meanwhile, the solar air that has passed through the floor has had its heat **absorbed** by the block and the 4-inch concrete slab laid over the block, causing it to radiate in a **controlled** manner up into the living areas. Additional heat is available from the atrium if all interior doors to that area are left open and the ceiling fan is turned on; this arrangement will cause hot atrium air to be **distributed** to the inner living areas. Heat loss is controlled with manually operated roll-down window quilts on all windows.

Back-up heat is available from a heatilator fireplace in the great room—drawing its combustion air from the outside—and electric resistance strips in the air conditioning/heating unit. This unit's duct system runs through the attic and reaches all rooms including the atrium.

In the summer mode, manually operated dampers in the collection wall/duct system are switched so that hot air at the top of the wall is exhausted outside by a separate duct fan. But the heating duct fan is also used on summer nights to draw cool air in and circulate it through the block and concrete slab floor. This will help keep the house cool during the next day. Heat gain is **controlled** in summer by fixed overhangs on all south-facing glass, and by an exhaust fan in the atrium. If windows in all rooms are left open, as well as interior atrium glass doors, this fan can change air in the house at the rate of once every six minutes. For peak cooling needs there is central air conditioning.

The insulation values for the house are R-30 for the roof and R-23 in the walls. All windows and glass doors are double glazed, and all entries are through air-lock vestibules.

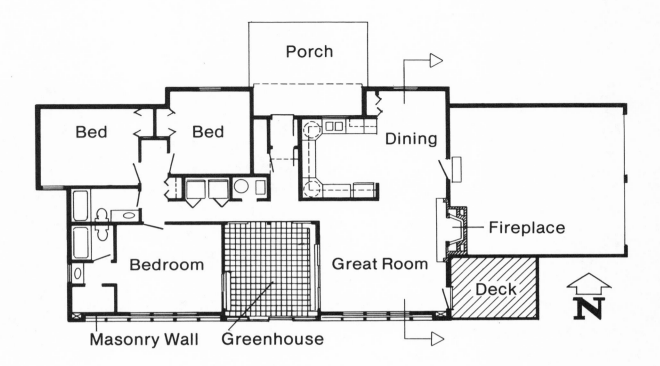

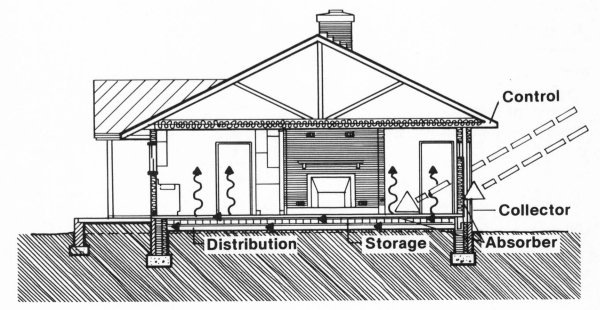

Builder: Millen Properties, Inc., Atlanta, GA

Designer: Paul Muldawer, Atlanta, GA

Solar Designer: Don Abrams, Atlanta, GA

Price: $55,000

Net Heated Area: 2039 ft²

Heat Load: 49.3 x 10⁶ BTU/yr

Degree Days: 2961

Solar Fraction: 51%

Auxiliary Heat: 4.08 BTU/DD/ft²

Passive Heating System(s): Direct gain, indirect gain, sun-tempering

Recognition Factors: Collector(s): South-facing double glazing, clerestory windows, 342 ft² **Absorber(s):** Concrete floor and wall, surface of water tubes **Storage:** Concrete floor and wall, water-filled tubes—**capacity:** 35,324 BTU/°F **Distribution:** Radiation, natural convection **Controls:** Overhangs, shading panels, water-tube covers, shading louvers

Back-up: Gas furnace (40,000 BTU/H)

Domestic Hot Water: 80-gallon storage

94

This compact 2-level house includes such design features as major glass areas, diagonal wood siding, and a vaulted clerestory. The building site slopes gently to the south away from the street, which runs along the high north boundary of the lot; a recreation area guaranteeing future solar access is on the low south boundary. Prevailing winter winds are deflected from the house by evergreens on the northwest and by shrubs adjacent to the north, east, and west walls of the house. Additionally, all sides of the lower floor, except the south, are buried, effectively blocking most infiltration to this level.

The lower level includes an entrance through the 2-car garage, a laundry room, and a playroom. The major living spaces are located on the upper level.

Three passive **collection** systems are used in this house. The first is 150 square feet of double-glazed clerestory windows. The second is a 120 square-foot double glass, direct solar heating system. The third is 60 square feet of double glass that heat water-filled tubes.

Absorption of heat for the direct system includes the surface of the slab in the lower level and the plaster surface of the north masonry wall of the upper level. **Storage** of this absorbed heat is in the mass of the masonry floor and wall. The 12-inch diameter water tubes both **absorb** and **store** heat.

Distribution of heat is by radiation from the masonry wall and concrete floor. Natural convection **distributes** heat from the water tubes. Cool air enters a vent in the bottom of the tube enclosure, contacts the warm tubes, is heated, and rises through a vent at the top of the tube enclosure into the living spaces above.

Control of the solar radiation is by fixed overhangs and seasonal shading panels that eliminate unwanted heat gains. The indirect gain system can be **controlled** by moving covers over the water tube modules to stop transfer of heat up into the living spaces. Throughout the summer months sun is blocked from reaching the tubes by fixed shading louvers above them.

Additional energy-conserving features of this house include: operable windows in high spaces to encourage natural ventilation during the cooling season; good wall and ceiling insulation; programmable thermostatic control of the back-up heating system; energy-saving appliance and fixtures; and an outside air source convection-type fireplace with glass doors.

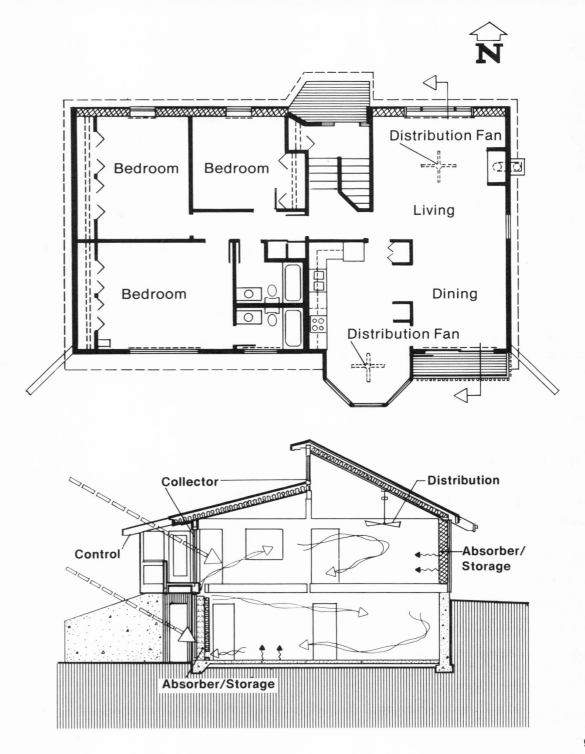

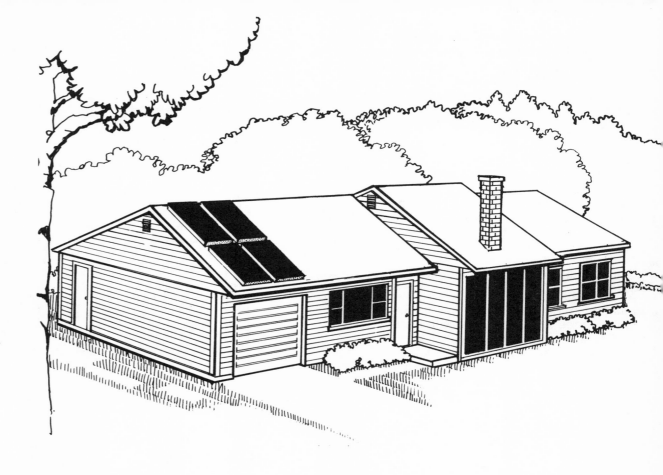

Snellville, GA

Builder: Hairston Enterprises, Inc., Snellville, GA

Designer: Sol Ahorrar Homes, Newman, GA

Solar Designer: B. Cruickshank, Atlanta, GA

Price: $52,900

Net Heated Area: 1175 ft²

Heat Load: 30.4 x 10⁶ BTU/yr

Degree Days: 3095

Solar Fraction: 65%

Auxiliary Heat: 2.85 BTU/DD/ft²

Passive Heating System(s): Sun-tempering, indirect gain

Recognition Factors: Collector(s): Double-glazed glass, single-glazed Trombe wall, 295 ft² **Absorber(s):** Concrete Trombe wall painted black **Storage:** Concrete Trombe wall—**capacity:** 3890 BTU/°F **Distribution:** Radiation, natural convection **Controls:** Insulating curtain, drapes, overhangs

Active Solar Heating: 120 ft² liquid flat-plate collectors, 500-gallon storage

Back-up: Gas furnace (64,000 BTU/H)

Domestic Cooling Type: Underground plastic cooling tubes, natural and induced ventilation

This economical 1-story home is part of a 50-unit subdivision. The developer has planted both deciduous and evergreen trees to provide summer shading and winter windbreaks on the previously treeless tract lot. Because cooling needs are very important for this southern location, the house plan features a garage and mechanical space on the west side that block the later afternoon sun from striking living areas of the house. Bedrooms are located on the east side to help keep them cool during summer nights. Insulation is well beyond the requirements of the mild local winters (R-38 ceiling, R-19 floor, R-22 walls, and a continuous vapor barrier with double foil), but it also serves to reduce the summer cooling loads. Cooling is also the objective of an experimental 500-foot long, 4-inch diameter plastic pipe, laid 4 feet underground in the back yard. It will provide cool earth-tempered air to the house.

A modest passive heating system is appropriate for this mild climate. The primary passive **collector** is just under 100 square feet of glazing over a Trombe wall on the south side of the great room. The **absorber** is the flat black paint of the poured concrete **storage** wall. **Distribution** from this system is by natural convection during the day and by radiation from the wall at night. **Control** of overheating is provided by a fixed building overhang.

96

The house also features an extensive array of energy-conserving appliances and equipment, including: an active solar system contributing to both space heat and domestic hot water needs, high-efficiency appliances, water flow restrictors, and high-efficiency heating, cooling, and lighting systems.

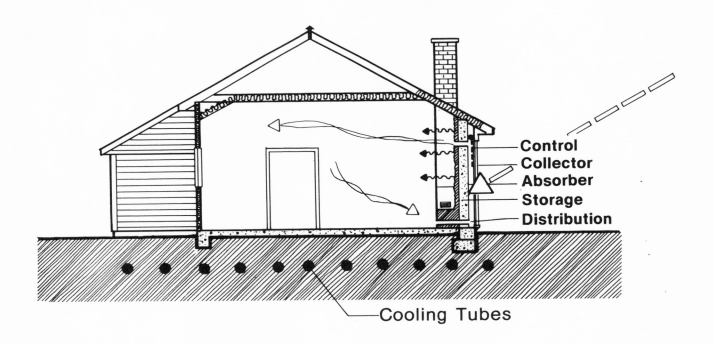

Control
Collector
Absorber
Storage
Distribution

Cooling Tubes

McCaysville, GA

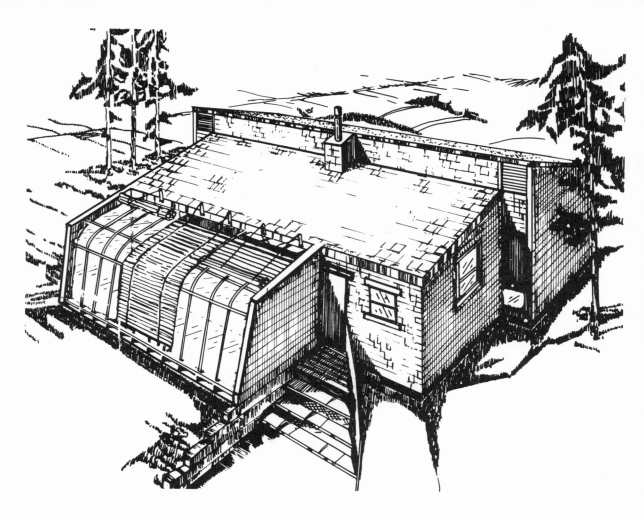

Builder: Walnut Town & Country, Epworth, GA

Designer: Richard Seedorf, Atlanta, GA

Solar Designer: Donald Abrams, Atlanta, GA

Price: $29,500

Net Heated Area: 1073 ft²

Heat Load: 26.8 x 10⁶ BTU/yr

Degree Days: 2961

Solar Fraction: 81%

Auxiliary Heat: 1.59 BTU/DD/ft²

Passive Heating System(s): Direct gain, isolated gain, indirect gain

Recognition Factors: Collector(s): South-facing glass, greenhouse, 376 ft² **Absorber(s):** Black 55-gallon drums, concrete floor **Storage:** Water-filled drums, masonry wall, concrete floor—**capacity:** 16,485 BTU/°F **Distribution:** Natural convection, radiation **Controls:** Moveable insulation panels, floor registers, backdraft dampers, shades

Back-up: Electric resistance heaters, woodburning stove

Passive Cooling Type: Induced ventilation

This design is an affordable, energy-efficient alternative to the mobile home, the prevalent budget-housing type of the area. It has been planned to include a number of energy-conserving features. It is well zoned, with living areas on the south and sleeping areas to the north. The south side of the heavily wooded lot has been cleared of native pines to permit better solar access, while on the east, north, and west sides of the lot additional plantings have been made to fend off winter winds.

Three types of passive systems are used. A sunken greenhouse that occupies two-thirds of the south wall **collects** sunlight to heat the house. Second, a wall of water-filled drums located under and adjacent to the living/dining space acts as an **absorber** and a **storage** medium. Finally, direct solar radiation through south-facing windows provides **collection** for two of the bedrooms, the kitchen, and the living/dining room.

There is a wood stove in the dining room and electric resistance heaters in each of the three bedrooms. **Storage** is generously sized for a house in Georgia's climatic zone and includes a total of 28 water-filled 55-gallon drums painted flat black; there is a concrete floor in the greenhouse as well. The drums are located in the greenhouse, in supply ducts under the floor of the living room, and also in the mass water wall adjacent to the living room/dining room. An 8-inch masonry wall in the center of the house between the living/dining area and the bedroom helps **control** temperature swings by providing **storage** for heat radiated from the wood stove.

Heat is **distributed** primarily by natural convection and radiation. The drums of water adjacent to the living and dining areas radiate their heat to those spaces. This warm air rises to the ceiling along the south wall and from the ceiling falls into the registers along the north wall. This cooler air then moves through under-floor ducts to the heated drums where the cycle begins again. Natural convection also **distributes** the radiant heat from the thermal storage walls and greenhouse water drums.

This house has a number of **control** devices. Nighttime heat loss through windows is minimized by moveable insulation panels. The concrete floor in the greenhouse and the concrete wall around the water drums are insulated to ensure that heat is returned to the house's living space. The natural convection circuit is **controlled** by the use of manual floor registers to prevent excessive heat build-up and by natural backdraft dampers to prevent cool air from flowing down to the heated drum storage area.

In warm weather, cooling is accomplished by cross-ventilation and by opening louvers in the ceiling, which allows hot air to rise and exit through the exhaust vent at each end of the house. Also, greenhouse heat gain can be cut by 80 percent with the manually operated roll-down shades.

In summary, the Walnut Town and Country House demonstrates a number of low-cost passive approaches in a compact, well-insulated house that should be an appealing alternative to budget-minded buyers.

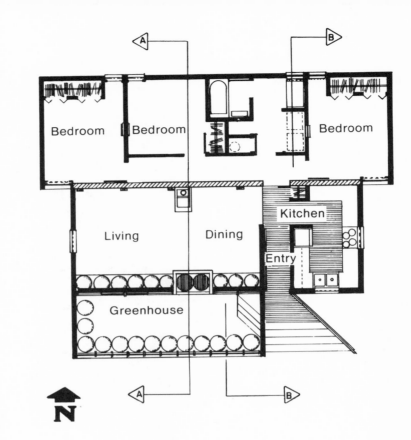

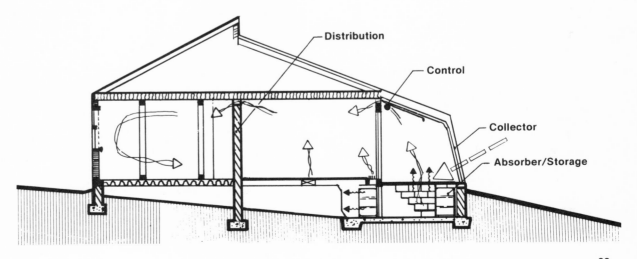

Huntsville, AL

Builder: The Southard Companies, Guntersville, AL

Designer: Jones & Herrin, Architects, Huntsville, AL

Solar Designer: Architectural Design Branch, Tennessee Valley Authority, Knoxville, TN

Price: $79,500

Net Heated Area: 2000 ft²

Heat Load: 56.2 x 10⁶ BTU/yr

Degree Days: 3302

Solar Fraction: 23%

Auxiliary Heat: 6.48 BTU/DD/ft²

Passive Heating System(s): Direct gain, indirect gain

Recognition Factors: Collector(s): South-facing glazing, 412 ft² **Absorber(s):** Concrete block walls, brick-paved floors **Storage:** Concrete block, Trombe wall, brick atrium floor—**capacity:** 19,630 BTU/°F **Distribution:** Radiation, natural and forced convection **Controls:** Insulating draperies and panels, sliding doors, vents

Back-up: Heat pump (63,000 BTU/H), electric resistance heaters, wood stove

Passive Cooling Type: Natural and induced ventilation

This compact 2-story house is part of a 144-unit development. The site is level, with deciduous trees to the south and evergreens to the north planted by the developer as buffers. The house, priced for middle- to upper-income buyers, is contemporary in style, featuring vaulted ceilings, a tight wall/roof envelope, triple glazing, and a dramatic atrium. The south windows face picturesque nearby mountain ridges. The garage and service rooms on the north buffer the living spaces from prevailing winter winds.

The passive system includes three distinct **collection** modes. The first is direct radiation through over 400 square feet of south-facing windows into all major rooms except the kitchen. The second is a pair of 2-story masonry Trombe walls. The third is a large central atrium.

Absorption and **storage** of solar energy in the directly heated spaces is accomplished by the concrete block walls of the dining room and atrium as well as in the brick-paved floor of the atrium. Concrete block wall serves as the **storage** mass in the ventless Trombe walls. Heat is **distributed** by radiation from the storage walls and floors.

Control mechanisms are used extensively to achieve the desired comfort ranges and to reduce heat losses. The atrium and the masonry walls are equipped with insulating draperies for use at night and during cloudy winter periods. The sliding glass doors that link the atrium and great room **control** convective heat flows between these spaces. Vents on the innovative "ice-house" roof are closed manually during the winter to trap heated air within the roof structure. Insulated panels, also operated manually, seal the clerestory vent when it is not needed in winter. A ceiling fan in the atrium recirculates warm air that has stratified, increasing comfort and preventing a waste of heat that has radiated from the storage walls and atrium floor.

Control mechanisms also assist the summer cooling process. Fixed louvers shade the south-facing glass from sunlight during summer. Glass doors in front of the Trombe mass walls open to reduce summer heat buildup. Sliding glass doors and operable windows in most rooms allow cross-ventilation which, along with well-placed clerestory exhaust fans, provide increased summer cooling through an induced chimney effect.

Aside from sophisticated approaches to passive cooling, ventilation, and control,

the designer has used back-up heating systems and well-chosen home appliances to save energy. An air-to-air heat pump moves heat from the upper levels of the house and from the area over the wood stove to the lower level. In this process, the heat pump circulator fan operates without activating the heat pump. The house will also include a dishwasher with an energy-saver cycle and a water heater with a programmable clock timer, all of which save energy with no extra effort on the part of the homeowner.

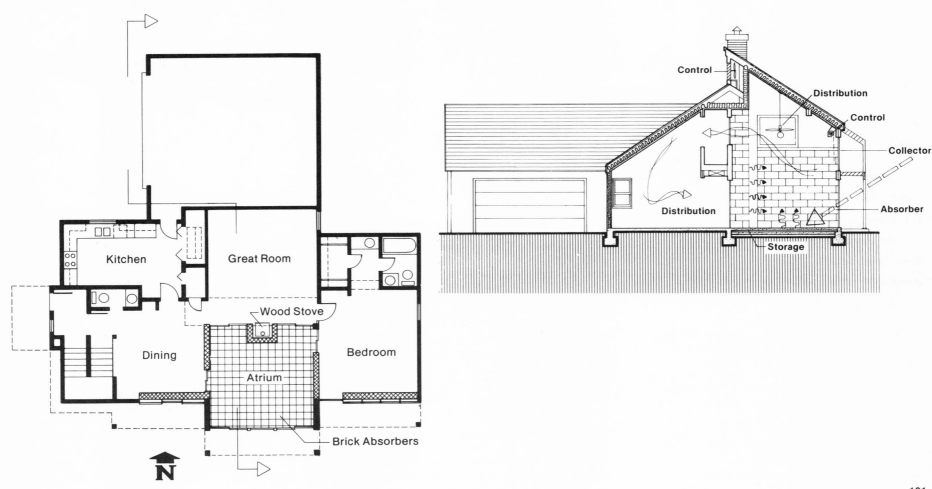

Prattville, AL

Builder: Simmons Builders, Prattville, AL

Designer: Chambless-Killingsworth & Associates, Montgomery, AL

Price: $80,000

Net Heated Area: 2066 ft²

Heat Load: 37.8 x 10⁶ BTU / yr

Degree Days: 2291

Solar Fraction: 37%

Auxiliary Heat: 5.16 BTU / DD / ft²

Passive Heating System(s): Direct gain, sun-tempering

Recognition Factors: Collector(s): South-facing double-glazed windows, 169 ft² **Absorber(s):** Floor quarry tile **Storage:** Concrete floor slab—**capacity:** 11,650 BTU / °F **Distribution:** Natural and forced convection, radiation **Controls:** Insulating shutters

Back-up: Gas-fired hot air furnace

Domestic Hot Water: 3 flat-plate collectors (58 ft²), 66-gallon storage

Passive Cooling Type: Natural ventilation

This home is a contemporary design with diagonal siding, stone accent walls, and a low-profile hip roof. The surrounding forest, new earth berms, and generous new landscaping contribute to the rustic flavor of the design, while helping to reduce cooling and heating costs in this hot southern climate.

The main solar collector is comprised of over 100 square feet of south-facing double glass in the den and living room. The windows located on the south wall of the master bedroom suite are also double glazed.

Tile floors in the den and living room **absorb** direct solar radiation, and the concrete slab under these tiles **stores** the heat. Radiant **distribution** from the floor is aided by natural convective air flow to provide even and comfortable heating of the house. Control of heat loss is accomplished by the use of bifolding insulating shutters on south-facing windows.

The return air for the furnace is preheated by the south-facing glass in the cupola. This high central space also enhances summer ventilation by permitting hot air to escape via north side louvers. These are sealed during the heating season by lowering a hinged insulating shutter. Cooling is also aided by overhangs to shade the glass and by a light-colored roof to reflect sunlight. The house also features a set of three roof-mounted, flat-plate active solar collectors for preheating domestic hot water.

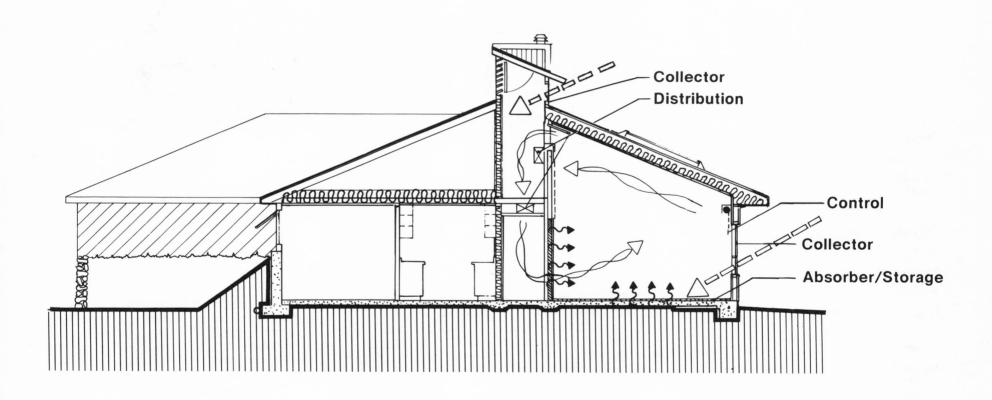

Collector

Distribution

Control

Collector

Absorber/Storage

103

Nashville, TN

Builder: Adanoroc Corporation, Nashville, TN

Designer: Adanoroc Corporation, Nashville, TN

Solar Designer: Watt Court Engineering Systems, Nashville, TN

Price: $64,900 to $68,500

Net Heated Area: 1138 ft²

Heat Load: 32.7 x 10⁶ BTU/yr

Degree Days: 3578

Solar Fraction: 42%

Auxiliary Heat: 4.60 BTU/DD/ft²

Passive Heating System(s): Sun-tempering, indirect gain

Recognition Factors: Collector(s): South-facing double glazing, 234 ft² **Absorber(s):** Mass wall surface **Storage:** Concrete mass wall—**capacity:** 4147 BTU/°F **Distribution:** Radiation, forced convection **Controls:** Draperies, shades, and Trombe wall shades, dampers

Back-up: Air-to-air heat pump (26,000 BTU/H)

Domestic Hot Water: 34.5 ft² liquid flat-plate collectors, 80-gallon storage tank

104

This 1-story condominium is part of a 123-unit development. It is the southeast end unit of an attached row of houses set on a southeast-northwest axis. The location is beneficial because the other houses in the row buffer this house from cold northwest winds. The house is also on the brow of a gentle south slope, where deciduous trees on its east and west sides block the early morning and late afternoon summer sun. The house is priced for middle-income buyers and is contemporary in style.

In contrast with most other passive designs, this house does not face south; its major collection wall is oriented at approximately 45 degrees east of south and its secondary collection wall is oriented at approximately 45 degrees west of south. Two passive **collection** modes are used. The first is 144 square feet of double glass in front of a concrete block Trombe wall on the southeast side of the great room. The second is 90 square feet of double glass to heat the kitchen on the southeast and both of the southwest-facing bedrooms.

Solar radiation striking the Trombe wall is **absorbed** by its blackened surface. Heat storage is provided by 144 cubic feet of grouted solid concrete block. The solar radiation **collected** by the windows in the kitchen is **absorbed** by floor and wall finishes, but these have minimal storage capacity. Because these kitchen windows are not oversized, overheating is not expected to be a problem.

Distribution of heat is by radiation and a forced-air system. Heat absorbed by the concrete block wall during the day eventually penetrates the wall and is radiated to the great room at night. The wall also plays a part in the house's conventional heating system. When the wall reaches a temperature of 80°F, air is drawn between its surface and its glass cover. The air is heated as it contacts the blackened surface, and is pulled by the heat pump fan through a duct along the top of the mass wall, to the back-up heat pump blower where it is **distributed** through floor ducts to all the rooms of the house.

Control of the operation of the mass wall is by a sophisticated group of automatic and manual mechanisms. An automatically operating reflective venetian blind set between the glass and the surface of the mass wall prevents overheating of the wall. A manually operated set of drapes on the room side of the mass wall prevents overheating of the great room. Automatic dampers close when the mass wall temperature exceeds 105°F to avoid ducting of high temperature air to the living space.

Besides passive heating, the house includes a number of energy-conserving features. A roof-mounted, liquid flat-plate solar collector with an 80-gallon storage tank provides one-half of domestic hot water needs. Water-conserving shower heads are used. The bathrooms and kitchen are lit by fluorescent lights. The building is well insulated and includes: an R-17 wall assembly, an R-31 ceiling assembly, and double-glass windows with insulating curtains. Finally, the building is constructed to be extremely resistant to infiltration.

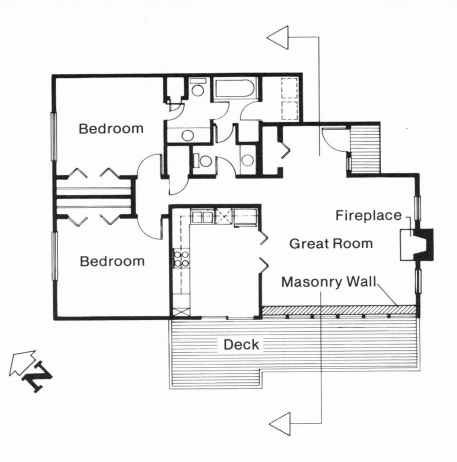

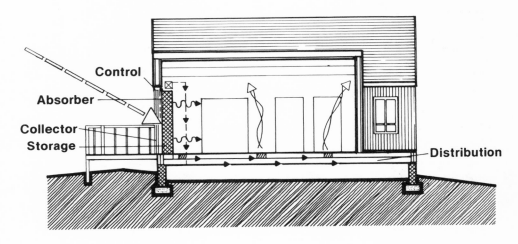

Builder: Winston Cox Admiral Construction Company, Oak Ridge, TN

Designer: Ron E. Barstow, Knoxville, TN

Solar Designer: Ron E. Barstow

Price: $85,000

Net Heated Area: 1939 ft²

Heat Load: 53.7 x 10⁶ BTU / yr

Degree Days: 3949

Solar Fraction: 83%

Auxiliary Heat: 1.13 BTU / DD / ft²

Passive Heating System(s): Direct gain, sun-tempering

Recognition Factors: Collector(s): Double-glazed windows, 548 ft² **Absorber(s):** Concrete brick floor **Storage:** Concrete brick floor, cement block wall —capacity: 65,474 BTU / °F **Distribution:** Radiation, natural and forced convection **Controls:** Insulating shutters, shades, overhangs

Back-up: Air-to-air heat pump (18,000 BTU / H), woodburning stove

This compact, contemporary home is part of a popular development in Oak Ridge, Tennessee. A pasture to the south and a tree-covered slope to the north constitute an ideal site for a solar building.

Collectors include over 500 square feet of double glazing. The **absorber** for the direct gain systems is the surface of a brick floor in the living room, in the front of the master bedroom, and in the greenhouse. A greenhouse and an isolated clerestory are primarily sun-tempered spaces and, by definition, use the room air as the **absorber**.

Storage for both collector systems is the first-floor slab and cement block walls. Charging of the **storage** masses associated with the clerestory occurs with the activation of a fan that forces air from this high space to the storage slabs and walls below. **Distribution** of heat from the storage is by radiation and natural convection. **Control** mechanisms include: manually operated, insulating shutters to decrease winter night heat loss; overhangs, manually operated reflective shades, and deciduous trees to minimize summer day heat gain; and a combination of operable windows and an attic fan to limit summer heat buildup. Earth berms buffer the winter winds and help to keep things cool in the summer.

The house also features several energy-conservation strategies. Over 3 inches of foam insulation on the exterior face of block walls and 12-inch fiberglass ceiling batts produce an effective thermal envelope. Extra insulation around both the refrigerator and the oven, water-conserving plumbing fixtures, and energy-conserving appliances are other energy savers that complete this design.

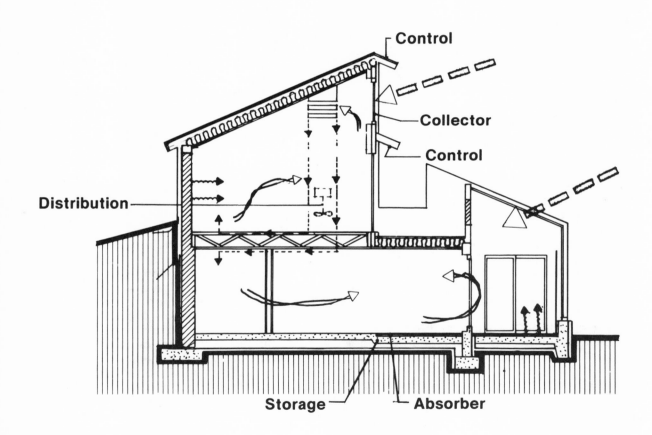

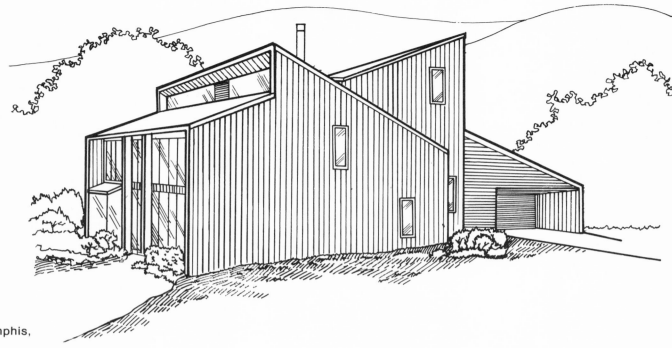

Memphis, TN

Builder: R. N. Stanley Construction Co., Memphis, TN

Designer: Solar Energy & Environmentally Designed Systems, Memphis, TN

Solar Designer: Solar Energy & Environmentally Designed Systems

Price: $90,000

Net Heated Area: 2560 ft²

Heat Load: 72.1 x 10⁶ BTU/yr

Degree Days: 3232

Solar Fraction: 78%

Auxiliary Heat: 1.95 BTU/DD/ft²

Passive Heating System(s): Direct gain, suntempered

Recognition Factors: Collector(s): Double-glazed windows, 655 ft² **Absorber(s):** Concrete and stone floor **Storage:** Concrete and stone floor— **capacity:** 21,388 BTU/°F **Distribution:** Radiation, natural and forced convection **Controls:** Overhangs, shades, fans, curtains

Back-up: Gas forced-air furnace (48,000 BTU/H)

This large contemporary home is designed from the ground up for passive solar energy collection and energy conservation. Its flared southern elevation, shaded by deciduous trees through the summer, presents a large area of glass for winter solar heat **collection.** The narrower northern side is nearly windowless and is buffered by three-foot earth berms, evergreens, and a well-placed carport. A 2- x 6-foot R-22 wall; R-30 ceiling; and R-4 moveable insulation over windows; and R-15 floor comprise the insulation envelope.

The passive solar heat **collection** systems include 200 square feet of south-facing, double glass opening on the exterior or looking into the greenhouse. **Absorption** and **storage** is in the concrete and stone floor of the greenhouse. In addition, overheated air in the house is controlled by being fan-forced into an insulated rock **storage** bed under the greenhouse floor. **Distribution** of heat is by radiation from the floor and by the natural convection of air in the greenhouse. **Distribution** of the heat stored in the rockbed is by activation of the fan. Heat loss is **controlled** by the moveable insulation on windows. A separate rockbed, under the carport, is used to precool air for circulation directly through the house and as a cool air source during the cooling season. **Control** of unwanted heat gain is provided by deciduous trees, overhangs, and manually operated roll-down exterior shades. In addition, exhaust fans at the top of the house induce air flows that ventilate the entire house. Winter air stratification is reduced by the use of high return-air registers feeding low supply-air registers.

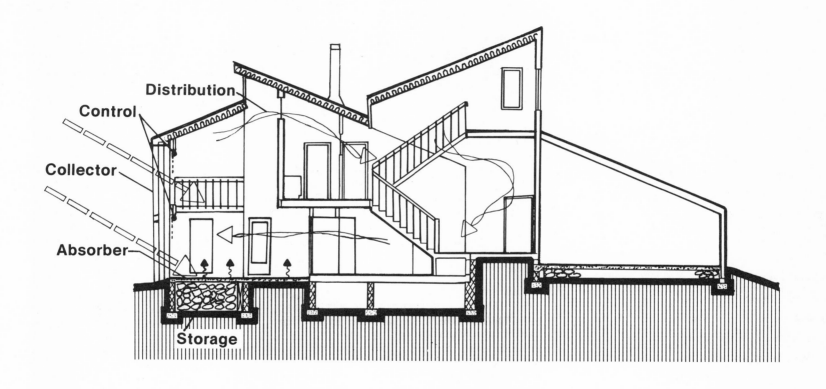

Distribution

Control

Collector

Absorber

Storage

109

Builder: Cliff Parrish, Franklin, TN

Designer: Gary L. Keckley, Nashville, TN

Solar Designer: Gary L. Keckley

Price: $150,000

Net Heated Area: 3537 ft²

Heat Load: 86.4 x 10⁶ BTU/yr

Degree Days: 3578

Solar Fraction: 98%

Auxiliary Heat: 0.16 BTU/DD/ft²

Passive Heating System(s): Sun-tempering, indirect gain (Trombe wall), isolated gain

Recognition Factors: Collector(s): South-facing double glazing, greenhouse glass, 1219 ft² **Absorber(s):** Greenhouse concrete floor, masonry Trombe walls **Storage:** Greenhouse concrete floor, masonry Trombe wall—**capacity:** 25,113 BTU/°F **Distribution:** Radiation, natural and forced convection **Controls:** Roll-down shade, insulated draperies, vents

Back-up: Air-to-air heat pump (45,000 BTU/H)

Domestic Hot Water: Liquid flat-plate collectors (77 ft²)

This spacious 2-story house is part of a small development priced for middle- and upper-income buyers. The house is located on a slight south slope that is shielded from prevailing winter winds by evergreens and shrubs to the north and northwest, and from summer sun by deciduous trees to the west.

It has zoning of spaces that permits solar gain. Downstairs, the most actively used spaces (kitchen, dinette, and family room) are concentrated in the center of the south side. Spaces receiving less use, the formal living room and dining room, are placed on the north side of the house, and service spaces (garage, pantry, and bedroom closets) act as thermal buffers at the windy corners. The upper floor is reserved for the children's bedrooms and playroom, allowing the owners to set back the heat in these areas when they are not occupied.

The house includes a list of other energy-conservation strategies that are important: (1) a recessed entry that reduces cold air infiltration; (2) wing walls to slow heat loss by promoting air turbulence and reducing

wind speed; (3) a steeply pitched roof with a storage area below it that buffers the upper-floor rooms; (4) an east-west building axis with a long south side and windowless east and west sides; (5) weatherstripped doors separating each of the three heating zones.

Three distinct passive **collection** systems are used. The first is direct radiation through south-facing double glass; the second is through double glass on several masonry Trombe walls, and the third is through greenhouse glass. **Absorption** and **storage** of solar energy from these systems is in the concrete floor of the greenhouse and in the darkened solid block walls of the Trombe system.

Distribution of heat from these systems is by radiation and natural convection. Solar radiation entering the house through south-facing windows is a source of early morning heat. Later in the morning the Trombe walls and greenhouse are warmed. By natural convection, air enters through vents low in the wall, becomes heated and rises up and out through vents high in these walls. After sunset, the heat stored in the mass of the Trombe walls and in the floor of the greenhouse continues to radiate into adjacent spaces until the next morning when the cycle begins again.

Heat loss is **controlled** by the use of insulated fixed glass; air-locks at all entries; 2-x 6-inch R-24, stud walls with a Mylar™ radiation barrier; an R-30 ceiling; and rigid insulation below and at the perimeter of the greenhouse slab and floor. Overheating is **controlled** by manual operation of an exterior, roll-down shade over the greenhouse, isolation of the skylight entry space, insulated draperies, exterior venting of the Trombe wall, and a fan-assisted ceiling vent in the greenhouse. A wood lattice shades the south walls from mid-May to mid-September.

Backing up this house's energy systems is a solar domestic hot water system and an air-to-air heat pump. The domestic hot water system includes 77 square feet of flat-plate collectors and a 52-gallon, quick-recovery, electric back-up. The air-to-air heat pump provides both cooling and back-up heating.

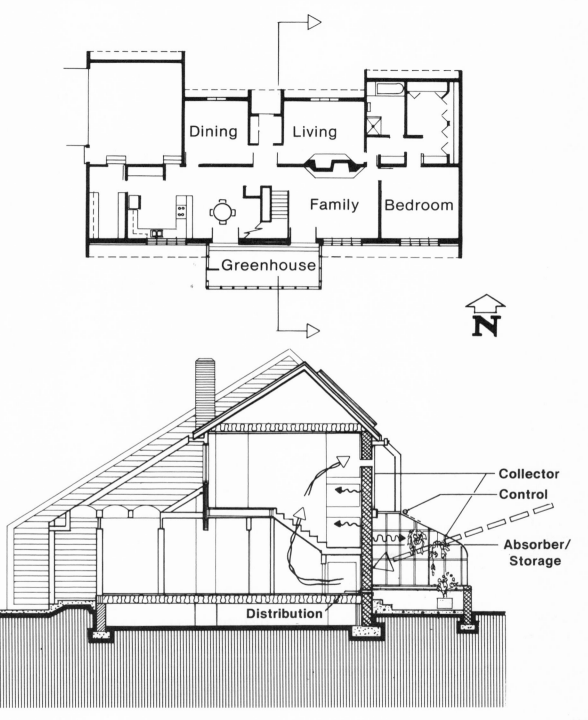

Pineville, LA

Builder: George Koncinsky, Builder, Alexandria, LA

Designer: George Koncinsky

Solar Designer: Southern Solar Systems, Alexandria, LA

Price: $135,000

Net Heated Area: 2294 ft²

Heat Load: 93.4×10^6 BTU/yr

Degree Days: 1921

Solar Fraction: 77%

Auxiliary Heat: 4.85 BTU/DD/ft²

Passive Heating System(s): Direct gain, isolated gain

Recognition Factors: Collector(s): South-facing double glazing, greenhouse glazing, 340 ft² **Absorber(s):** Greenhouse mass wall and floor, concrete floor **Storage:** Greenhouse mass wall and floor, concrete floor—**capacity:** 8,061 BTU/°F **Distribution:** Radiation, natural convection **Controls:** Insulated curtains, roof overhang, rolling shutters

Active Solar Heating: 202 ft² active hydronic collectors, 650-gallon storage tank

Back-up: Electric resistance heaters (62,300 BTU/H), water-to-air heat pump

Domestic Hot Water: Part of active solar system

This traditional saltbox design is part of a 100-unit subdivision. North-side pine trees and a garage act as a winter wind buffer. South-side trees have been removed to allow solar access.

Passive solar **collectors** include over 100 square feet of south-facing double glass. **Absorbers** and **storage** are the masonry wall and slab floor of the greenhouse. **Storage** for the living and dining rooms is a small area of concrete slab floor. **Distribution** is by radiation from the greenhouse masonry wall and natural convection of the air in the lower-floor to the upper-floor spaces. **Control** of heat loss is by operable insulated curtains. Heat gain is **controlled** by overhangs and operable ledge rolling shutters on south-facing win-dows and by vertical fins adjacent to east and west windows.

The house also features an extensive active solar system using roof-mounted, flat-plate liquid collectors. Heat collected from these solar panels is retained in a large storage tank, where it is used to preheat domestic hot water and as a heat sink for the water source heat pump.

Insulation values of R-17 in the walls and R-30 in the roof, including a vapor barrier, are adequate for the region. All three entries have unheated air-locks. Storage rooms, mechanical spaces, and closets are all unheated zones along the perimeter of the general living area. The floor plan and operable windows on east and west sides provide cross-ventilation and heat circulation.

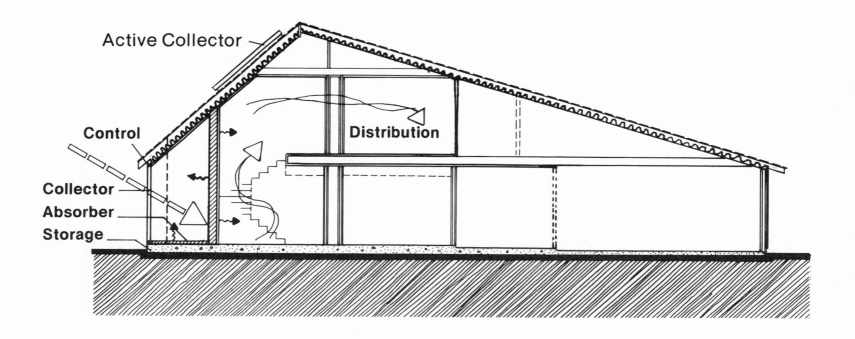

Active Collector

Control

Distribution

Collector

Absorber

Storage

Builder: Donald C. Oster & Associates, Inc., Kenner, LA

Designer: William Higgins, Cambridge, MA

Solar Designer: William Higgins

Price: $135,000

Net Heated Area: 2299 ft²

Heat Load: 33.6 x 10⁶ BTU / yr

Degree Days: 1385

Solar Fraction: 79%

Auxiliary Heat: 2.05 BTU / DD / ft²

Passive Heating System(s): Direct gain, sun-tempering, isolated gain (atrium)

Recognition Factors: Collector(s): Double-glazing, 664 ft² **Absorber(s):** Vinyl floor cover, brick paving **Storage:** Concrete floors, mass brick wall—**capacity:** 8148 BTU / °F **Distribution:** Radiation, convection **Controls:** Sliding doors, roll-down shades, insulated draperies, overhangs

Back-up: Electric hot-air furnace (68,000 BTU / H)

Domestic Hot Water: 60 ft² liquid flat-plate collectors

This large, 4-bedroom home has a traditional 2-story plan that includes extensive use of brick and siding, a vaulted sunlit entry, and natural ventilation. The plan exhibits functional zoning with a 2-car garage placed on the northwest corner to deflect prevailing winter winds and to protect the recessed front entrance. A separate heating zone for the second-floor bedrooms and study can be closed off when these areas are unoccupied, and a southern orientation allows heating of all major living spaces.

The house has an above-average insulation package for Louisiana. Walls are insulated to R-16 and the roof to R-33. All windows are double glazed and all window perimeters and other exterior penetrations for doors, wires, and pipes are sealed with insulating foam. The few windows with east and west exposures have operable exterior shutters for summer shading, and most windows open for natural ventilation. The operable clerestory windows are particularly helpful in promoting warm weather ventilation. The house includes three types of passive heating systems. Direct solar heat **collection** occurs in the breakfast room where the sun is **absorbed** by the vinyl floor cover and is **stored** in the concrete floor. Solar heat is also **collected** in the central atrium, which has brick paving on a 4-inch concrete slab for **absorption** and **storage**. The extensive clerestory windows and full-height windows in the dining and great rooms are used to **collect** solar energy but without any direct storage medium. **Distribution** of heat is by simple radiation and natural convection. **Control** of this air flow is by operation of the sliding glass linking the atrium to adjacent rooms. **Control** of potential summer overheating is by manually operated roll-down shades over the atrium and by fixed overhangs at all south windows.

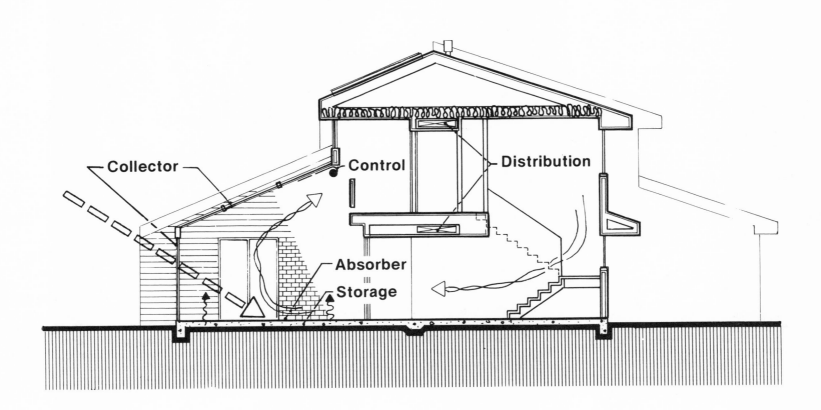

North Little Rock, AR

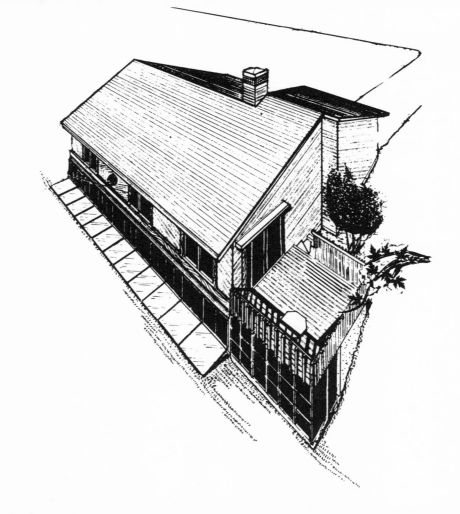

Builder: Winrock Homes, Inc., North Little Rock, AR

Designer: Arkansas Ark Builders, Inc., Little Rock, AR

Solar Designer: Bob Bland, Little Rock, AR

Price: $68,900

Net Heated Area: 1515 ft²

Heat Load: 24.4 x 10⁶ BTU/yr

Degree Days: 3219

Solar Fraction: 58%

Auxiliary Heat: 2.08 BTU/DD/ft²

Passive Heating System(s): Direct gain, isolated gain, indirect gain, sun-tempering

Recognition Factors: Collector(s): Double-glazed windows, greenhouse glass, 372 ft² **Absorber(s):** Black-painted metal sheets in thermosiphon ducts, ceramic tile floor **Storage:** Concrete storage slab, concrete block walls, rock storage bin—**capacity:** 26,856 BTU/°F **Distribution:** Radiation, convection **Controls:** Baseboard registers, moveable insulation panels, dampers, overhang

Back-up: Woodburning fireplace, gas furnace (40,000 BTU/H)

116

To further enhance the marketability of the best selling model in his large non-solar development, the developer converted the model into a passive solar house by adding a relatively inexpensive thermosiphon air collection system and a greenhouse. The change was made by adding a collection system to the south wall of the house, where the first floor is 4 feet above grade. (It is a grade on the north side, and there is no basement level.)

Added to the lower part of the south wall was a band of 24 double-glazed windows that project out approximately 8 inches from the main wall. This creates **collection** duct space leading to baseboard registers in the floor above. A sheet of expanded metal lath, painted black, is suspended in these ducts to **absorb** the solar energy. A 3-foot deep, 5-foot wide rock **storage** bin (600 cubic feet) was dug out and enclosed behind the thermosiphon duct spaces for the length of the house. Without the aid of fans the solar-heated air rises naturally to the baseboard registers on the first floor above. The baseboard registers may be closed to allow for daytime charging of the storage bin behind the collector. At night, an automatic damper closes the thermosiphon duct and the baseboard registers open. Cool air from the first-floor spaces is ducted under the house to the underside of the storage bin. From there, it flows through storage, extracting heat for supply again through the baseboard registers.

The thermosiphon system is supplemented by the **collection** of direct radiation through the south-facing windows (108 square feet). Heat is **absorbed** by a ceramic tile floor that covers the concrete storage slab. In the winter, heat loss is minimized by the moveable insulation panels on all the windows. Overheating in summer is controlled by the overhang of the south roof.

A 110-square foot greenhouse is located below the deck and uses a 24-inch deep bed of moist soil for heat storage. Air heated in the greenhouse is conveyed to registers in the north side of the dining room by means of a manually controlled damper system. In addition to the solar heat systems, the house has a centrally located woodburning fireplace on the first floor that contains a preheated coil for the conventional domestic water heater.

A number of other energy-conserving features are also included in the design. The house was sited with deciduous trees on the east and west to block low altitude summer afternoon sun. There is no glazing on the east and west elevation and minimal glazing on the north, but it is generous on the south elevation. Although all windows are single glazed, they can be closed off at night with sliding panels filled with urethane foam (R-10).

Exterior walls are constructed of 2- x 6-inch studs with 6-inch fiberglass plus 1-inch rigid insulation, for a total R-value of 23. There is also an aluminum foil windbreak on the exterior face of the studs to act as a wind infiltration barrier. Similarly, a 6 mil polyethylene vapor barrier is located on the inside face of the studs and ceiling joists. Twelve inches of fiberglass batts are installed in the ceiling joists (R-36), and a

thermal break of 1⅝-inch urethane foam has been installed between the house floor construction and the garage and deck floors.

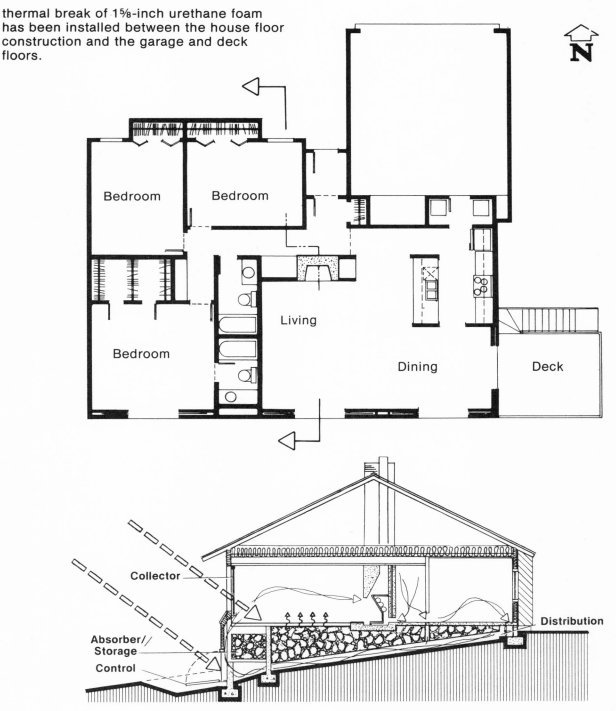

Hot Springs Village, AR

Builder: Village Homes, Inc.

Designer: James Lambeth Studio, Fayetteville, AR

Solar Designer: James Lambeth Studio

Price: $75,000

Net Heated Area: 1745 ft²

Heat Load: 80.0 x 10⁶ BTU / yr

Degree Days: 3220

Solar Fraction: 70%

Auxiliary Heat: 4.32 BTU / DD / ft²

Passive Heating System(s): Direct gain, indirect gain

Recognition Factors: Collector(s): South-facing glazing, 578 ft² **Absorber(s):** Water in tubes **Storage:** Water in tubes—**capacity:** 14,637 BTU / °F **Distribution:** Convection, radiation **Controls:** Drapes, overhangs

Back-up: Electric air-to-air heat pump (27,000 BTU / H)

Energy conservation receives great emphasis in the design of this custom house. Earth is bermed to a depth of 5 feet above floor level along the north wall. Inside, closets and a corridor run along the north wall, allowing all other rooms a southern exposure and generous natural lighting. The roof slopes to deflect cold winter winds over the house. For insulation, there are 12-inch fiberglass batts (R-40) in the roof, 8-inch batts (R-28) in the exposed south wall, and 6-inch batts in the floor joists (R-21). All solar energy is **collected** through south-facing windows or glass doors, 40 percent of which allow sunlight directly into the rooms for immediate warmth. Water tubes that **absorb** sunlight and **store** it as heat are located just inside the rest of the south-

facing glazing. In the central section of the house, there are 10 tubes 18 inches in diameter and 10 feet high, and in the bedrooms in the east and west wings 16 tubes 12 inches in diameter and 8 feet high. All of these tubes provide absorption and storage.

Gradually throughout the day and into the night the heat is **distributed** by radiation from the water tubes into all of the living spaces. At night, drapes are drawn across the windows to **control** heat loss to the outside. High-altitude sun cannot enter the house because it is blocked by a 4-inch roof overhang; while cooling ventilation flows through the house from the south sliding doors to windows in the north wall.

118

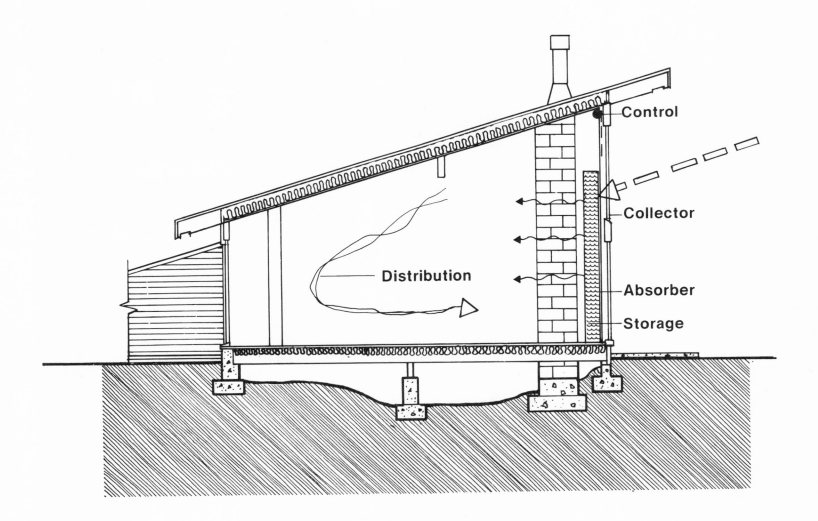

Control

Collector

Distribution

Absorber

Storage

119

College Station, TX

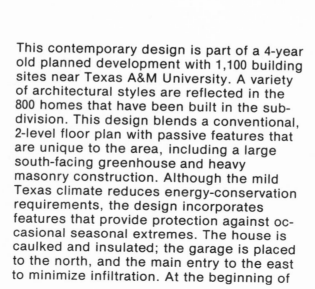

Builder: Dwayne Rhea Construction, Inc., College Station, TX

Designer: Entek Associates, Inc., College Station, TX

Solar Designer: Paul H. Woods

Price: $76,000

Net Heated Area: 1744 ft²

Heat Load: 36.0 x 10⁶ BTU/yr

Degree Days: 1617

Solar Fraction: 50%

Auxiliary Heat: 6.24 BTU/DD/ft²

Passive Heating System(s): Isolated gain

Recognition Factors: Collector(s): South-facing greenhouse glazing, 467 ft² **Absorber(s):** Concrete floor and wall **Storage:** Concrete floor and wall—**capacity:** not available **Distribution:** Radiation, natural and forced convection **Controls:** Moveable insulating panels, vents, roof overhangs, aluminum shade screens

Back-up: Electric heaters (24,000 BTU/H)

Domestic Hot Water: Liquid flat-plate collectors (38 ft²), 80-gallon storage

120

This contemporary design is part of a 4-year old planned development with 1,100 building sites near Texas A&M University. A variety of architectural styles are reflected in the 800 homes that have been built in the subdivision. This design blends a conventional, 2-level floor plan with passive features that are unique to the area, including a large south-facing greenhouse and heavy masonry construction. Although the mild Texas climate reduces energy-conservation requirements, the design incorporates features that provide protection against occasional seasonal extremes. The house is caulked and insulated; the garage is placed to the north, and the main entry to the east to minimize infiltration. At the beginning of

the cooling season, the greenhouse can be converted to an open porch by raising and latching the hinged exterior windows.

During the winter solar heat is **collected** through single-glazed windows in the first story greenhouse, and through windows of the second-story porches which also act as greenhouses. The concrete slab floor in the greenhouse and the interior and exterior masonry walls **absorb** and **store** the solar heat during the day. At night, heat is distributed as it is radiated back into the family room, dining room, and bedrooms. Manually activated ceiling fans on both levels assist the **distribution** of solar heat.

In this warm climate summer cooling is an important design consideration. The cooling needs of this house are met in the spring by raising the exterior hinged glass panels in the greenhouse and attaching them to the ceiling, thus creating an open porch on the south side of the house. Opening the French doors onto the greenhouse/porch, the second story awning windows and the north windows permit cooling of the house by natural cross-ventilation. The ceiling fans can be used to assist air movement. The attic is ventilated by an exhaust fan and by soffit and continuous ridge vents. When a back-up heat pump system is used as an air conditioner during the summer, all interior doors and windows are closed. The masonry storage elements are protected from solar gain in the summer by roof overhangs, vine and evergreen plantings, and aluminum shade screens on all windows.

Domestic water is heated by a Cole™ flat-plate solar collector system that uses water as a heat transfer medium. Freeze protection is provided by a pump that circulates water when the collector temperature is below 40°F.

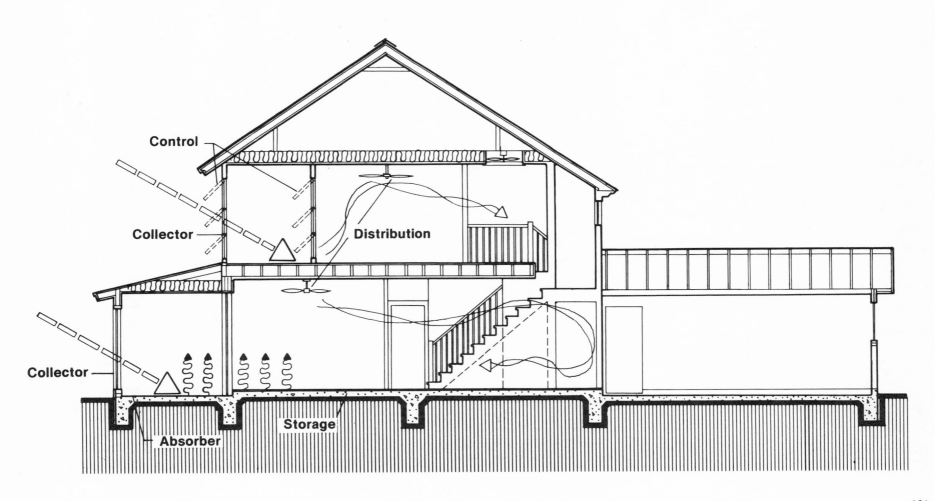

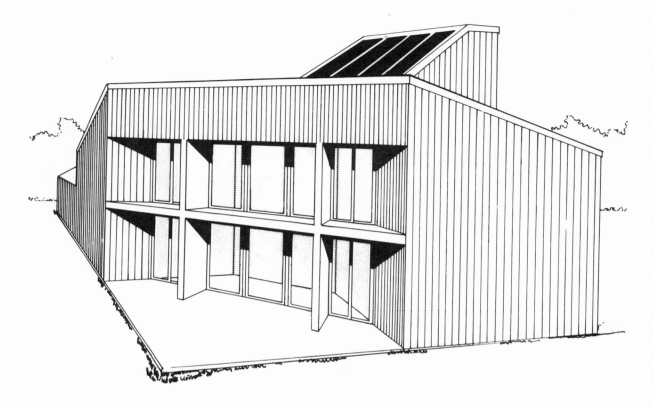

Builder: CTC Enterprises, Inc., Woodlands, TX

Designer: Michael Garrison, Architect, Austin, TX

Solar Designer: Michael Garrison

Price: $84,000

Net Heated Area: 1757 ft²

Heat Load: 20.8 x 10⁶ BTU/yr

Degree Days: 1414

Solar Fraction: 67%

Auxiliary Heat: 2.91 BTU/DD/ft²

Passive Heating System(s): Isolated gain

Recognition Factors: Collector(s): Greenhouse glazing, 210 ft² **Absorber(s):** Concrete mass wall and clay floor **Storage:** Concrete mass wall and clay floor; rock storage bin—**capacity:** 7709 BTU/°F **Distribution:** Radiation, convection, fan **Controls:** Dampers, shades, overhangs, thermostats

Back-up: Air-to-air heat pump (37,565 BTU/H)

Domestic Hot Water: Liquid flat-plate collectors (36 ft²)

Passive Cooling Type: Stack effect, solar chimney

An oblong hexagonal tower with a contemporary cupola is the salient feature of this 2-story house in southeast Texas. The longer sides of the hexagon face due north and south, sandwiching the house's "core spaces": stairs, mechanical room, bathrooms, entry, and a greenhouse. Bedroom spaces and the living room fill out the hexagon. From the northwest side of the hexagon, the dining room, kitchen, and garage are strung out from the living room, removing kitchen heating loads from the main living spaces and blocking prevailing winter winds from the house.

There are only a few windows on the north and east elevations, with none on the west to prevent summer afternoon overheating. South dining room and kitchen windows are recessed under roof overhangs for summer shading. The bulk of the south-facing glazing occurs at the two-story greenhouse that takes up the entire south face of the hexagon. The back wall of the greenhouse is 5½ feet inside the glazing and is 8-inch thick concrete. Solar energy **collected** by the greenhouse in winter is **absorbed** and **stored** by the mass wall and clay tile floor. Each bedroom and the living room open into the greenhouse through sets of sliding glass doors (the second-floor rooms open into balconies in the greenhouse space), and **distribution** of warm air from the greenhouse into these rooms is by natural convection. Under the stairs behind the mass wall is a rock **storage** bin. Warm air at the top of the greenhouse is blown into the rock bin by a thermostatically **controlled** fan for long-term storage.

At night, or on cloudy days, the mass wall radiates heat back into the greenhouse, which now acts as a buffer space, separating the warm living spaces from the cold outdoors. Also, preheated air from the rock storage is drawn up through the back-up heat pump for **distribution** through a conventional hot air duct system. Return air is drawn into a plenum beneath the rocks and then up for preheating. All fans and dampers are **controlled** by thermostats.

The greenhouse glazing is shaded by an egg-crate fin system in summer, while allowing the windows to be opened. There is a narrow aperture between the green-house and the louvered cupola so that heated air in the greenhouse can rise and exhaust itself, pulling warm house air outside. This process is assisted by an attic fan at the base of the cupola when necessary.

Insulation is adequate for this climate with 9-inch batts over the ceiling (R-26) and 4-inch batts in the wall (R-13). In addition, the wood siding is nailed over vertical strips, creating passages that are open at the bottom and top (protected by the eave). As the sun heats the wall, the air in the space rises and exhausts at the top, cooling the house wall.

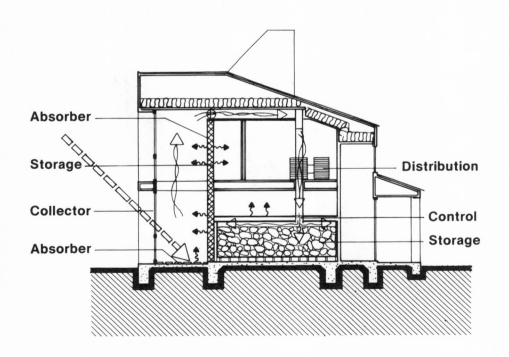

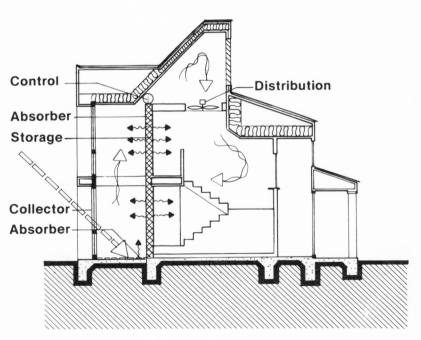

Mid-America

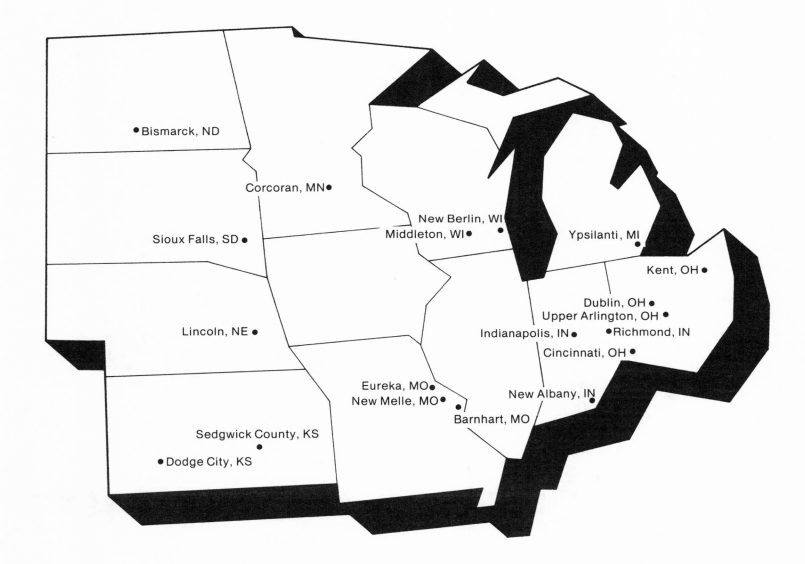

Bismarck, ND

Corcoran, MN•

New Berlin, WI•

Middleton, WI•

Ypsilanti, MI•

Sioux Falls, SD•

Kent, OH •

Dublin, OH •

Upper Arlington, OH •

Lincoln, NE•

Indianapolis, IN•   •Richmond, IN

Cincinnati, OH •

Eureka, MO•

New Melle, MO•

New Albany, IN•

Barnhart, MO•

Sedgwick County, KS•

•Dodge City, KS

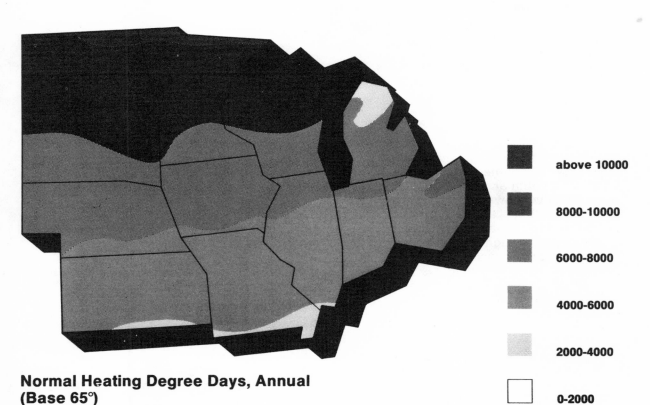

**Normal Heating Degree Days, Annual
(Base 65°)**

above 10000

8000-10000

6000-8000

4000-6000

2000-4000

0-2000

The Regional Solar Energy Center for Mid-America is:

Mid-American Solar Energy Complex
8140 26th Ave. S.
Bloomington, MN 55420
(612) 853-0400

The states served by it are:

Illinois
Indiana
Iowa
Kansas
Michigan
Minnesota
Missouri
Nebraska
North Dakota
Ohio
South Dakota
Wisconsin

Dublin, OH

Builder: Solartherm Building Systems, Columbus, OH

Designer: Joseph Kawecki, Columbus, OH

Solar Designer: Joseph Kawecki

Price: $90,000

Net Heated Area: 1828 ft²

Heat Load: 64.7 x 10⁶ BTU/yr

Degree Days: 5702

Solar Fraction: 41%

Auxiliary Heat: 3.64 BTU/DD/ft²

Passive Heating System(s): Direct gain, isolated gain

Recognition Factors: Collector(s): Double-glazed panels, sliding glass doors, greenhouse glazing, 524 ft² **Absorber(s):** Greenhouse masonry wall, tile-covered concrete floor slab **Storage:** Masonry wall, concrete floors—**capacity:** 13,416 BTU/°F **Distribution:** Radiation, natural and forced convection **Controls:** Thermostats, insulated blinds and shutters, overhangs

Back-up: Electric resistance heater (20,000 BTU/H), woodburning stove

126

The primary solar **collector** for this modern 3-bedroom home is the 2-story atrium. Its facade has 10 double-glazed acrylic panels facing due south and a pair of sliding glass doors, with windows above them, that face southwest. Upper- and lower-level rooms to the west of the greenhouse **collect** solar heat directly through their windows. In the great room on the lower level, sandwiched double-glazed sliding windows, with a 6-inch air cavity, face south, and a pair of sliding glass doors face southeast. The two bedrooms above the great room have triple-glazed windows facing south and sand-wiched double-glazed slider windows—with an 8-inch cavity—facing southeast. The master bedroom to the east of the green-house on the upper level receives sun through operable windows that face onto

the greenhouse and double-glazed sliding doors leading onto a wooden sundeck. The workroom below the master bedroom and the room adjacent to it are connected to the greenhouse by sliding doors and receive some radiation through them.

Absorption and **storage** of heat within the greenhouse is in a 2-story high, 12-inch thick masonry wall, and a tile covered, 4-inch concrete slab floor. Heat is **absorbed** and **stored** in the "alternate" room by a similar flooring, and in the workroom by a bare concrete slab. There is no thermal storage capacity in the great room or any of the bedrooms.

Heat is **distributed** by radiation from the storage masses, and by natural and forced

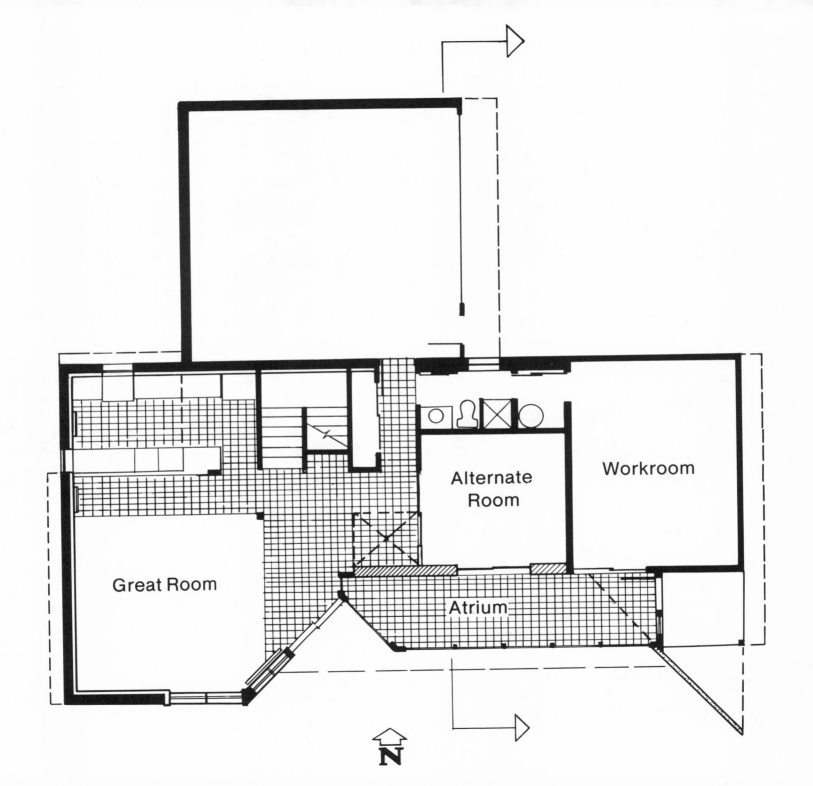

Great Room

Alternate
Room

Workroom

Atrium

N

127

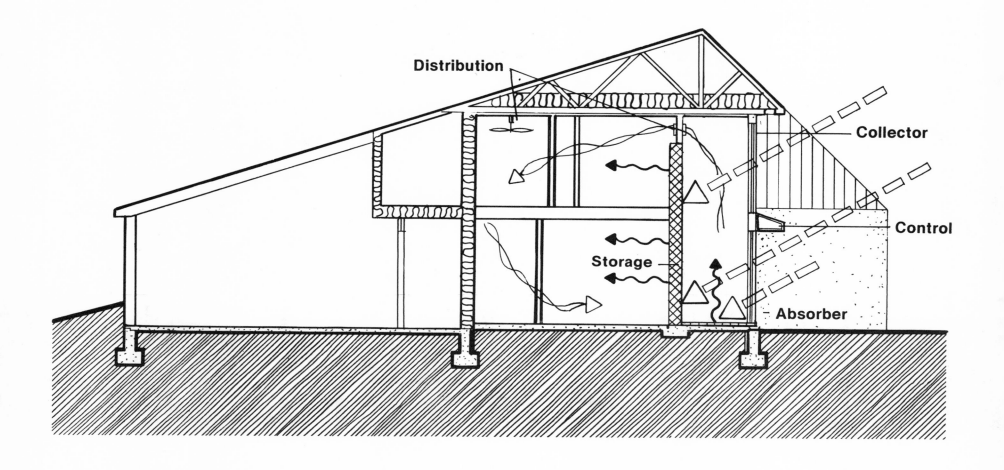

Distribution

Collector

Control

Storage

Absorber

convection. During winter days, greenhouse heat is drawn into the loft on the upper level by a pair of thermostatically **controlled** fans. The heat is drawn into the hallway and blown down the stairwell by a 56-inch ceiling fan located above the stairwell. Cool air is drawn back into the atrium for re-heating through opened glass doors

in the "alternate" room below. At night these doors are closed and the loft fans shut off. If the insulated drape is lowered over the greenhouse side of the mass wall, the wall will radiate heat into the living areas. For colder nights there is a woodburning stove on the lower level. Above the stove is a 5-foot square opening in the loft

floor to allow its heat to rise to the upper level. Nighttime heat in the bedrooms is supplied primarily by electric baseboard heaters, though some heat from solar masses may pass through opened doors and adjustable grilles above the doors.

During the summer, doors and windows on the southwest wall of the greenhouse can be opened to ventilate that area; also, there is a ceiling vent that allows heat to convect into the attic and exhaust through roof vents. A similar vent is located inside the loft ceiling. For peak summer heat, there are removeable window air conditioners for the three bedrooms. Heat gain is controlled by fixed overhangs on all windows, and at upper and lower levels of the greenhouse. Within the air cavity of the double-glazed slider windows there are retractable foil shades to reflect sunlight. On the triple-glazed bedroom windows there are interior hinged wooden shutters.

High earth berming and vegetation on the west and north sides protect the house from prevailing northeast winds. The attached garage that covers the air-lock entry system also acts as an effective wind buffer. Insulation values are high with walls rated at R-38 and ceilings at R-50.

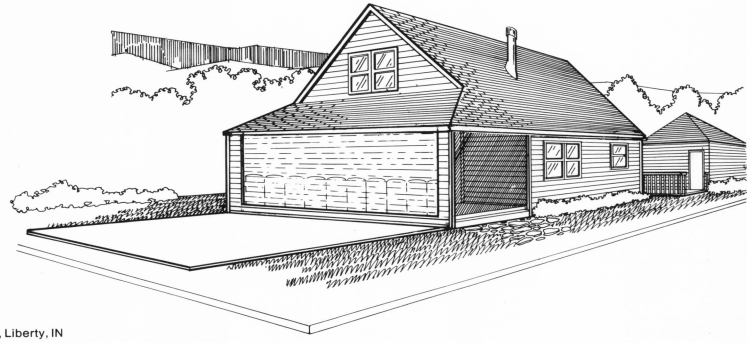

Builder: Miles-Richmond, Inc., Liberty, IN

Designer: Fuller Moore, Architect, Oxford, OH

Solar Designer: Fuller Moore, Architect

Price: $40,000

Net Heated Area: 1005 ft²

Heat Load: 39.8 x 10⁶ BTU / yr

Degree Days: 5611

Solar Fraction: 63%

Auxiliary Heat: 2.59 BTU / DD / ft²

Passive Heating System(s): Isolated gain, sun-tempering

Recognition Factors: Collector(s): Corrugated fiberglass greenhouse glazing, 256 ft² **Absorber(s):** 55-gallon steel drums **Storage:** Water in glass tubes, water in steel drums—**capacity:** 5747 BTU / °F **Distribution:** Radiation, natural and forced convection **Controls:** Sliding glass panels, insulating shades, thermostat

Back-up: 51,000 BTU / H wood stove, 30,600 BTU / H electric resistance baseboard heaters

Passive Cooling Type: Earth tubes, convection, mechanical assistance

130

Within a context of tight energy management controls for all new construction, the City of Richmond is beginning to assist in the development of lots along the alleys of its center city for residential use. Although houses are built by individual developers, the city assists in acquiring lots and assembling appropriate zoning and building / energy standards.

This house, the first in the program, uses a greenhouse and a water wall to contribute to its energy requirements. It is located on a 4,000-square foot lot at the intersection of two alleys.

Houses to the west deflect prevailing winter winds as well as late afternoon sunlight, while to the east, a park across the alley

permits early morning winter sun to warm the house. The house is located towards the north property line so there is clear land to the south and across the alley to allow unobstructed solar access.

The very compact, 2-story, traditional gable roof design is in character with other houses in the neighborhood. The house has a fan-shaped greenhouse along the south elevation with a porch on both sides, tucked behind the diagonal greenhouse walls. The porches, one open and one screened, promote effective ventilation in the summer.

Heavy insulation is used throughout. The floor joists above the crawl space include R-17 fiberglass batts, while R-11 batts are

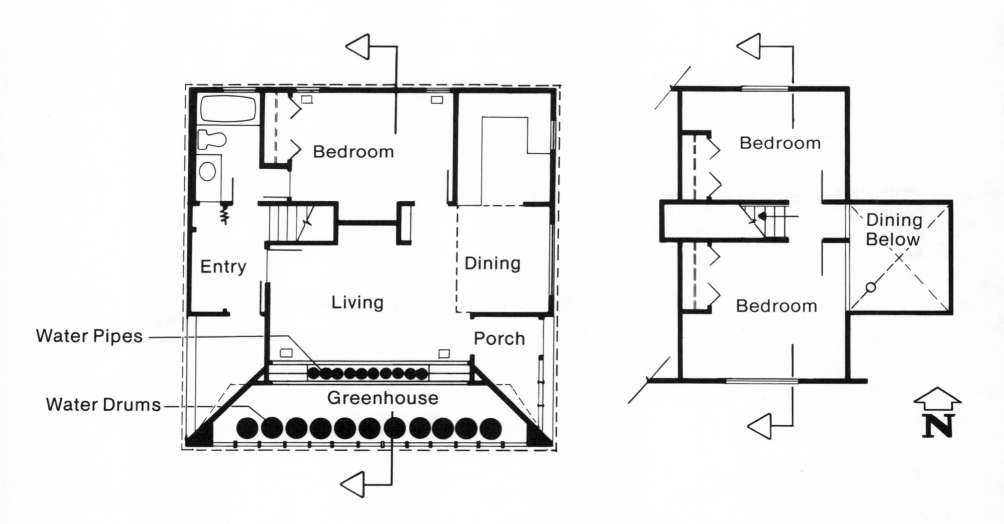

Water Pipes

Water Drums

Bedroom

Entry

Living

Porch

Dining

Greenhouse

Bedroom

Dining Below

Bedroom

N

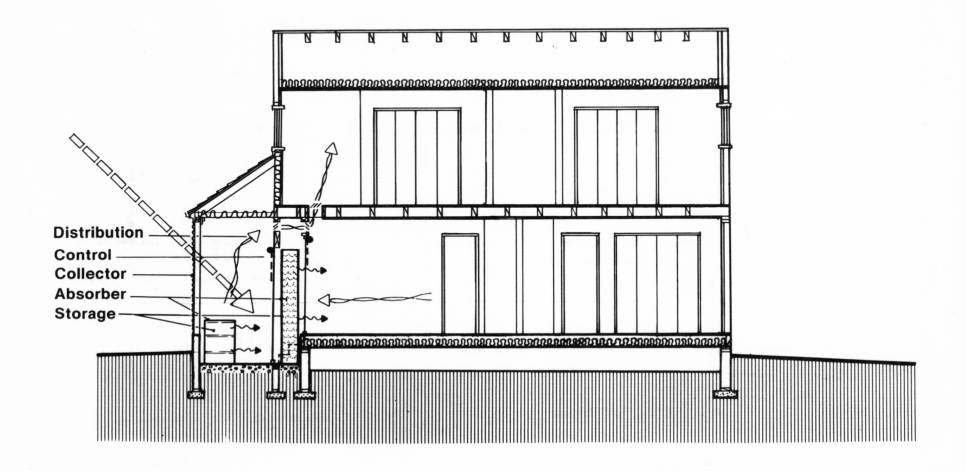

Distribution
Control
Collector
Absorber
Storage

installed in the floor of this crawl space wall. Building walls have R-11 batts plus ½-inch foil-faced urethane for a total of R-21. Roof insulation achieves value of R-28. All windows are triple glazed and have reflective roll-down insulating shades, providing a combined value of R-7.

The greenhouse, which is 2 feet below the lower floor level, encloses a water wall. Sunlight is **collected** in the greenhouse through 190 square feet of corrugated fiber-glass glazing. Just inside the greenhouse are 11 water-filled 55-gallon drums to **absorb** and **store** the solar energy. Five feet away is the living room water wall that consists of a row of 10 open water-filled fiberglass tubes that also **absorb** and **store** the sun's heat. To each side of the water wall is an open 3-foot wide set of stairs up the living room that also allows a flow of heated air to be **distributed** from the greenhouse. Four sliding glass door panels enclose the water wall. They can be arranged so that the tubes are closed off from the living room or from the greenhouse, or from both (or the open wall is closed off). Each panel is equipped with a roll-down insulating shade, and above each set of sliding panels and glass tubes there are operable through wall vents. All of these arrangements make it possible to carefully **control** the amount of heat passing from the greenhouse to storage and to the living area.

Additional **controls** consist of an attic fan, six operable floor vents in the upper floor (three of which are fan-assisted), four operable floor vents on the lower floor, and six operable vents between the crawl space and the greenhouse.

In the winter, sun is collected in the greenhouse, heating the water in the drums and the tubes. The sliding panels are adjusted by day to **control** the amount of convection from the greenhouse and convection induced by the tubes. Vents to the upper floor are open or closed as necessary to heat the upper floor. At night, the insulating shades are lowered to cover the greenhouse glazing and the water wall, while the water wall panels are positioned to isolate the tubes from the greenhouse if necessary. The tubes radiate stored heat to the interior and also induce convection to heat the second floor.

In the summer cooling mode, the floor vents to the crawl space are opened during warm water as part of the cooling mode. Two air intakes located at the northwest corner of the lot are connected to the crawl space by PVC pipes that are buried 4 feet deep. During the day, the sliding panels (with insulating shades down) are moved to isolate the water tubes from the greenhouse. Heat radiates from the first floor living spaces to warm the water in the tubes. At the same time, the attic fan can be activated to draw air from outside through the crawl space and up to the attic where it is exhausted. The air is cooled by its 55-foot underground run into the crawl space. At night the panels are reversed so that the tubes are isolated from the living room and opened to the greenhouse.

Middleton, WI

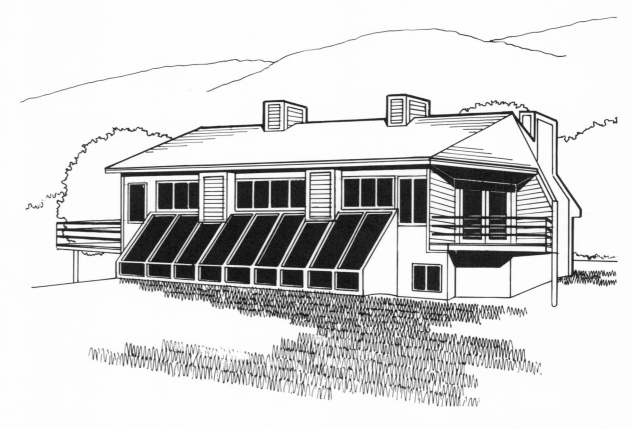

Builder: Northland Country Homes, Inc., Middleton, WI

Designer: North Design Architecture/Engineering/Planning, Middleton, MI

Solar Designer: Bruce D. Kieffer

Price: $79,500

Net Heated Area: 1788 ft²

Heat Load: 83.5 x 10⁶ BTU/yr

Degree Days: 7721

Solar Fraction: 52%

Auxiliary Heat: 2.95 BTU/DD/ft²

Passive Heating System(s): Indirect gain, isolated gain, sun-tempering

Recognition Factors: Collector(s): South-facing double glazing, 343 ft² **Absorber(s):** Greenhouse concrete slab floor, water tube surface, concrete block wall **Storage:** Greenhouse concrete slab floor, water wall, concrete block wall—**capacity:** 9600 BTU/°F **Distribution:** Radiation, natural convection **Controls:** Vents, registers, operable thermal doors, fixed overhangs, insulated shade

Back-up: Gas furnace (64,000 BTU/H)

Passive Cooling Type: Earth-cooled underground pipes, natural ventilation

This compact, 2-story, rectangular house is set into a south slope. It has mixed coniferous planting on its north side for protection from prevailing winter winds and a species of rapidly growing maple on its west side that will shade it from the hot, late afternoon, summer sun. Earth berms and the garage on the north and west sides will also deflect winter winds away from the entry and the upper floor spaces. The house faces 13 degrees east of south to encourage quick heat intake.

An innovative plan reduces heating needs by two methods. First, an inverted floor plan is used. This plan places active spaces (living room, dining room, family room, and kitchen) on the upper, entry floor and the

quiet spaces (bedrooms, utility room, and laundry) on the partially, below-grade, lower floor. This strong break with conventional house planning half buries the bedrooms and service areas in a cool, viewless part of the house, while placing the view-related, daytime kitchen, family room, living and dining rooms at the sunny top of the house. Second, rooms are placed for solar orientation. The lower floor bedrooms all receive direct sun while service functions—closets, bathrooms, laundry and utility—are relegated to a buried rear placement. The more active rooms of the upper-floor kitchen, family room, and dining room also are on the warm south side while a bathroom, stairway, and living room are on the cooler north side.

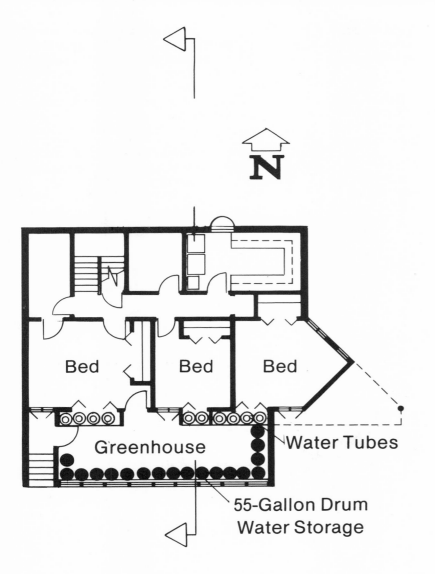

Bed

Bed

Bed

Greenhouse

Water Tubes

55-Gallon Drum
Water Storage

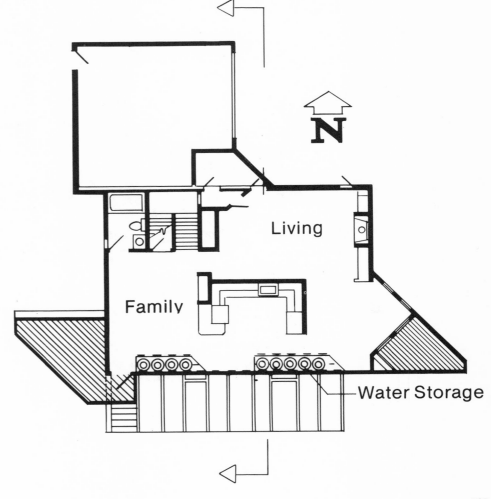

Living

Family

Water Storage

An extremely well-insulated building envelope is another energy asset. The wall construction has a composite R-value of 24, including: 2 x 6's with R-19 fiberglass plus 1-inch Styrofoam™ sheathing and a 4 mil vapor barrier. The roof has an R-value of 42 including 1 foot of blown cellulose and a 6 mil vapor barrier.

Two passive **collection** methods are used: (1) approximately 100 square feet of south-facing double glass **collects** heat for all major living spaces on both floors except the living room; (2) approximately 250 square feet of 40 degrees sloping, tempered, double glass, form the roof of a greenhouse that occupies over 27 feet of the lower-floor south wall.

Absorbers include two major surface areas: a concrete floor slab in the greenhouse is the first, and the south faces of the 12-inch and 18-inch diameter vertical water tubes form the second absorber.

Storage for the direct radiation is the 3-inch concrete floor slab in the greenhouse as well as the 154 cubic feet of water in the water tubes. Twenty-two 55-gallon drums are used for **storage** of indirect radiation and as extra thermal mass to dampen temperature fluctuations in the greenhouse. An insulated, 8-inch concrete block wall in the greenhouse and the carpet-covered concrete slab on the lower floor also help store heat and dampen temperature variations.

Radiation and natural convection **distribute** heat throughout the house. During winter daylight hours, sunlight penetrating the glass warms the south side surfaces directly in its path. These surfaces then warm the

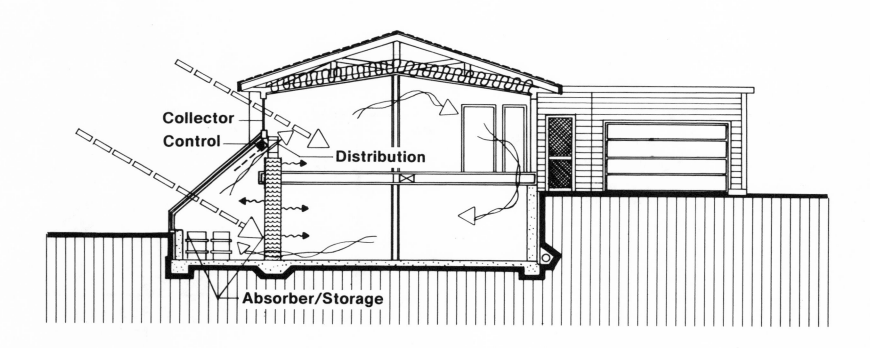

air which comes in contact with them, causing that air to rise and be replaced by cool air settling on the north side. This winter daytime convection current allows heat collected in the lower-floor sunspace to be circulated throughout the upper-floor living spaces. During the winter evening, a similar convection current occurs. Heat stored in the lower-floor water tubes is released to the air; this air also rises to the upper floor providing a night-long source of warmth. In addition, radiation from these water tubes provides heat for the adjacent lower-floor bedrooms, when insulated, bi-folding doors are open.

The strongest point of the **distribution** system is its excellent ability to respond to a normal daily-use pattern. This **control** is accommodated by both the plan of the house, a manually operated system of vents and registers, and a full complement of other control devices, including: (1) operable low and high vents designed to capture breezes and keep the sunspace from overheating during the summer; (2) operable, thermal doors on the south side of the water-tube wall to prevent unwanted summer heat gain; (3) bi-fold doors and the bedroom side of the water tubes control radiation; (4) fixed overhangs to provide 100 percent shading of south-facing glass from May through August; (5) a north-side underground tube that provides cool earth-tempered air to the house during the summer; (6) a high south-side induction vent linked to the attic and four wind turbines mounted on two thermal chimneys for venting of warm air during summer; (7) manually moveable, shade insulation (R-5) on all south-facing glass including the greenhouse to prevent heat loss during winter nights.

Completing this house's package of energy-conserving systems is a carefully selected group of conventional appliances. Included are: a refrigerator with a switch for de-activating its automatic defrost cycle; a pilotless gas oven/range; a dishwasher with a cycle for air drying; a range hood that exhausts heat to the outdoors during the summer and recirculates it through a filter during the winter; separate switching and a backdraft prevention bag on the bathroom exhaust fan. Also part of the design is a back-up furnace with an automatic flue damper, electric ignition, and an outside combustion of air source and a circulating air fireplace with an outside combustion air source, and tight-fitting glass doors.

Corcoran, MN

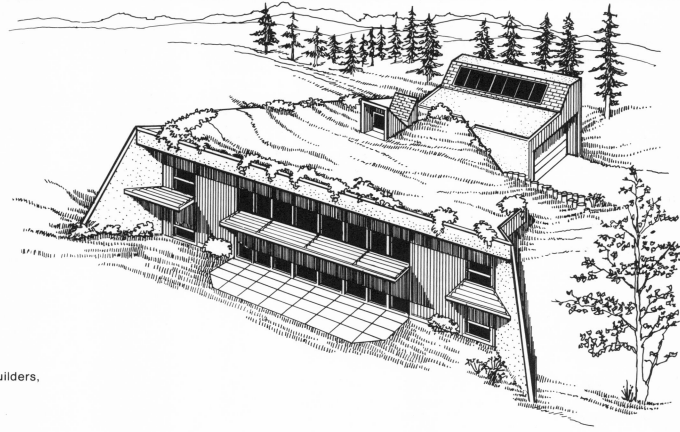

Builder: Berg and Associates, Design/Builders, Plymouth, MN

Designer: Berg and Associates

Solar Designer: Berg and Associates

Price: $120,000

Net Heated Area: 1665 ft²

Heat Load: 76.5 x 10⁶ BTU/yr

Degree Days: 8054

Solar Fraction: 83%

Auxiliary Heat: 0.99 BTU/DD/ft²

Passive Heating System(s): Direct gain, indirect gain, isolated gain

Recognition Factors: Collector(s): South-facing panels, glazing, 560 ft² **Absorber(s):** Concrete block wall, concrete floor **Storage:** Concrete block wall, concrete floor—**capacity:** 45,116 BTU/°F **Distribution:** Radiation, natural and forced convection **Controls:** Moveable insulation on Trombe walls, roof overhang

Back-up: Electric resistance heaters (30,000 BTU/H)

This contemporary, 2-story house is part of a 17-unit development. The house is buffered from winter winds by evergreen vegetation to the northwest and from the heat of early morning and late afternoon summer sun by deciduous vegetation to the southwest and southeast. Half of its wall area is sheltered by extensive earth berms; the roof is also partially earth covered. The house is heavily insulated, even for a building in the cold Minnesota climate. The main roof of the building has an R-value of 50. Above grade walls have an R-value of 19. The doors have a value of R-10, and windows are triple glazed.

The building's energy consumption is also minimized by an innovative floor plan and the use of buffer spaces. The living areas with different heating needs have been placed on different levels. The upper floor consists of a master bedroom, two additional bedrooms, a bathroom, and storage space. The lower floor includes most of the daytime living spaces: the living room, family room, kitchen, bath, and a large atrium. The garage, entry, and foyer are at an intermediate level. Each room has a separate electric resistance heating unit with individual thermostatic control. The occupants have the option of providing auxiliary heating to the lower level during the day and to the upper level at night.

The house has a well-integrated passive heating system. Three passive **collection** types are used: (1) over 70 square feet of triple glass on the south walls of the family room, living room, and two bedrooms provide direct heating of these rooms; (2) near-

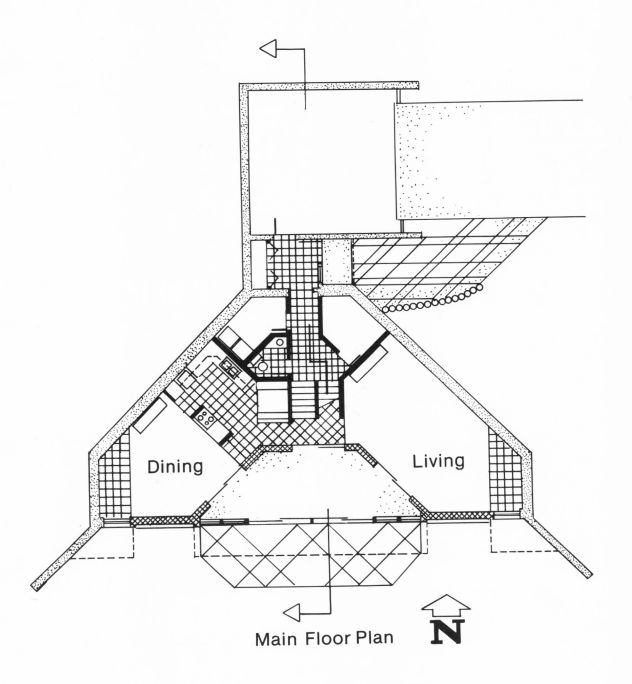

Dining

Living

Main Floor Plan

N

ly 200 square feet of Kalwall™ glazing is used on two radiant Trombe walls; (3) nearly 300 hundred square feet of triple glass on the south side of a 2-story atrium heat the rest of the house.

Heat is **absorbed** and **stored** in the first system by a massive brick floor and a solid concrete block wall. The other two systems **absorb** and **store** their heat in over 850 cubic feet of concrete wall and floor. Heat is **distributed** by natural convection and radiation, assisted by a fan located at the top of the atrium. Control of solar heat gain, heat loss, and ventilation is essential to maintaining indoor comfort. Automatic roll-

down insulation on the outside of the Trombe wall **controls** nighttime heat loss during the winter. Baffles that deflect warm fan-blown air from the atrium down into the center of the house during winter can also be moved to a summer position that aides ventilation. The summer position of the baffles, the open clerestory windows, and the scoop shaped roof above creates a "venturi effect" for natural suction of warm air up and out of this high area during the summer. A 4 foot 6 inch roof overhang and a similarly sized intermediate louvered overhang located over all south windows diminishes summer heat gains.

Manual dampers located above and below the Trombe glazing permit ventilation and avoid heat build-up during summer months.

The house also includes an extensive array of energy saving appliances: water conserving bath and toilet fixtures; an energy efficient water heater; an energy saving refrigerator; a microwave oven; and fluorescent light fixtures. In addition, a 7-panel active solar domestic water heating collector array is mounted on the garage roof. This system's efficiency is enhanced by a white stone roof in front of the collectors that acts as a reflector.

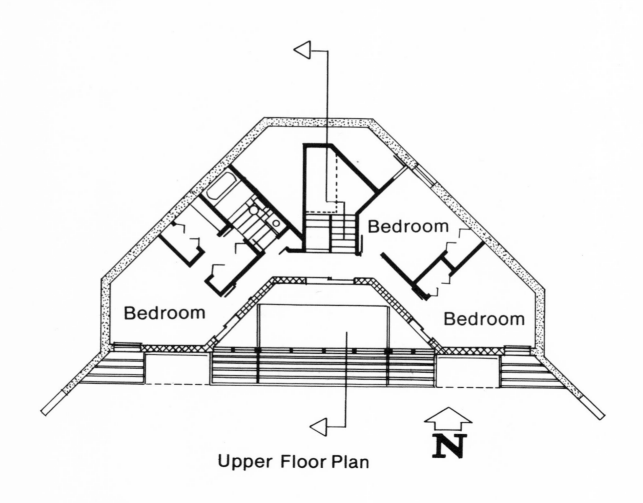

Upper Floor Plan

N

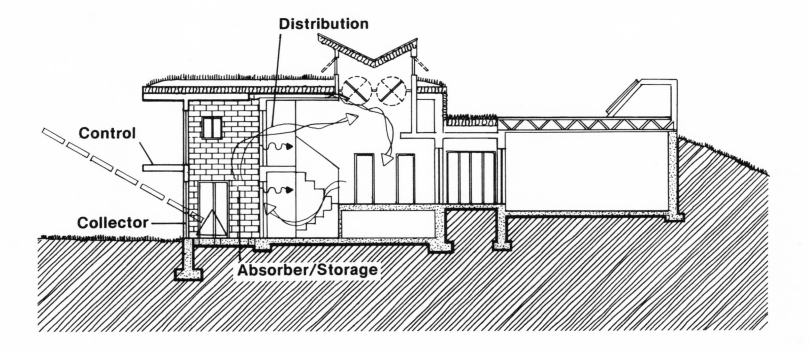

Distribution

Control

Collector

Absorber/Storage

Lincoln, NE

Builder: Peterson Construction Company, Lincoln, NE

Designer: The Clark Enersen Partners, Lincoln, NE

Solar Designer: The Clark Enersen Partners

Price: $75,000

Net Heated Area: 2487 ft²

Heat Load: 81.3 x 10⁶ BTU / yr

Degree Days: 5864

Solar Fraction: 73%

Auxiliary Heat: 1.50 BTU/DD/ft²

Passive Heating System(s): Direct gain

Recognition Factors: Collector(s): South-facing glass, 426 ft² **Absorber(s):** Water-filled thermal storage tubes, mass floors and walls **Storage:** Brick and concrete thermal walls and floors, water-filled thermal storage tubes—**capacity:** 22,869 BTU/°F **Distribution:** Radiation and natural convection **Controls:** Automatic and manual moveable insulation, overhangs, and awnings

Back-up: 40,000 BTU/H gas furnace

Evergreen trees to the northwest protect this Lincoln, NE home from harsh winter winds, and the garage and storage areas on the west side of the house provide additional buffers. To cut winter heat loss, windows have been kept to a minimum on north, east, and west sides of the house. Walls are insulated to R-20, the roof to R-33.

Passive solar elements have been integrated into every major room of this 1-story house. South-facing windows **collect** direct sunlight for the front living areas. Heat is **absorbed** and **stored** in the living room by 5-foot high 1½ foot diameter water-filled tubes placed immediately inside the south-facing glass and by brick walls and floors. Spaces between these water tubes allow solar radiation to reach the 8-inch brick storage wall on the north, east, and west living room walls. Kalwall™ glazed clere-

story windows channel sunlight to additional water-filled heat **storage** tubes along the living room's north wall.

Solar heat stored in the brick walls and water tubes is **distributed** into the room by radiation and natural convection.

A woodburning stove by the north living room wall is used for back-up heat. The nearby water tubes will also absorb excess heat from the wood stove.

Two Kalwall™ clerestory windows channel sunlight to the back bedrooms. This design is one of the few methods that permits sunlight to penetrate directly to rooms on the north side of a building. The angle of the clerestory shafts enables sunlight to reach the bedrooms in the winter but blocks it during the summer.

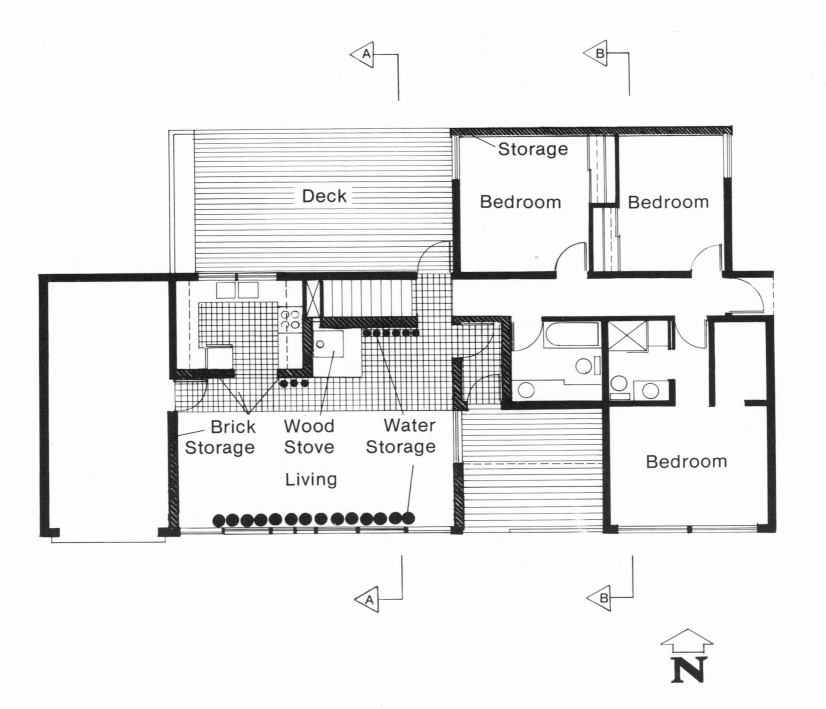

Deck

Storage

Bedroom

Bedroom

Brick
Storage

Wood
Stove

Water
Storage

Living

Bedroom

A

B

A

B

N

143

Brick walls and concrete floors in the bedrooms also serve as storage mass for solar heat. Light **collected** by the clerestory shafts strikes the north walls, is **absorbed** at the surface and **stored** in the walls' mass. The heat is **distributed** by radiation from the brick walls and by natural convection.

A vestibule located between the living room and front bedroom is both an air-lock entry and a heat collection area with brick thermal storage walls on the east, west, and north sides. The greenhouse shares one common wall with the living room, front bedroom, and bathroom, and provides heat to these areas.

The auxiliary distribution system gives a mechanical assist to the natural **distribution** processes of convection and radiation. Stratified air is returned from the ceiling of the east living room wall to the furnace. In winter, solar energy preheats the air returning to the furnace before distribution to the other rooms.

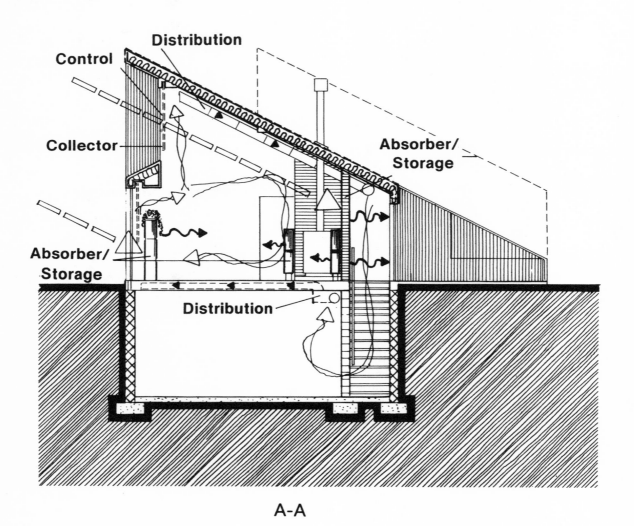

A-A

In the return air system, damper positions are reversed between seasons to draw conditioned air from different sides of the house. In the summer, return air is drawn through perimeter floor registers in the cool north end of the house and recirculated. In the winter, return air comes from the warm south rooms.

Moveable insulation for the living room glazing and the clerestory is automatically **controlled**. During the winter it will open in the day and close at night. This is reversed in summer. All other windows have manually operated awnings. During spring and fall, the moveable insulation can be manually positioned to **control** solar gain when

necessary. Insulated glass on the south wall is operable to allow summer ventilation across the living space.

Southeast deciduous trees channel summer breezes for cooling and provide some summer shade. Vents in the south wall take advantage of the prevailing southeast summer winds.

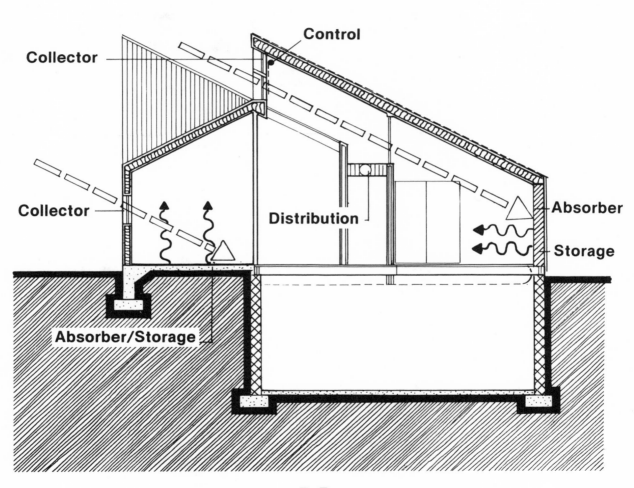

B-B

Cincinnati, OH

Builder: Louis S. Ionna III & Associates, Inc., Cincinnati, OH

Designer: Fuller Moore, Architect, Oxford, OH

Solar Designer: Fuller Moore

Price: $82,500

Net Heated Area: 1600 ft²

Heat Load: 45.5 x 10⁶ BTU/yr

Degree Days: 4834

Solar Fraction: 82%

Auxiliary Heat: 1.04 BTU/DD/ft²

Passive Heating System(s): Direct gain, isolated gain, indirect gain

Recognition Factors: Collector(s): Double-glazed, south-facing greenhouse windows, sliding glass doors, 521 ft² **Absorber(s):** Black aluminum in plenum area, water drum surfaces, darkened surface of water wall. **Storage:** 55-gallon water-filled drums, water wall—**capacity:** 6000 BTU/°F **Distribution:** Natural and forced convection, radiation **Controls:** Thermostat, damper, roll-down insulating shade

Back-up: 50,000 BTU/H woodburning stove, electric baseboard heaters

Domestic Hot Water: Preheating coil in the greenhouse and heat exchanger on woodburning stove

Passive Cooling Type: Earth pipes, ground cooling, natural and induced ventilation

This 3-bedroom house is designed to accommodate the local climate's wide range of seasonal temperatures (12°F winter and 92°F summer), as well as a normal daily fluctuation of about 27°F. The rustic contemporary styling is typical of other custom homes in the area. The landscaping includes evergreens to the west for wind protection, with deciduous trees to the northwest and east. There are no significant solar obstructions.

Energy-conserving features are central to the success of this solar design. These include R-40 insulation in the attic and R-22 in the exterior stud walls. In addition, there is double glazing on all windows including the greenhouse. Particular attention was paid to caulking and weatherstripping in an effort to further reduce heat loss.

The primary solar **collector** in this house is a greenhouse that extends nearly the entire length and height of the south wall. Sun-light is also **collected** in a plenum area above the greenhouse that runs the entire length of the roofline. Both the plenum and the greenhouse are tilted at a 60-degree angle.

The sunlight **collected** by the greenhouse is **absorbed** and **stored** as heat in two ways: 1) by a series of 13 water-filled 55-gallon drums arranged along the south wall of the greenhouse, which is partially below grade; and 2) by a water wall that separates the greenhouse from the upper floor of the living area. The water wall is a series of 4-inch diameter water-filled tubes set between exposed studs and single glazed on both sides. Reflective surfaces on the end walls of the greenhouse reflect addi-additional light onto the dark surface of the water wall.

A natural convective **distribution** loop is formed during the day when heated air rises in the greenhouse and flows into the living room, which is on the upper floor. This heat flow is **controlled** by opening either or both of a pair of sliding glass doors (one on either side of the water wall) that connect the greenhouse and the upper floor. These doors also admit direct radiation that immediately heats the room air when the sun is shining. As the air reaches the north wall it becomes cooler, and therefore heavier. Losing buoyancy, it sinks down the rear stairwell into the sleeping areas and from there siphons back into the greenhouse, via bedroom windows, for reheating. In moderately cool weather, this convective loop plus radiant heat from the water wall are expected to be all that's needed to warm the house.

At night heat loss from the greenhouse is controlled by a roll-down insulating shade with an R-value of 6.5.

On colder winter days, the solar plenum above the greenhouse will be used to further heat the greenhouse air. The stove is also equipped with a heat exchanger used to preheat domestic water. In addition to the stove, there are "last resort" electric baseboard heaters on the south wall of the lower level.

The passive cooling mode is a matter of inducing convection by the chimney effect and allowing cross-ventilation by opening windows. For strictly passive cooling, the greenhouse is sealed off from the rest of the house, and the insulating shade is lowered to prevent the sun from heating the water wall or the barrels.

Essential to the cooling effect, though, is attaining the lowest possible temperature in the lower level. To this end, the designer has accented the effect of having the area below grade cooled by running four 6-inch diameter PVC corrugated air tubes approximately 6 feet underground near the foundation.

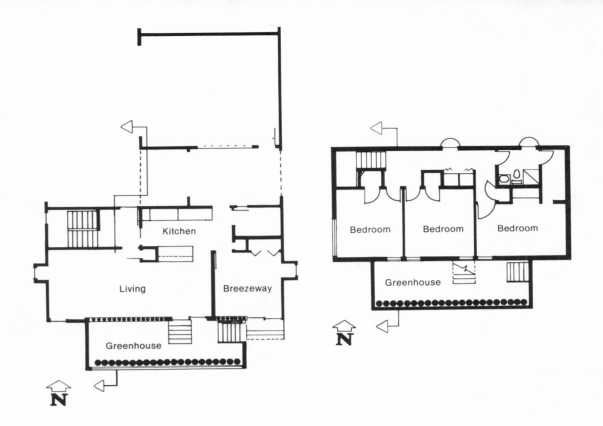

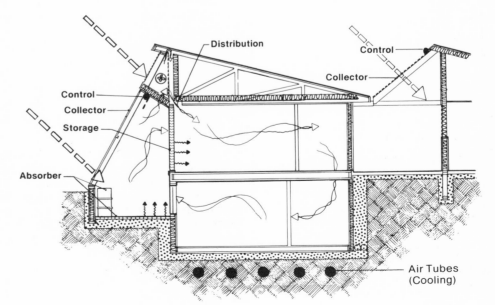

Builder: Huth Westwood Builders, Akron, OH

Designer: Environmental Design Alternatives, Kent, OH

Solar Designer: Environmental Design Alternatives

Price: $130,000

Net Heated Area: 2158 ft²

Heat Load: 76.2 x 10⁶ BTU/yr

Degree Days: 6037

Solar Fraction: 46%

Auxiliary Heat: 3.14 BTU/DD/ft²

Passive Heating System(s): Isolated gain, sun-tempering

Recognition Factors: Collector(s): Single- and double-glazed windows and doors, 423 ft² **Absorber(s):** Water tubes, ceramic tile floor **Storage:** Water tubes and mass floors—**capacity:** 16,345 BTU/°F **Distribution:** Radiation, natural and forced convection **Controls:** Insulating shutters, fixed and retractable overhangs

Back-up: Woodburning stove, gas heat

This modern 3-bedroom home features a double-glazed solar greenhouse that **collects** solar radiation. Sheltered inside the greenhouse is a single-glazed **collection** area that admits sunlight directly into the family room. This combination of passive collection modes allows immediate heating of the family room as soon as the sun shines, while the greenhouse provides a buffer and heat storage zone that will allow for a controlled circulation of heated air into the family room.

The kitchen and two upper-level bedrooms also have double-glazed apertures designed to collect solar radiation. There is also a west-facing pair of sliding glass doors admitting direct sunlight to the dining room. Just behind the collection areas, for the bedrooms and family room, there are Kalwall™ water tubes that **absorb** and **store** heat. In the dining room and kitchen ceramic tiles **absorb** for the 4-inch concrete slab **storage** floor that they cover.

Distribution of heat occurs by radiation from storage and natural convective flows, as well as by forced air distribution from the back-up furnace. Heated air from storage elements on the lower level pass to the upper level via the open staircase at the north wall, assisting in the heating of that area at night. For the most part, natural convection distributes heat within each room individually. The exceptions are the lower-level living room and upper-level bedroom in the northwest corner, which rely almost entirely on the gas furnace for heat. Back-up heat is available from a woodburning stove in the family room, and from the furnace, which has supply and return air grilles in all rooms, including the greenhouse. Heat loss is **controlled** by moveable insulating shutters on all glazed areas except the greenhouse.

Summer cooling is a matter of opening windows to create cross flows of fresh air. Upper-level collectors are shaded by fixed roof overhangs; the lower-level collectors have moveable overhangs that are adjusted seasonally. Heat that builds up indoors is exhausted through the attic by a 2-speed, manually operated fan in the ceiling of the upper-level hallway.

Interior temperature stability is maintained with the help of partial earth berming on all walls, and winter wind infiltration has been reduced by using the garage as an air-lock entryway. Insulation in the walls is 3-inch urethane foam and in the roof 12 inches of poured cellulose.

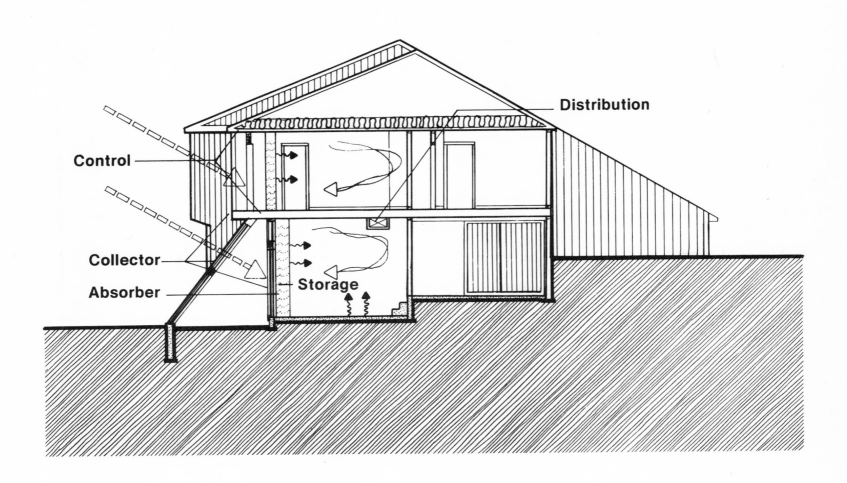

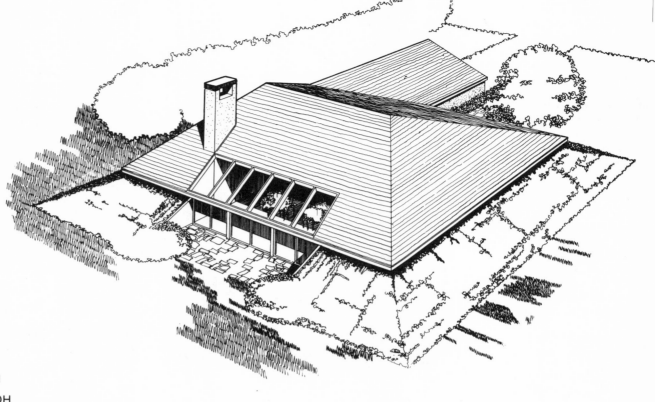

Builder: H.R. Ranson, Inc., Columbus, OH

Designer: Walter S. Withers, Worthington, OH

Solar Designer: James M. Pabst, Columbus, OH

Price: $150,000

Net Heated Area: 2894 ft²

Heat Load: 68.7 x 10⁶ BTU / yr

Degree Days: 5660

Solar Fraction: 52%

Auxiliary Heat: 2.03 BTU / DD / ft²

Passive Heating System(s): Isolated gain

Recognition Factors: Collector(s): Double-glazed atrium glass, 336 ft² **Absorber(s):** Concrete slab floor, poured concrete walls **Storage:** Concrete slab floors, poured concrete walls—**capacity:** 9600 BTU / °F **Distribution:** Radiation, natural and forced convection **Controls:** Dampers, ducts, insulating panels, thermostat

Back-up: Woodburning stove, electric resistance mats

The prominent design feature of this 3-bed-room house is the extensive earth berming on the east and west sides, which wraps around to partially berm the north and south walls as well. Sunlight is available to the living areas primarily through windows and sliding glass doors that face onto an atrium.

The primary **collector** in this single-level home is the double-glazed atrium, set into the south side of the building. At the north wall of the atrium there are also windows and sliding glass doors **collecting** light for the living spaces; this glass is also double.

The outermost collectors of the atrium—the skylights and sliding doors—pass solar radiation to be **absorbed** and **stored** by the 8-inch concrete slab floor within, and by the 8-inch poured concrete walls partially surrounding the atrium. All wall absorber surfaces in the atrium are stucco. The 4-inch slab floor in the living and dining rooms will also **absorb** and **store** heat.

Distribution involves radiation from storage masses and natural convection, but is for the most part by forced convection. In the winter mode, the dampers in the rafters between the skylight and vertical glass of the atrium are kept closed so that heated air can gather in the ceiling. A plenum in the ceiling has nine thermostatically **controlled** dampers: five supply air and four exhaust it.

When heat is required, the supply air dampers open so that hot air can be drawn into the attic duct system by the furnace in the storage room. A manually operated damper within the central supply duct is moved to the open position, which allows the hot plenum air to reach the furnace. The furnace then **distributes** the air to all rooms through sub-slab ducts. Three separate sub-slab ducts allow cool air to be drawn back into the atrium from the living and dining areas for re-heating.

During extreme cold or at night, when the air being drawn from the atrium plenum is not hot enough to satisfy the house thermostat, electric coils within the furnace supply additional heat to meet the demand. To reduce dependency on the coils, there is a woodburning stove in the atrium. This stove shares the chimney used by the conventional fireplace in the family room. Additional back-up heat is available from electric resistance mats in the atrium slab floor. The mats are thermostatically adjustable, but are designed to be used only if the temperature in the atrium drops below 50°F.

The atrium's heat loss is **controlled** at night by manually operated insulating panels (R-10) that cover all exterior exposed glass. Roof insulation for the atrium is rated at R-30. Blown insulation for the living area ceiling is R-50. The location of utility areas in the exposed (unbermed) northwest corner and the air-lock entry also help to buffer living areas from winter drafts.

In the summer mode, the dampers in the eaves are opened; this allows cool air to be drawn in as hot air is vented through open exhaust grilles to an air box in the plenum. There, it can either convect out naturally or be drawn out by a manually operated fan.

Air is continually mixed in the living areas by shifting the damper in the central supply duct to the closed position so that the furnace can circulate without drawing on hot plenum air. Insulation panels can also be used to shade the atrium storage masses.

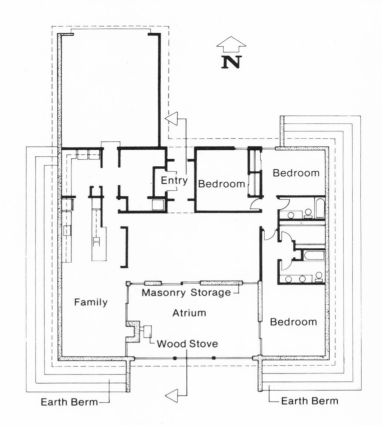

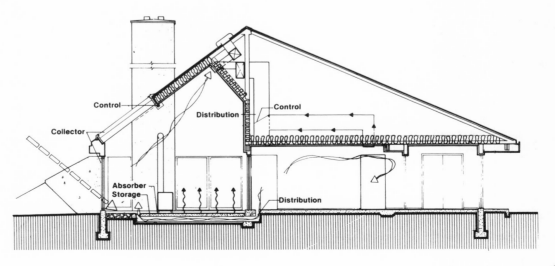

New Albany, IN

Builder: George W. Rosenbarger, New Albany, IN

Designer: Jim Rosenbarger, New Albany, IN

Solar Designer: Terry W. White, P.E., Terry White, Engineer, New Albany, IN

Price: $78,500

Net Heated Area: 1800 ft²

Heat Load: 45.4 x 10⁶ BTU/yr

Degree Days: 4636

Solar Fraction: 64%

Auxiliary Heat: 1.91 BTU/DD/ft²

Passive Heating System(s): Isolated gain, sun-tempering, direct gain

Recognition Factors: Collector(s): Greenhouse glass, glass doors and windows, 511 ft² **Absorber(s):** Concrete mass wall and tile-covered concrete slab floor **Storage:** Concrete mass wall and slab floor—**capacity:** 16,312 BTU/°F **Distribution:** Radiation, natural and forced convection **Controls:** Canvas shades, fixed overhangs

Back-up: Woodburning stove and electric furnace

Passive Cooling Type: Exhaust fan in attic and natural ventilation

152

In this house, solar radiation is **collected** by a greenhouse. Sunlight also directly enters the living space through glass doors at the rear of the greenhouse. In a raised extension of the greenhouse just to the west, there is a double-glazed sliding door and two fixed windows above it **collecting** solar radiation. In the living room to the far west, there are three double-glazed windows that collect heat and light for that area and the dining room behind it.

Heat is **absorbed** and **stored** in the greenhouse by a solid 2-story concrete block wall, and a 4-inch concrete slab floor surfaced with quarry tile pavers. This same type of floor is used to **absorb** and **store** heat in the living room as well.

Distribution of heat is by radiation from storage masses together with both natural and forced convection. During winter days, heat that gathers at the top of the greenhouse can pass onto the second floor either through a window in the bedroom or over an open hallway with railings on either side. Behind the hallway, in the ceiling area of a 2-story kitchen, a 36-inch ceiling fan pushes heated air down to the lower level. Cooled air travels back into the greenhouse for re-heating through connecting doors. For back-up heat at night and during extreme cold, there is a woodburning stove located in the living room beside a 12-inch masonry wall that stores heat. In addition, there is a furnace and duct system that makes continuous air flow available to all rooms.

To help cut heat loss, there is a 7-foot earth berm on the northwest corner of the house;

insulation values are R-19 for the walls and R-30 for the roof. Wind infiltration has been minimized by locating the garage and evergreen vegetation to the northwest where they can buffer winter breezes.

In the summer mode, canvas shades can be pulled to block out radiation entering through the greenhouse and to prevent it from being absorbed by the masonry wall. Fixed overhangs shade all other collectors.

Heat that does build up in the greenhouse can be exhausted through the attic and roof monitor by an attic fan in the raised section of the greenhouse. Natural ventilation of the living areas is achieved by opening east, west, and south windows. For peak cooling needs there is central air conditioning.

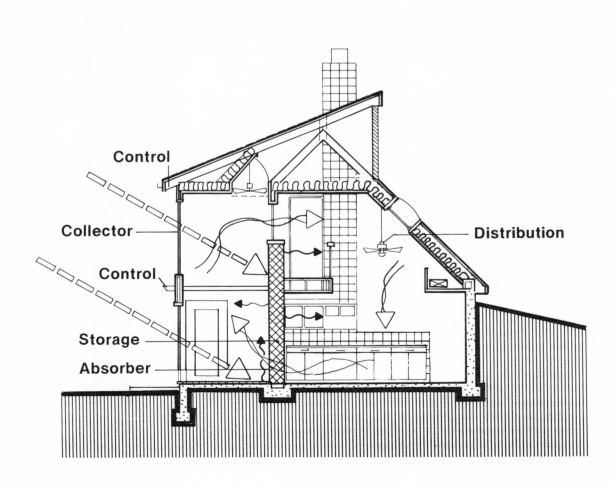

Control

Collector

Control

Storage

Absorber

Distribution

Builder: Barnard Brothers, Inc., Indianapolis, IN

Designer: Sun Design Group, Indianapolis, IN

Solar Designer: Sun Design Group

Price: $80,000

Net Heated Area: 1553 ft²

Heat Load: 55.0 x 10⁶ BTU / yr

Degree Days: 5679

Solar Fraction: 24%

Auxiliary Heat: 4.72 BTU / DD / ft²

Passive Heating System(s): Sun-tempering, indirect gain

Recognition Factors: Collector(s): South-facing windows, 156 ft² **Absorber(s):** Glass tubes **Storage:** Water in glass tubes, concrete tube enclosures—**capacity:** 11,000 BTU / °F **Distribution:** Radiation, forced and natural convection **Controls:** Louvers, window shades, attic fan

Back-up: 24,000 BTU / H electric air-to-air heat pump

Domestic Hot Water: 43 ft² air flat-plate collectors, air-to-water coil heat exchanger

Bedrooms in this compact 2-story house are located below grade, while the major living spaces are at grade. The garage is located to the north to block cold winter winds.

In winter, 40 percent of the **collected** sunlight passes through windows to warm the rooms directly. The rest is **absorbed** and **stored** by 14 water-filled tubes, located in pairs along the side of the house, just inside and at a 45° angle to the windows. Each pair of tubes is surrounded in back and on both sides by a plastered "U" shaped, 6-inch thick concrete wall, with a 6-

inch air space between the tubes and back wall. Grille vents at the top and bottom of the wall allow convection. As the tubes radiate heat to the concrete for storage, convection currents carry heat from the tubes up the air space and **distribute** it into the living spaces. The concrete wall radiates heat to the spaces more gradually than the tubes would themselves. A ceiling fan circulates air as needed. There is also an attic fan to exhaust air in warm weather conditions. All windows are double glazed and have insulating shades (for a total of R-15) to **control** night heat loss.

Total insulating value of the frame walls, with 3½-inch glass fiber batts and 1-inch foam sheathing, is R-21, and with an additional 3½-inch insulation at the stairs, wall insulation there is R-32. The roof, with 12-inch batts, is R-41. Windows are minimal on the north, east, and west elevations. Additionally, a horizontal trellis extends out from the south wall; it has wood slats built in at an angle to block high-altitude sun while permitting low-altitude sun to enter.

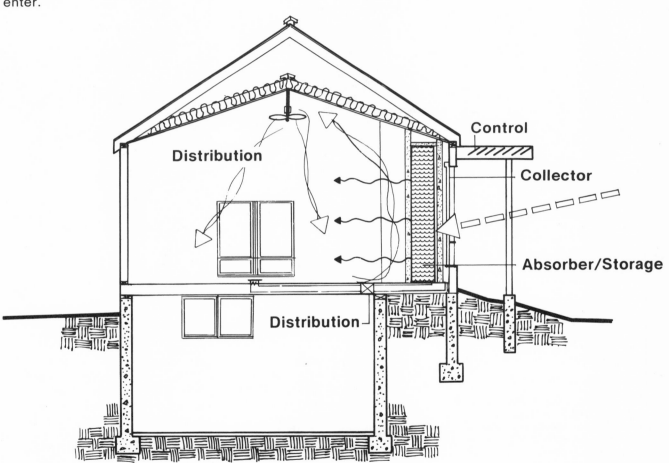

Control

Collector

Distribution

Absorber/Storage

Distribution

Ypsilanti, MI

Builder: Holtzman and Silverman, Southfield, MI

Designer: Turner Brooks, Starksboro, VT

Solar Designer: Turner Brooks

Price: $123,000

Net Heated Area: 2460 ft²

Heat Load: 134 x 10⁶ BTU / yr

Degree Days: 6909

Solar Fraction: 51%

Auxiliary Heat: 3.91 BTU / DD / ft²

Passive Heating System(s): Isolated gain

Recognition Factors: Collector(s): Window glazing, cyroacrylic greenhouse panels, 600 ft² **Absorber(s):** Concrete floor, masonry mass wall **Storage:** Concrete floor, masonry mass wall—**capacity:** 14,300 BTU / °F **Distribution:** Radiation, natural and forced convection **Controls:** Interior greenhouse windows and doors, window insulating shades

Back-up: 88,000 BTU / H gas furnace

Passive Cooling Type: Night ventilation, induced ventilation

A full-height greenhouse is the dominant feature of this long 2-story house. The greenhouse which is the primary solar **collector**, is 45 feet long and serves as an entrance gallery for the lower-floor family and dining rooms. Its exterior wall juts out so that the interior width varies from 4 to 8 feet. Double acrylic panels glaze the greenhouse and account for 85 percent of the exterior glazing. The greenhouse floor is 6-inch concrete with a 1-inch flagstone finish to **absorb** and **store** the solar energy. Behind the greenhouse is a mass wall for additional **absorption** and **storage** built of 4-inch brick and 8-inch block with mortar-filled voids; the interior of this wall is plastered. Wood windows with insulating glass penetrate the mass wall to light living spaces on both floors.

The construction of the remainder of the house is energy conserving with 2- x 6-inch stud wall construction and R-21 fiberglass batts; R-39 fiberglass batts are used in the ceiling trusses. A continuous polyethylene vapor barrier on the inside face of the studs and on the underside of the roof trusses serves to block wind infiltration. All entrances are constructed as air-locks for the same reason. Primary access from the front is through an air-lock into the greenhouse and then into the family room. Access from the garage to the house is also through the greenhouse. Another air-lock entry gives access to the kitchen on the north side of the house. The few exterior windows that do not face into the greenhouse are triple glazed and are equipped with pull-down shades that bring the total value up to R-15.

For solar **collection**, insulating shades of the greenhouse windows are raised on winter mornings to admit sunlight which is **absorbed** by the mass floor and wall. As the greenhouse warms, any of the interior greenhouse doors and windows may be opened as required to permit heat to be **distributed** directly into the living spaces by convective flow. In addition, heat radiates from the mass wall into the house, and if necessary, an interior greenhouse fan can be activated to **distribute** warm air from the upper level of the greenhouse through ducts to two second-floor bedrooms. At night, with the insulating shades closed to **control** heat loss to the outside, the mass wall and mass floor continue to reradiate heat into the rooms. However, as the greenhouse cools further, the interior windows and doors are closed to **control** any heat losses to the greenhouse.

In summer, the greenhouse insulating shades are closed all day and the doors and windows are shut to insulate the greenhouse as a buffer space. A greenhouse ceiling fan automatically exhausts hot air if needed. Exterior windows are operable, allowing ventilation through the house. By controlling the shades, doors and interior windows, space temperatures are modulated throughout the changes of season.

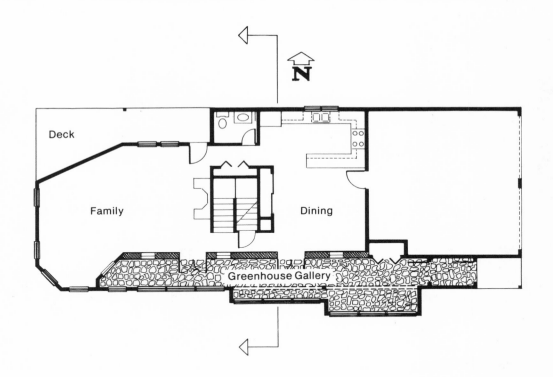

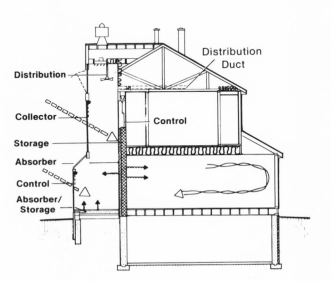

Builder: Trustway Homes, Inc., Milwaukee, WI

Designer: Ray Prell & Associates, Brookfield, WI

Solar Designer: Roger Schiller, Trustway Homes, Inc.

Price: $65,000

Net Heated Area: 1900 ft²

Heat Load: 72.0 x 10⁶ BTU/yr

Degree Days: 7635

Solar Fraction: 50%

Auxiliary Heat: 2.50 BTU/DD/ft²

Passive Heating System(s): Sun-tempering, direct gain

Recognition Factors: Collector(s): South-facing double glazing, 250 ft² **Absorber(s):** Tile surface, brick walls **Storage:** Concrete mass floor, brick mass wall—**capacity:** 19,000 BTU/°F **Distribution:** Radiation, convection **Controls:** Insulated shades, overhangs

Back-up: Gas-fired boiler (62,000 BTU/H)

Passive Cooling Type: Natural and induced ventilation

This 2-story home, built in a model subdivision, shows that only minor changes from conventional planning and construction are needed to incorporate passive solar features. The garage and service rooms act to buffer winter winds from the northwest. Minimal openings on the north, east, and west walls, and a well-insulated and sealed building envelope all reduce the need for heat energy. A significant portion of these heat needs are met by a passive **collection** system that includes south-facing double glass, part of which makes up a direct passive system, with the remainder providing heat to bedrooms that have no storage mass. **Absorbers** for the direct system are the surfaces of the quarry tile floors and brick walls located in south-facing rooms.

Storage is in the concrete slab below the quarry tile and in the body of the thick brick wall. **Distribution** is primarily by radiation from these walls and floors with natural convection occurring as air comes in contact with these warm surfaces. Heat loss at night is **controlled** by using roll-down insulating shades over all glass.

Other features that save energy and contribute to comfort in the house include: an operable clerestory window in the living room to aid natural ventilation in the summer, a flue damper and a spark ignition on the furnace, water-saving shower heads and water closets, and an energy-efficient, air-circulating fireplace.

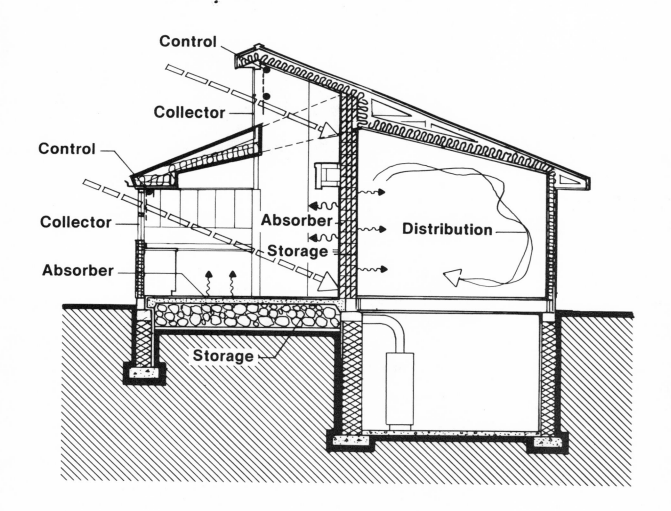

Control

Collector

Control

Collector

Absorber

Absorber

Storage

Distribution

Storage

Bismarck, ND

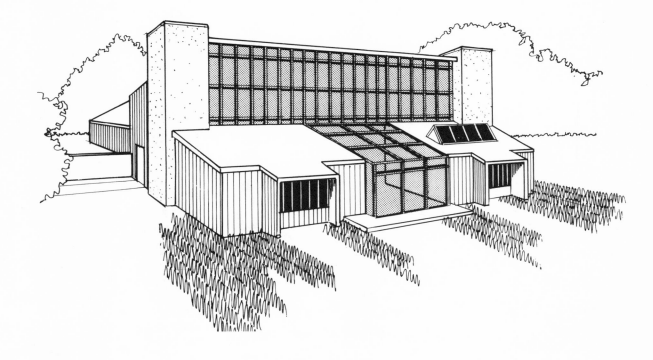

Builder: Bismarck-Mandan Home Builders Associates, Bismarck, ND

Designer: Don J. Jiran, Architects and Planners, Bismarck, ND

Solar Designer: Ken Schwartz Engineering, Inc.

Price: $100,000

Net Heated Area: 1860 ft²

Heat Load: 149.1 x 10⁶ BTU/yr

Degree Days: 8923

Solar Fraction: 48%

Auxiliary Heat: 4.69 BTU/DD/ft²

Passive Heating System(s): Isolated gain, indirect gain

Recognition Factors: Collector(s): South-facing glass, greenhouse glazing, 593 ft² **Absorber(s):** Mass wall surface **Storage:** Concrete block mass wall—**capacity:** 18,068 BTU/°F **Distribution:** Radiation, convection **Controls:** Insulating drapes, wall vents, overhangs

Back-up: Gas furnace, fireplace

Domestic Hot Water: Flate-plate collectors, 48 ft²

160

The site of this home is near a small ridge of a south knoll. The home, which has natural redwood siding, fits in well with the other houses in this contemporary subdivision.

Winters in this area of North Dakota are extremely cold, but there is an abundance of sunshine. Temperatures drop well below freezing for months at a time and are combined with high wind speeds.

Earth berms and fir trees are located on the north and west sides of the house to dampen winter winds. Garage and closets are placed on the north to serve as buffers for the heated spaces and there is little glass on the north exposure. Fins on outer walls protect windows from winter winds. The insulation value is R-40 for the roof,

and R-26 for the walls; an air-lock on the south is used as the main entry.

There are three distinct **collection** systems in operation in the home. The main system is a 2½-story mass wall running through the middle of the house. The upper level of the wall is fronted with triple glazing. Sunlight enters through the south glazing, strikes the darkened surface of the wall, and is **absorbed** and **stored** as heat.

On the lower level, sunlight enters through the front rooms and strikes the unglazed lower portion of the storage wall. There it is **absorbed** and **stored** as heat in the mass of the wall.

The greenhouse is located in the front center of the house and doubles as an air-

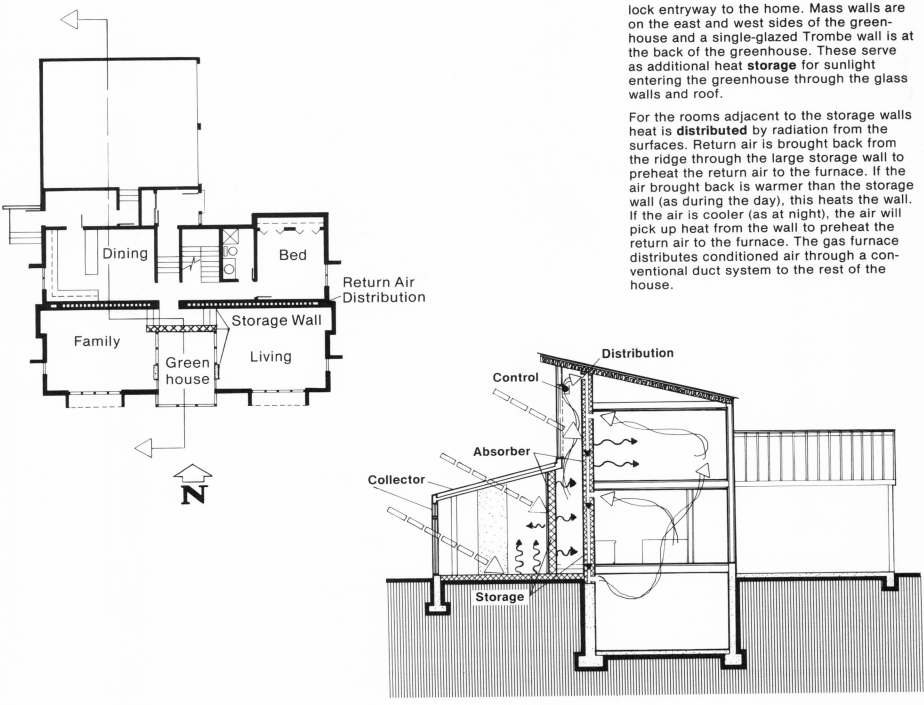

lock entryway to the home. Mass walls are on the east and west sides of the greenhouse and a single-glazed Trombe wall is at the back of the greenhouse. These serve as additional heat **storage** for sunlight entering the greenhouse through the glass walls and roof.

For the rooms adjacent to the storage walls heat is **distributed** by radiation from the surfaces. Return air is brought back from the ridge through the large storage wall to preheat the return air to the furnace. If the air brought back is warmer than the storage wall (as during the day), this heats the wall. If the air is cooler (as at night), the air will pick up heat from the wall to preheat the return air to the furnace. The gas furnace distributes conditioned air through a conventional duct system to the rest of the house.

Dining

Bed

Return Air Distribution

Storage Wall

Family

Green house

Living

N

Distribution

Control

Absorber

Collector

Storage

Builder: Dick Sorum Construction, Renner, SD

Designer: The Spitznagel Partners, Inc., Sioux Falls, SD

Price: $100,000

Net Heated Area: 2074 ft²

Heat Load: 125.7 x 10⁶ BTU/yr

Degree Days: 7839

Solar Fraction: 33%

Auxiliary Heat: 5.12 BTU/DD/ft²

Passive Heating System(s): Isolated gain, direct gain

Recognition Factors: Collector(s): Greenhouse glazing, south-facing double glazing, 364 ft² **Absorber(s):** Water storage tank surface, concrete slab floors, masonry wall **Storage:** Water storage tank, concrete slab floors, masonry wall —**capacity:** 16,028 BTU/°F **Distribution:** Radiation, natural and forced convection **Controls:** Vents, dampers, roll-down insulating curtain and shades, greenhouse overhang

Back-up: Gas forced-air heating system

This split-level, 3-bedroom passive solar design in South Dakota is a modification of a conventional home with high market appeal. The house is built into a south-facing slope that provides earth berming for the lower level. A windbreak wall on the north, an airlock entry, high activity areas zoned to the south, and insulation R-values of 31 in walls and 40 in ceilings are additional energy-conservation features. All windows are double or triple glazed and have moveable insulation.

A south-facing greenhouse is the first solar **collection** area. During the day, heat is **absorbed** and **stored** in a water storage tank, in the concrete slab floor, and in a dark masonry wall faced with brick on the living room side. The masonry wall has floor and ceiling air vents and the high vents are equipped with backdraft dampers. As the house begins to cool in the evening, the storage walls and floor **distribute** radiant heat into the greenhouse and living room. Circulation between the two rooms is by natural convection. When temperatures at the cathedral ceiling of the living room are high enough, a thermostat activates the low-speed blower of the back-up forced air heating system, and solar-heated air is **distributed** throughout the house via the conventional furnace ductwork and vents. Air is returned to the greenhouse through the lower thermocirculation vents in the masonry wall.

At night, heat loss from the greenhouse is **controlled** by closing an automatic roll-down insulating curtain.

The second **collector** is the double-glazed, south-facing windows in the kitchen and family room. Heat is **absorbed** in the quarry tile floor and **stored** in the 6-inch concrete slab, which later radiates it back into the rooms for **distribution.** Because of the open floor plan, solar heat collected and stored in the kitchen and family room circulates through the lower level and through the upper level when bedroom doors are open. Windows in these rooms are protected from heat loss by manually operated insulating shades.

During the summer, the greenhouse is ventilated by operable upper and lower windows; overhangs, insulating curtains, and shades protect all south-facing glazing from heat gain. Cross-ventilation is induced when windows are opened throughout the house

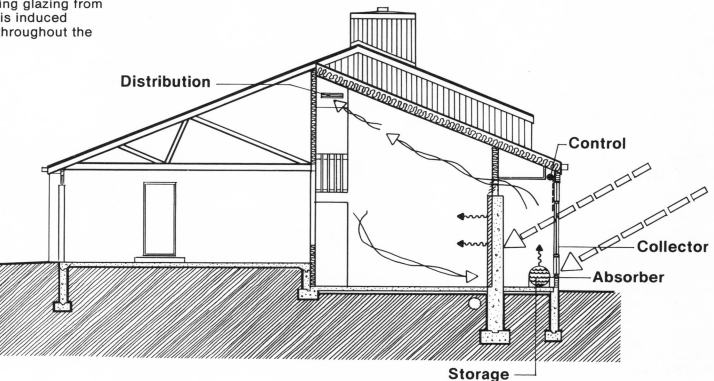

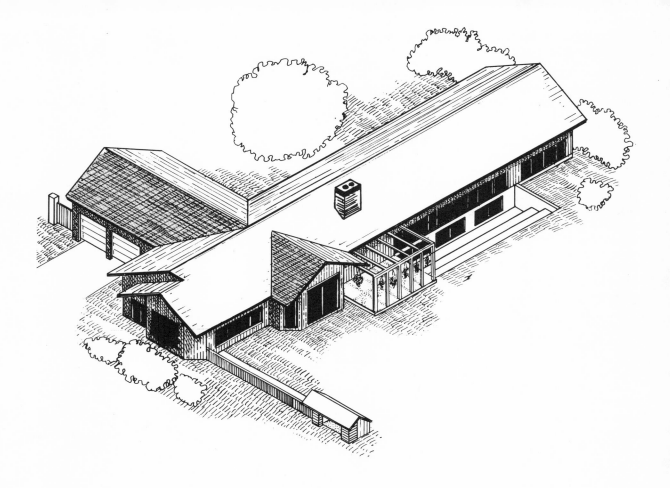

Sedgwick County, KS

Builder: John M. Roberts, Wichita, KS

Designer: Allen and Mahone, Watertown, MA

Solar Designer: Allen and Mahone

Price: $132,000

Net Heated Area: 3411 ft²

Heat Load: 98.9 x 10⁶ BTU/yr

Degree Days: 4620

Solar Fraction: 63%

Auxiliary Heat: 2.33 BTU/DD/ft²

Passive Heating System(s): Direct gain, indirect gain

Recognition Factors: Collector(s): South-facing glass, 469 ft² **Absorber(s):** Darkened north wall surface, ceramic tile floor **Storage:** Tile and concrete mass floor, thermal mass walls—**capacity:** 10,300 BTU/°F **Distribution:** Radiation, natural convection **Controls:** Window quilts, fixed overhang, removable louvers, canvas shade

To the casual observer, this large, simply designed home would appear to be of standard ranch-style construction. It was specifically designed to be compatible with other non-solar homes in its subdivision.

The home is located 3½ miles east of Kansas City, an area subject to temperature extremes, with hot, humid summers and cold winters. The flat topography allows cold winter winds to penetrate from the northwest. To protect the major living spaces from these winter winds, closets and secondary spaces are located on north

walls of the house. A garage on the north and a garden wall to the west act as additional buffers. There are at present no trees or shrubs on the level, 160 x 125 foot lot, which was originally part of a wheat field. Landscaping will be left to the buyer.

The home is divided into four **collection/ storage/ living** zones: the living/dining area, the family room, the three bedrooms, and the basement. Sunlight radiates directly into all of these except for the bedrooms. All areas have mass thermal **storage** walls and floors. The walls are 8-inch solid concrete blocks faced with plaster. The floors are 6-inch concrete slabs covered with ceramic tile.

Sunlight **collects** in the three direct gain living areas by passing through double-paned glass on the south wall. Heat is **absorbed** by the plaster on the walls and ceramic tile on the floor and is **stored** in the concrete mass of the walls and floors. Stored heat is **distributed** as it radiates from the thermal mass into the rooms; it is circulated within the rooms by natural convection.

For the bedrooms, sunlight enters and is collected in the south-facing hallway where it strikes the mass wall and floor and is **absorbed** and **stored** by the masonry. Heat then radiates into the bedrooms where it is **distributed** by a convective loop. An operable **control** transom above the doors also allows heated air to circulate from the hallway to the bedrooms, but heat can also be admitted simply by opening the doors whenever privacy is not required.

The solar system **control** requires some minimal occupant operation. Major south windows are insulated at night with Window Quilts™. These are manually operated roller shades with side tracks to reduce air leaks. They are available commercially.

In summer, heat gain is reduced through shading of the south glass by fixed overhangs. The lower areas of the larger windows also receive shading from removable louvers; these are stored during winter months.

The trellis over the patio is fitted with manually retractable shades. This **control** feature allows the owner to shade the family room windows, preventing heat gain, or to allow the sun to enter when heating is desired.

Insulation is R-19 in the exterior walls and R-30 in the ceiling. The number of east and west windows is minimized to prevent winter heat loss. An air-lock entry is located to the southwest.

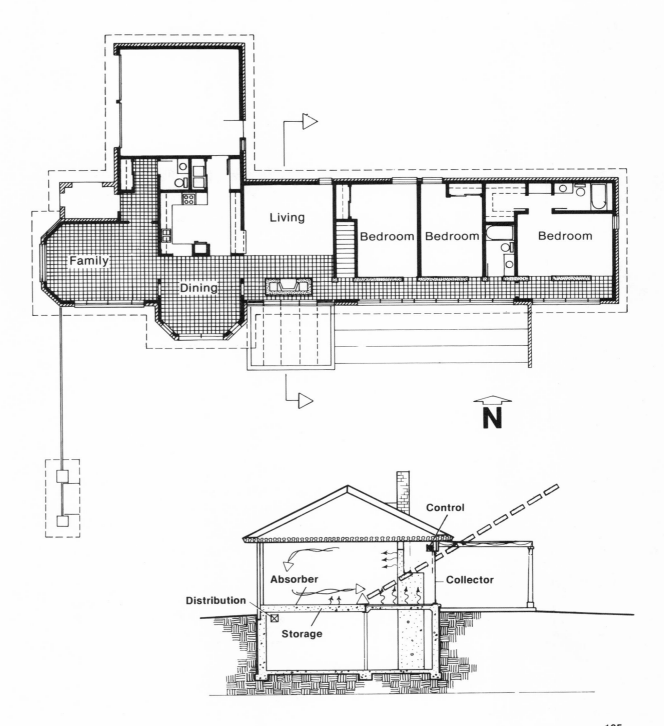

N

165

Builder: Country Club Heights Developers, Dodge City, KS

Designer: G.L. Weaver, Dodge City, KS

Solar Designer: Kansas Energy and Environment Lab, Inc., Wichita, KS

Price: $105,000

Net Heated Area: 2496 ft²

Heat Load: 90.6 x 10⁶ BTU/yr

Degree Days: 4986

Solar Fraction: 31%

Auxiliary Heat: 5.05 BTU/DD/ft²

Passive Heating System(s): Indirect gain, isolated gain, sun-tempering

Recognition Factors: Collector(s): South-facing panels, glazing, 250 ft² **Absorber(s):** Concrete slab floor and wall, concrete Trombe wall **Storage:** Concrete slab floor and wall, concrete Trombe wall—**capacity:** 6953 BTU/°F **Distribution:** Radiation, natural convection **Controls:** Moveable greenhouse glazing, vents, roof overhangs

Back-up: Natural gas furnace (52,000 BTU/H), wood stove

Passive Cooling Type: Convection, stack effect

Country Club Heights Developers, Inc., of Dodge City, Kansas, have developed a simple southwestern style 1-story passive house for a climate with extreme annual temperature swings. This locally popular style has been designed to maximize natural lighting and solar gain, while minimizing heat loss.

The house uses three main solar heating systems. The first is a Kalwall™ glazed greenhouse that **collects** solar heat. Its concrete wall and concrete slab floor **absorb** and **store** this heat. Heated air is **distributed** into the living space from the greenhouse through the one-way vents high in the wall, and natural convection recirculates cooled air back to the greenhouse through a vent lower in the wall.

During the summer, the glazing is replaced by screens, and the manually **controlled** vents high in the wall allow cool breezes to enter. If the lower vent is closed, warm air is expelled into the greenhouse. Insulation in the greenhouse roof also reduces solar gain in the summer.

The Kalwall™-glazed concrete Trombe wall provides the second form of solar heating. The masonry storage wall that is central to this Trombe system is an extension of the greenhouse storage wall. The Trombe system provides heat to the eastern half of the great room.

The double-glazed clerestory windows serving the kitchen and bedrooms on the north are the third passive heating system. They add natural light and some solar gain. Manually operated moveable insulation for these windows **controls** unwanted heat loss. Roof overhangs above the three solar heating systems deter heat gain in the summer.

Back-up heat for the house is provided by a gas furnace and a wood stove; cooling is provided by a conventional electric system.

Several other design features moderate the effects of temperature extremes on the building heating and cooling loads. Sheltered courtyards with full-height walls on the north and east protect the building from winter winds, while the roof slope also deflects the northwestern wind. The main entrance is through an air-lock, and the service entrance opens from the garage into the utility room.

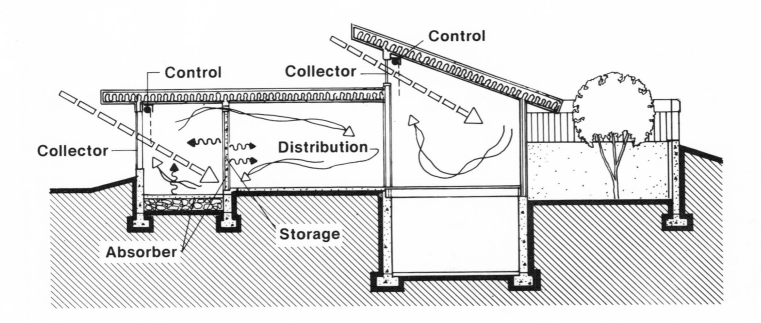

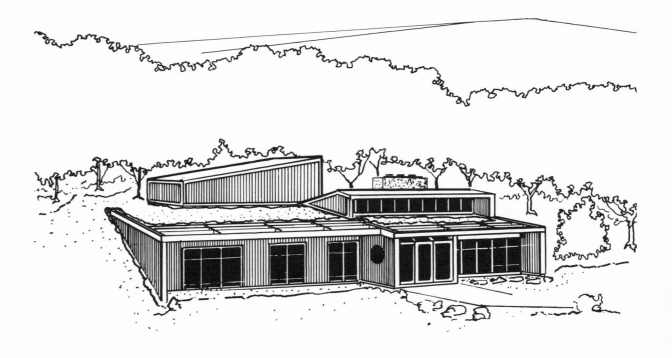

Eureka, MO

Builder: G. T. Kinnikin and Associates, House Springs, MO

Designer: Robert Lutz Architects, St. Louis, MO

Solar Designer: Ener-Tech, Inc., St. Louis, MO

Price: $115,000

Net Heated Area: 1783 ft²

Heat Load: 47.8 x 10⁶ BTU/yr

Degree Days: 4900

Solar Fraction: 58%

Auxiliary Heat: 2.27 BTU/DD/ft²

Passive Heating System(s): Indirect gain (Trombe wall)

Recognition Factors: Collector(s): Double-glazed windows, reflective white marble chips, 292 ft² **Absorber(s):** Dark concrete Trombe wall **Storage:** Concrete Trombe wall—**capacity:** 54,264 BTU/°F **Distribution:** Radiation, natural convection **Controls:** Moveable insulation, overhangs, vents

Back-up: Electric resistance heating, fireplace

Passive Cooling Type: Earth sheltering, convection

Nestled into the south-facing slope on a 3-acre, wooded site, this energy-efficient home is earth sheltered on the north, east, and west sides by earth berms. St. Louis winters are fairly brisk, with occasional periods of extreme cold. Prevailing winter winds are from the northwest. Summers are not excessively warm. The main concern is to moderate winter heating loads. The underground massing, sod roof, and earth berms greatly decrease the building's winter heat loss and reduce the summer cooling load as well.

Trees on a ridge to the north of the home provide winter wind protection. The garage, built on the same ridge, also helps to protect the house. Garage and asphalt pavement uphill from the home divert drainage to either side of the site. Drainage is accomplished by placing double draintile at

the foundation. The sloped roof provides quick water runoff.

The rustic style of this 1-story house is similar to most of the surrounding houses. The front is trimmed in cedar with some visible stone work. The rooms have been carefully placed. The main living spaces are located on the south side of the house for exposure to the sun, while on the north side unheated storage areas and closets act as buffers. All windows face south. The underground design of the house greatly moderates temperature fluctuations inside.

Each of the three bedrooms and the living/dining area receive heat collected through the south-facing windows. Each of the four main rooms (three bedrooms and living room/dining area) also has an individual Trombe wall using part of the south window **collection** space. Each wall is constructed of 16-inch thick concrete. White marble chips are placed under each double-glazed window to reflect additional sunlight onto the wall. Heat is **absorbed** by the darkened surface of the wall and **stored** in the concrete. Heat is **distributed** into the rooms by radiation, and within the room by natural convection.

A fireplace is used as the major source of back-up heat. Combustion air for the fireplace is ducted from the outside to prevent loss of warm interior air. The concrete mass of the fireplace provides heat **absorption** and **storage** for wood combustion heat and for sunlight **collected** by a clerestory window. Electric resistance heating is also provided, and it can be operated in the individual room to allow supplemental heating only where needed.

Moveable insulation is provided on all windows to control night heat loss. All Trombe walls are vented to the outside to allow manual exhaust of excess heat. Overhangs on each window reduce heat gain to the home in summer. Most windows can be opened for summer cooling. The clerestory on the east side of the home may be opened to induce summer venting. There is an air-lock entry into the home that reduces the magnitude of air changes, helping to reduce both heating and cooling loads.

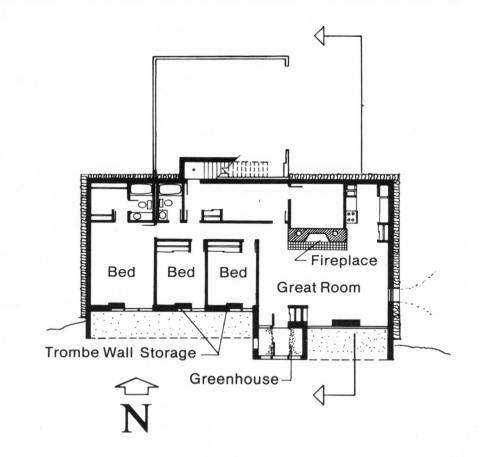

Bed Bed Bed

Fireplace

Great Room

Trombe Wall Storage

Greenhouse

N

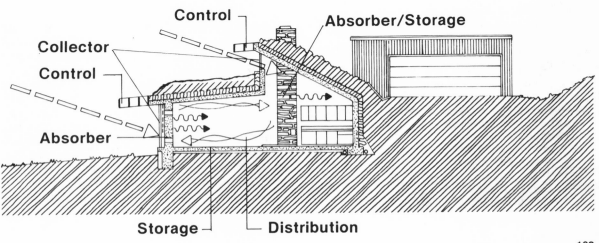

Control

Collector

Control

Absorber/Storage

Absorber

Storage   Distribution

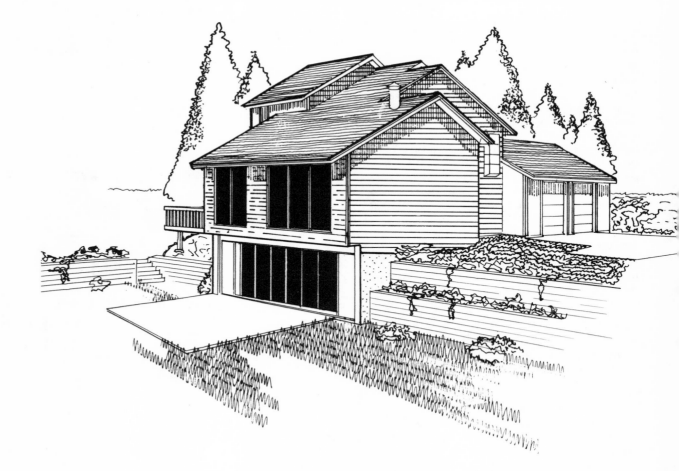

Builder: N.O. Brown Development Company, St. Louis, MO

Designer: N.O. Brown Development Company

Solar Designer: N.O. Brown Development Company

Price: $89,000

Net Heated Area: 2050 ft²

Heat Load: 62.6 x. 10⁶ BTU/yr

Degree Days: 4900

Solar Fraction: 53%

Auxiliary Heat: 2.03 BTU/DD/ft²

Passive Heating System(s): Sun-tempering, indirect gain

Recognition Factors: Collector(s): Double-glazed panels, 293 ft² **Absorber(s):** Water-filled polyethylene containers **Storage:** Water-filled polyethylene containers—**capacity:** 4725 BTU/°F **Distribution:** Radiation, natural and forced convection **Controls:** Return air registers, rolldown shades, overhangs

Back-up: 51,000 BTU heat pump, wood stove

Domestic Hot Water: Optional DHW pre-heat

Cooling Load: 12.79 x 10⁶ BTU/yr

170

A large, water Trombe wall is the dominant passive solar feature of this house, which is part of a custom development. Solar radiation is **collected** through double-glazed panels on the south face of the basement wall and is **absorbed** and **stored** by the 120 polyethylene 5-gallon containers located in an enclosed space that is separated from the rest of the basement by three insulated walls. Heated air is **distributed** from the water wall as it rises through registers in the living room floor and circulates to a return air register at the top of the stairwell; from there it is drawn by fan to the bottom of the water wall to be heated again.

Another fan, which can be controlled either thermostatically or manually, has been installed in the registers to **control** first-floor overheating.

Supplemental **collection** is provided by direct radiation through the double-glazed living room/dining room windows. During summer, an attic fan is used to exhaust hot air to the outside, and both the water wall and direct south windows are shaded by overhangs.

The 2-story plan, which has a low surface-to-volume ratio, is sited on a moderate south-facing slope. Earth is bermed on the north, east, and west sides to envelop the basement and to serve as a winter wind deflector. A stand of pines planted to the northwest acts as an additional wind buffer. The building has R-30 insulation in the ceilings and R-18 insulation in the walls and features details to eliminate wind infiltration such as: sill plates installed over sealant and siding/foundation wall joints sealed with polyurethane foam.

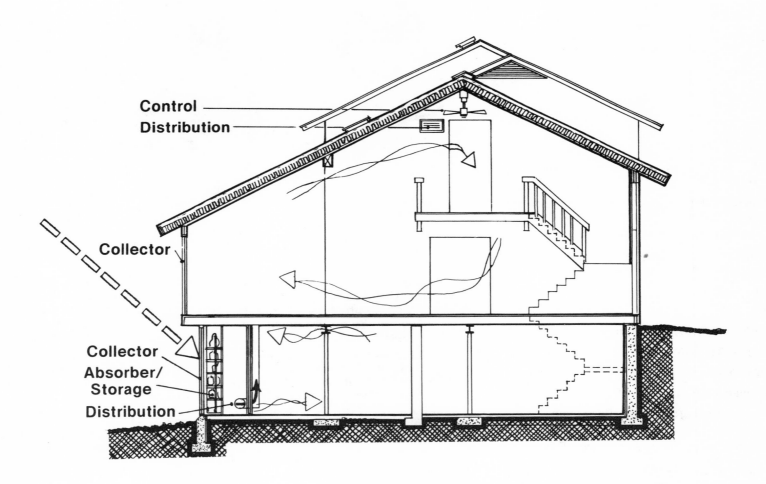

Control

Distribution

Collector

Collector

Absorber/
Storage

Distribution

Barnhart, MO

Builder: Parkton Development Company, Barnhart, MO

Designer: Londe-Rarke-Michels, Inc., St. Louis, MO

Solar Designer: Tim Michels, St. Louis, MO

Price: $62,000

Net Heated Area: 2800 ft²

Heat Load: 49.0 x 10⁶ BTU / yr

Degree Days: 4900

Solar Fraction: 63%

Auxiliary Heat: 1.29 BTU / DD / ft²

Passive Heating System(s): Direct gain

Recognition Factors: Collector(s): South-facing double glazing, 297 ft² **Absorber(s):** Ceramic tile over concrete slab, concrete wall surface **Storage:** Concrete floor and walls—**capacity:** 65,000 BTU / °F **Distribution:** Radiation, natural and forced ventilation **Controls:** Insulating shades, overhang, trellis, vents

Back-up: Gas furnace

172

This passive solar house is an adaptation of a model home for a large development. It is built into a south slope so that its upper level is at grade on the north. The wall construction is 2- x 6-inch studs with 6-inch fiberglass batts and ¾-inch polystyrene sheathing, while below grade walls are 8-inch concrete with 2-inch polystyrene. A continuous strip of butyl rubber sheet is attached to the exterior wall at the first-floor sill plate to reduce air infiltration. Twelve-inch fiberglass batts insulate the roof.

With the exception of a few north-facing windows, glazing (297 square feet) is confined to the south side. All windows are double glazed and are equipped with manually operated roll-down insulating shades.

The winter sun is **collected** directly through the south windows to heat the floor of the major living spaces. Dark-colored ceramic tile flooring **absorbs** the radiation, and the 8-inch concrete slab **stores** most of the heat for radiant distribution to the living spaces at night, when the insulating shades have shut off the windows, minimizing heat losses.

Overheating is prevented in the summer by a roof overhang that shades the second floor and by a trellis that extends about 5 feet from the upper floor, supporting a deciduous vine growth. Additionally, an attic fan draws air from the living spaces and exhausts it through a continuous roof vent.

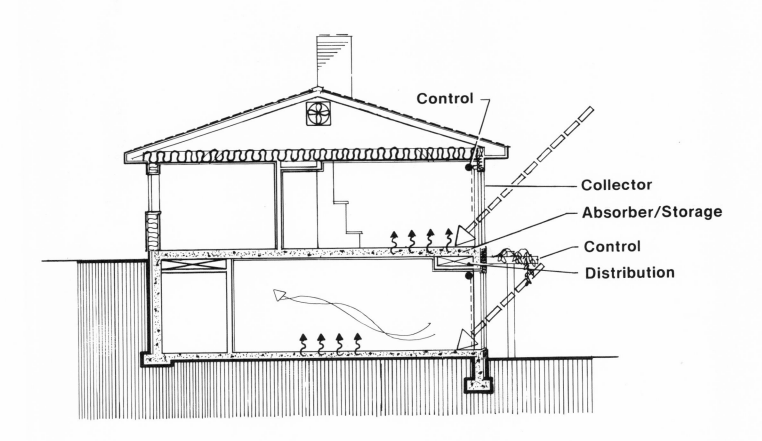

Control

Collector

Absorber/Storage

Control

Distribution

West

Port Townsend, WA

Eagle River, AK ●
Mat-su Borough, AK ●

Springfield, OR
Eugene, OR
Winston, OR

Bozeman, MT

Pocatello, ID

Cheyenne, WY

Truckee, CA

Walden, CO
Boulder, CO   Aurora, CO

Santa Rosa, CA
Davis, CA
Elk Grove, CA
Lockford, CA

Riverton, UT

Carbondale, CO

Redwood City, CA

Grand Junction, CO

Colorado
Springs, CO

Santa Fe, NM

West Sedona, AZ

Manzano Springs, NM

Tucson, AZ

above 10000

8000-10000

6000-8000

4000-6000

2000-4000

0-2000

Normal Heating Degree Days, Annual (Base 65°)

The Regional Solar Energy Center for the West is:

Western SUN
Pioneer Park Bldg.
Suite 800
715 S.W. Morrison
Portland, OR 97205
(503) 241-1222

The states served by it are:

Alaska
Arizona
California
Colorado
Hawaii
Idaho
Montana
Nevada
New Mexico
Oregon
Utah
Washington
Wyoming

Carbondale, CO

Builder: West Sopris Creek Builders

Designer: Sunshine Design, Carbondale, CO

Solar Designer: Sunshine Design

Price: $97,500

Net Heated Area: 1646 ft²

Heat Load: 48.0 x 10⁶ BTU/yr

Degree Days: 7339

Solar Fraction: 56%

Auxiliary Heat: 1.69 BTU/DD/ft²

Passive Heating System(s): Direct gain, indirect gain (Trombe wall), isolated gain

Recognition Factors: Collector(s): South-facing glazing, greenhouse glazing, skylight, 348 ft² **Absorber(s):** Concrete floor slab, Trombe wall surface **Storage:** Concrete floor slab, concrete Trombe wall, mass hearth—**capacity:** 12,870 BTU/°F **Distribution:** Radiation, natural and forced convection **Controls:** Trombe wall shade, insulated shutters and curtains, vents, roll-down shades

Active Solar Heating: See DHW

Back-up: Electric resistance heater (32,000 BTU/H), woodburning stove

Domestic Hot Water: 46 ft² flat-plate collectors, 82-gallon storage

A majestic view of mountain peaks to the south is a by-product of the passive solar design for this contemporary single-level home in Carbondale, Colorado. This area is experiencing a boom in its coal-mining industry, and the home is designed and priced for the typical buyer, a miner with a wife and two children. The gable roof design with attached garage is similar to the other conventional homes in the development. The extensive south-facing glass required for solar **collection** in this house is, because of the mountain view, a feature of many other local homes.

Energy-conservation features are emphasized for this cold winter climate. Insulation in the north and other walls has R-values of 35 and 25, respectively. The R-value of ceiling insulation is 39. All windows are wood frame with insulating glass, and all have

moveable insulating shutters, quilted curtains, or reflective shades. The main entry is through an unheated air-lock vestibule, and other entries are through buffer areas. The attached garage is located on the northwest as protection from prevailing winter winds. Inside, the living areas have been placed in the sunny south part of the house and support areas are located along the north wall. This design also includes an enclosed interior greenhouse for heat collection in the southeast corner, and a "sunscoop™" skylight above the central masonry wall and hearth.

Four different passive solar heating systems are simply and efficiently combined in this house. In the winter heating mode, 12-inch concrete block Trombe walls in the bedrooms and dining room **absorb** and **store** heat collected through south-facing glazing during the day. These walls are painted dark brown on the glazing side and are finished with stucco on the living side. Floor and ceiling vents in the walls permit convective circulation to **distribute** solar-heated air from the walls to the rooms. Also, heat stored in the Trombe walls is later re-radiated into the interior. In the evening when external temperatures drop, multilayer insulating curtains are automatically closed on the glazed side of the Trombe walls to **control** heat loss; they will open again automatically in the morning. These Insulating Curtain Walls™ are activated by a **control** system that has outdoor temperature and photocell sensors, and in-cludes manual overrides. The **control** mode setting is changed twice a year, once at the beginning of the summer, and again at the beginning of winter. All other windows are equipped with insulating shutters or roll-down shades that are manually operated.

In the greenhouse, aluminized Mylar™ shades on the living side of exterior glazing are opened each morning to permit solar **collection**. Heat is **absorbed** and **stored** in the 4-inch thick mass concrete floor and in mass planters, all of which are painted or stained dark brown. Opening the sliding glass doors and windows communicating with central living spaces allows circulation for **distribution** of solar-heated air from the greenhouse. At night, interior greenhouse doors and windows are closed, isolating this space from the rest of the house; the reflective roller shades, which have tight-fitting side tracks, are manually closed, which adds substantially to the insulating value of the exterior glazing, and the **control** of heat loss.

A third passive system combines a "sunscoop™" skylight collector and a central concrete mass wall and hearth. The sunscoop is created by cantilevering part of the north roof out over the south roof peak, and glazing from the top of the cantilever

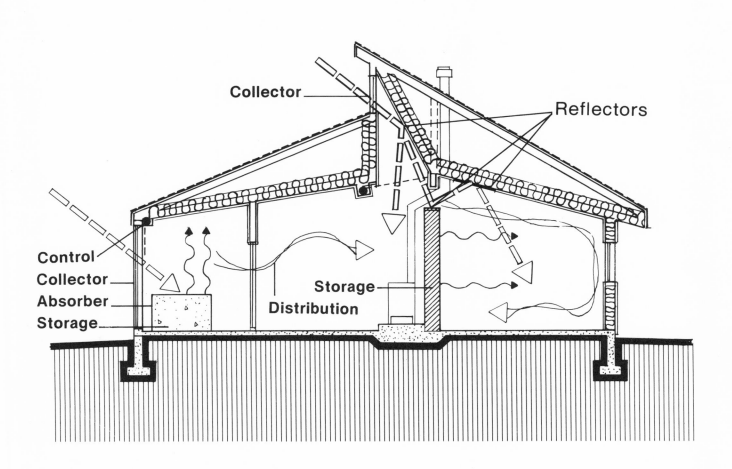

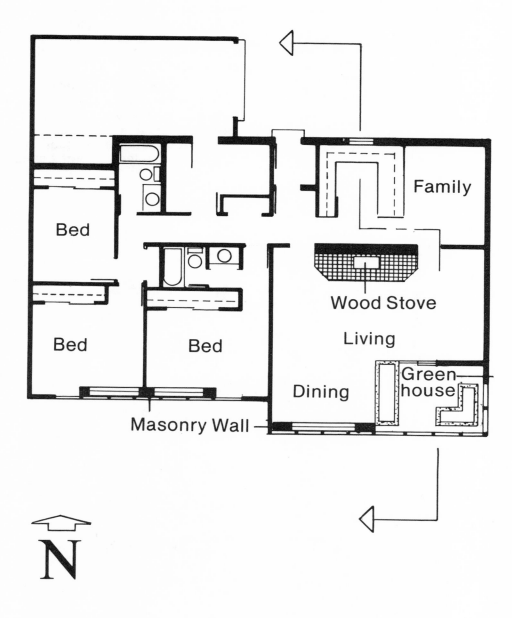

Family

Bed

Bed

Bed

Wood Stove

Living

Dining

Green house

Masonry Wall

N

down to the roof. This design produces a tilt angle that is optimum for winter heat **collection**. Inside the house, a reflective surface is constructed behind the glazing by extending plywood from the roof peak down to the ceiling level, and facing the plywood with mirrors. Sunlight passing through the skylight strikes the mirrored surface and is reflected onto the masonry wall and hearth directly below, where it is **absorbed** and **stored** as heat. The top surface of the wall is also faced with mirrors, and further reflects incoming light onto the kitchen ceiling. Heat stored in the wall and hearth during the day is later re-radiated for **distribution** into the kitchen and dining rooms. At night, an insulating window quilt is automatically drawn across the aperture beneath the sunscoop at ceiling level. Controls for this automatic shade are identical to those used for the Trombe wall insulating curtains.

In the fourth passive system, sunlight that is **collected** through exterior glazing and Trombe wall windows strikes bedroom and dining room floors directly. But because the bedroom floors are carpeted, they have less storage capacity. The dining room floor is a dark brown, 4-inch concrete slab that **absorbs** and **stores** solar heat for later release. **Control** of these passive heating elements is achieved by automatic closure of Trombe wall insulating curtains during winter nights and summer days.

Distribution of solar and back-up heat in winter is assisted by through-wall fans that draw warm air from the living space to the sleeping space.

In the summer, the interior greenhouse door and windows are closed during the day and the reflective greenhouse shades are left down. These shades will transmit about 20 percent of the incident light, so this space will not be unpleasantly dark. Venting the greenhouse is partially accomplished by opening the exterior door. An exhaust fan also contributes to ventilation; it is controlled by a cooling thermostat and does not require owner operations.

Opening all moveable insulation and windows throughout the house at night induces natural cross-ventilation and permits stored heat to be exhausted. Ridge and soffit vents cool the attic, and a turbine roof exhaust vent enhances natural summer ventilation. In the winter, an insulated cover is placed over the turbine inlet.

This design includes an active solar water heating system that has two flat-plate collection panels mounted on the roof. The system uses a propylene glycol solution as the heat transfer medium and a double-walled heat exchanger. It is expected to provide an average of 43 percent of the domestic hot water needs for a family of four persons.

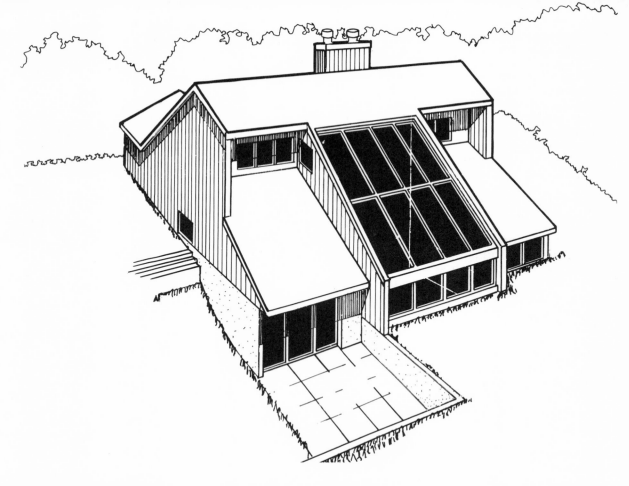

Aurora, CO

Builder: Wexford Corporation, Englewood, CO

Designer: Seracuse Lawler & Partners, Inc., Denver, CO

Solar Designer: Seracuse Lawler & Partners, Inc.

Price: $70,000

Net Heated Area: 1514 ft²

Heat Load: 110.5 x 10⁶ BTU/yr

Degree Days: 6277

Solar Fraction: 75%

Auxiliary Heat: 2.86 BTU/DD/ft²

Passive Heating System(s): Direct gain

Recognition Factors: Collector(s): South-facing panels, sliding glass doors, 504 ft² **Absorber(s):** Concrete slab floor covered with brick pavers, masonry wall **Storage:** Concrete slab floor, brick pavers, masonry wall—**capacity:** 17,443 BTU/°F **Distribution:** Radiation, forced and natural convection **Controls:** Operable curtain, vents, thermostats

Back-up: Gas furnace (65,000 BTU/H), woodburning stove

Domestic Hot Water: Optional

South-facing **collectors** have been provided for all major living areas of this 3-bedroom solar design. Each of the two upper-level bedrooms has four windows for heating individual storage masses, while the first-floor master bedroom has three windows and no storage. There are three sliding glass doors **collecting** heat in the dining room. The family room, located between the dining room and master bedroom, has eight vertical glass **collectors** and a sloping roof made entirely of Kalwall Sunwall™ panels. These panels have an R-value of 4.1, which is increased to R-10 with the use of integrated roll-out window quilts at night. All windows are double glazed and have fixed overhangs.

In the family room, there are two surfaces capable of **absorbing** and **storing** a significant amount of heat: an 8-inch concrete slab floor covered with brick pavers, and the 8-inch masonry wall at the north end of the room. The dining room has only the brick-covered slab floor. In the upstairs bedroom there are large brick-covered window sills **absorbing** heat for the 6-inch concrete **storage** slab beneath.

Backing up these solar systems in the winter and at night are a woodburning stove (within the masonry wall of the family room) and a gas furnace. The furnace is equipped with an air handler that can operate independently of the heater to evenly

distribute heat radiated from storage masses. This is accomplished by the return air intake in the ridge above the family room where heated air, which gathers there by natural convection, is drawn down into the furnace by the air handler and supplied to the rest of the house through floor and wall registers. Because the stove's flue closely parallels this air intake tube within the chimney, use of the stove will significantly raise the temperature of air being drawn down for distribution. As the stove draws its combustion air from the outside, its use will not diminish internal pressure. During extreme cold, the gas heater will activate automatically until the thermostat is satisfied. Heat loss at night is **controlled** by the window quilts that cover the Kalwall™ panels, sliding insulation panels on the upper-level bedroom windows, and conventional draperies on all other vertical glass.

In summer, when the temperature in the family room rises above 78°F, a thermostat will open a motorized damper in the ridge to exhaust hot air. The damper also opens if the outside thermostat indicates outside temperature to be about 68°F. To aid in ventilation, there is a manually opened electric fan box within the plenum with intake vents along the top of the skylight. When the window quilts are drawn to prevent solar gain, there is an air space left between them and the glazing. The fan draws the hot air out from this space, which in turn draws cooler air in from vents at the bottom of the glazing. Overheating is further **controlled** by use of the same moveable insulation and draperies used to control heat loss.

Earth berming has been used on all sides to help stabilize interior temperature. To reduce wind infiltration, buffer spaces (closets, utility spaces, etc.) have been located along the north wall of the house; the garage on the northwest side protects against prevailing northwest winds. Attic insulation is R-38, and walls are R-19.

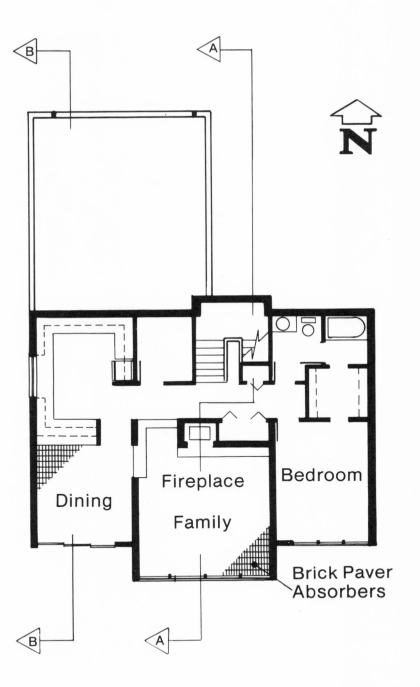

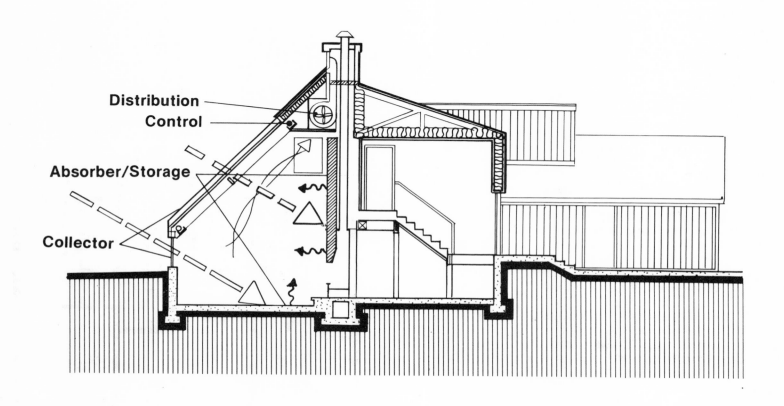

Distribution

Control

Absorber/Storage

Collector

A-A

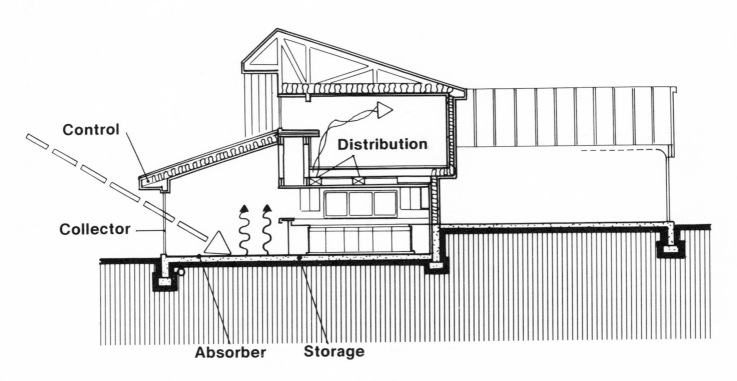

Control

Distribution

Collector

Absorber   **Storage**

B-B

West Sedona, AZ

Builder: Gary E. Wagley, General Contractor, Sedona, AZ

Designer: Sun System Engineering, West Sedona, AZ

Solar Designer: Jim Raney, Sedona, AZ

Price: $93,000

Net Heated Area: 1377 ft²

Heat Load: 45.3 x 10⁶ BTU/yr

Degree Days: 3702

Solar Fraction: 84%

Auxiliary Heat: 1.49 BTU/DD/ft²

Passive Heating System(s): Direct gain, indirect gain, sun-tempering

Recognition Factors: Collector(s): Double-glazed windows, 280 ft² **Absorber(s):** Tile floors and mass walls **Storage:** Masonry walls, concrete slab—**capacity:** 46,074 BTU/°F **Distribution:** Radiant, natural and forced convection **Controls:** Insulated shutters, fixed overhangs, exterior sun shading, earth berming, clerestory vent

Back-up: Electric furnace and woodburning stove

Domestic Hot Water: Two flat-plate collectors, roof-mounted, 82-gallon glass-lined tank

Passive Cooling Type: Natural and induced ventilation, night-sky radiation

184

The site is in north central Arizona where climate is characterized by light rainfall, very light winds, and large daily temperature swings. The structure is a rustic contemporary design situated on a south-sloping rectangular lot replete with indigenous vegetation. The house has been built into the slope so that it is earth-bermed on three sides. The main entry is on the north side where there is least exposure to prevailing southwest winds. The entry sytem is an air-lock vestibule located adjacent to a covered entry court which is additionally buffered by the carport and entry landscaping. Landscaping is also used to protect the west side from light winds, hot sun, and winter storms. To aid in this effect, the architect has located closets and utility areas along the interior of this west wall and omitted windows. There is only one window on the east side and it, too, has protective vegetation to reduce wind infiltration.

Double-glazed windows along the south wall of the house **collect** sunlight for the lower level: the living room, dining room and kitchen. On the upper level, the **collectors** are south-facing, fixed, double-glazed clerestory windows above the bedrooms. Domestic water is preheated by two roof-mounted flat-plate collectors.

Each passive collector transfers direct and indirect radiation to storage masses located on both levels. Direct radiation is **absorbed** and **stored** on the lower level by a floor of tile pavers covering a 6-inch concrete slab, and by 8-inch masonry walls along the east, west, and north sides of the interior. The sun's heat is directly **absorbed** and **stored** in the upper level by 8-inch masonry walls.

The efficiency of this structure's heating system is enhanced by the extensive use of forced **distribution**. A system of ducts and

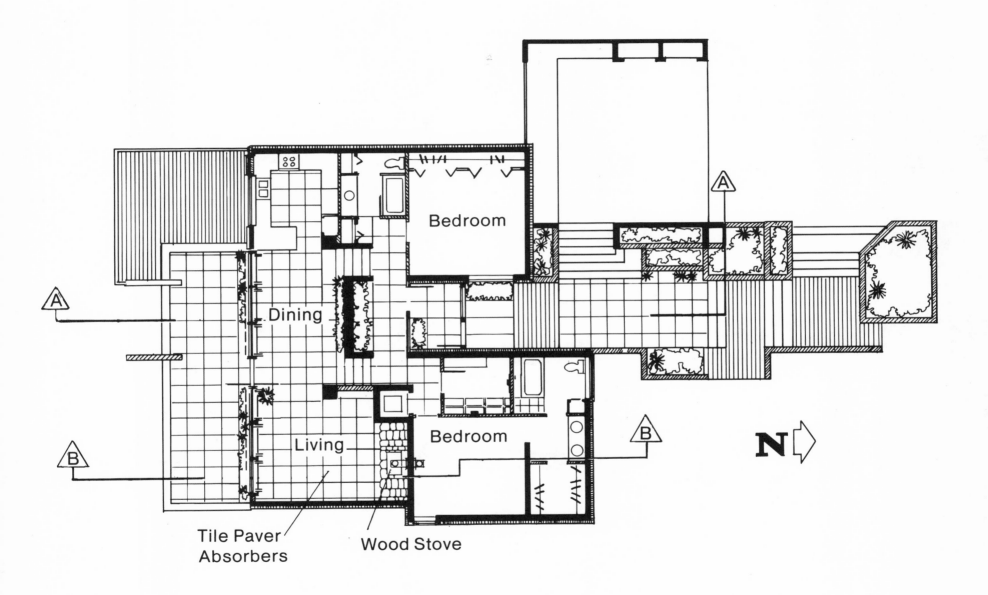

Tile Paver
Absorbers

Wood Stove

registers in the walls, ceilings, and floors connects to a central blower on the upper level. For back-up heating this blower has an integrated electric element. Except for moderate weather conditions, when natural convection and ventilation are adequate, this multi-phase **distribution** system is used in all seasons. In the winter mode the system operates in two stages. In moderate cold the first stage is activated automatically when the house thermostat demands heat and the ceiling sensor indicates that air in the clerestory is 12 degrees above the house thermostat. This turns on the furnace air handler which pulls the air down through ceiling vents and blows it back through

floor registers in all rooms. This operation continues until either the thermostat is satisfied or the ceiling sensor indicates that air in the clerestory is down to 8 degrees above the house thermostat. If the house thermostat requires heat when the ceiling temperature is less than 8 degrees warmer, the second stage becomes operational. In this stage the back-up electric element within the furnace heats the air before it is blown back out the floor registers. The element will stay on until the house thermostat is satisfied or the temperature difference between the house and ceiling reaches 12 degrees again. In this back-up stage the owner has the option of firing up the

woodburning stove located at the north wall of the living room when he notices that the back-up element indicator lamp is on. The stove draws its combustion air directly from the outside so that its use will not waste heated air from the house.

The duct system in the winter phase can also recirculate air from the clothes dryer through a filtered damper assembly, providing much needed winter moisture as well as heat.

All collectors are controlled by manually operated moveable insulation. On clerestory windows there are 1½-inch foam in-

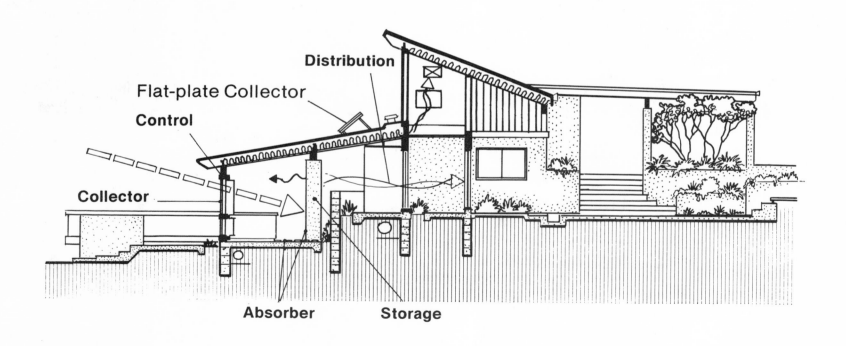

Distribution

Flat-plate Collector

Control

Collector

Absorber   **Storage**

sulation shutters, split horizontally (4-foot tops and 2-foot bottoms). During summer days the top section is left closed to prevent direct radiation to storage masses while the bottom section can be left open for natural lighting. For the dining room and living room windows there are interior 1½-inch foam insulation shutters split vertically, and exterior pull-down shades for filtering light. Kitchen windows have exterior insulated shutters, and all south walls have fixed overhangs.

For summer cooling, windows are left open at night so that by natural convection heat is exhausted through vents in the clere-

story. A fan can be turned on to increase the rate of this flow. During the day the moveable insulation covers collector windows to prevent direct radiation from heating the storage masses. If this is done, storage masses will cool interior air.

For more severe hot weather an evaporative cooler located outside the east wall is brought into operation by switching manual slide-in dampers and bypassing the furnace air handler. In this mode the fan in the cooler pumps cool humidified air into the subslab ducts and up through the floor registers. This air is then drawn up as hot air is exhausted by the fan, through the

clerestory exhaust damper. Both this damper and the evaporative cooler are sealed off in the winter phase.

The roofs are vaulted and light-colored to reflect heat and light. Insulation in the roof is R-32; wall insulation averages R-19.

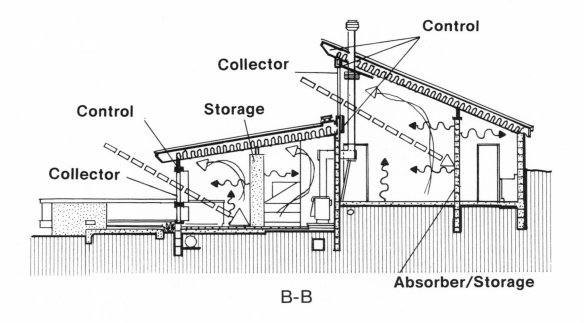

B-B

Winston, OR

Builder: James L. Richey, Jr., Building Contractor, Winston, OR

Designer: Sunwood Building and Design, Roseburg, OR

Solar Designer: Sunwood Building and Design

Price: $75,000

Net Heated Area: 1652 ft²

Heat Load: 70.6 x 10⁶ BTU / yr

Degree Days: 4496

Solar Fraction: 30%

Auxiliary Heat: 6.69 BTU / DD / ft²

Passive Heating System(s): Direct gain

Recognition Factors: Collector(s): Double-glazed windows, 246 ft² **Absorber(s):** Concrete floor, mass walls, brick tile floor **Storage:** Concrete floor, concrete block walls—**capacity:** 17,183 BTU/°F **Distribution:** Radiation, natural and forced convection **Controls:** Window shutters, thermostat, overhang, moveable insulation

Back-up: Electric furnace, wood stove

Domestic Hot Water: Active solar closed loop

188

The Cape Cod home has great appeal to buyers, and this example of that popular style has been successfully modified to include a passive solar energy system. This system is simple and reliable. Sunlight is **collected** through double-glazed windows on the home's south-facing walls and through skylights on the south-facing roof. A total of 246 square feet of openings is used for solar **collection.**

The sun's energy is **absorbed** by the brick tile floor surface and the surface of a concrete block wall that is located inside the home. Heat from the absorber surfaces is carried through the brick tiles into the concrete floor slab and also into the concrete block wall to be **stored.** The concrete blocks are covered with concrete in order to increase their storage capacity.

Heat stored in the mass of the floor and walls is **distributed** as it radiates to the living space when the indoor air temperature goes down. A ¼-horsepower blower in the ducting system draws heat from the ridge of the home and redistributes it to the rest of the living space. When the heat storage mass gives up all its heat to the living space, a differential thermostat turns on the back-up electric furnace which distributes heat throughout the duct system. There is also a wood stove.

When the sun sets, the homeowner covers the skylights with wood shutters that are filled with rigid insulation; insulating curtains are lowered over the south-facing windows. These moveable devices **control** heat loss.

The home has been built so that conversion to a heat pump back-up system could be made easily. The electric furnace is designed to accept a heat pump coil, and all compressor pipes have been installed.

In order to prevent heating the house in the summertime, the skylights are covered by insulated shutters during the daytime, and the shades on the windows are adjusted to keep out direct sunlight. During summer nights, the skylight shutters are opened and the shades are folded up. This allows interior heat to radiate out.

Overhangs shade the windows from the high summer sun. Openings on the north and south side of the home allow cross-ventilation. An exhaust fan at the home's upper level can be used to help create cooling drafts.

Most of the domestic hot water is pre-heated by the sun. The south-facing roof supports three active solar collectors. A solution of water and antifreeze is pumped through the collectors to a double-walled heat exchanger in the storage tank and then back to the collector. In the heat exchanger, the antifreeze transfers its heat to a supply of potable water. This preheated water then supplies a conventional electric domestic hot water tank.

Many details of the design make the home energy conserving. Most of the lower floor is located below grade and is also partially earth-bermed. This moderates the temperature extremes by surrounding the living space on the lower floor with the constant temperature of earth below the frost line. Windows and doors are weather-stripped.

All exterior walls are insulated to at least R-19. The roof is insulated to R-30. All windows can be covered with moveable insulation at night. Storage, utility, and bathrooms are located on the north wall to shield the living space. The concrete slab and perimeter are insulated with 2-inch rigid foam.

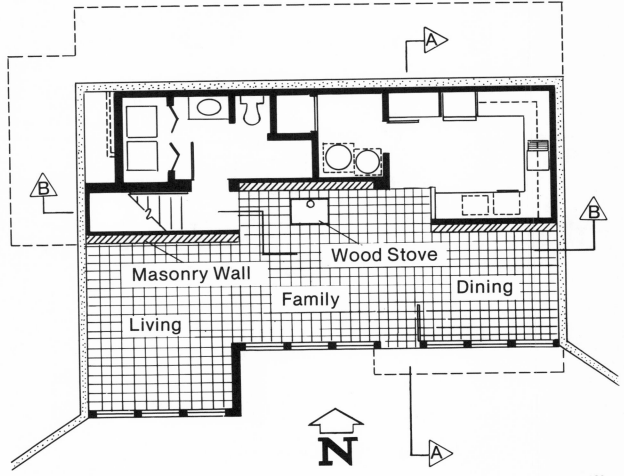

Masonry Wall

Wood Stove

Family

Dining

Living

N

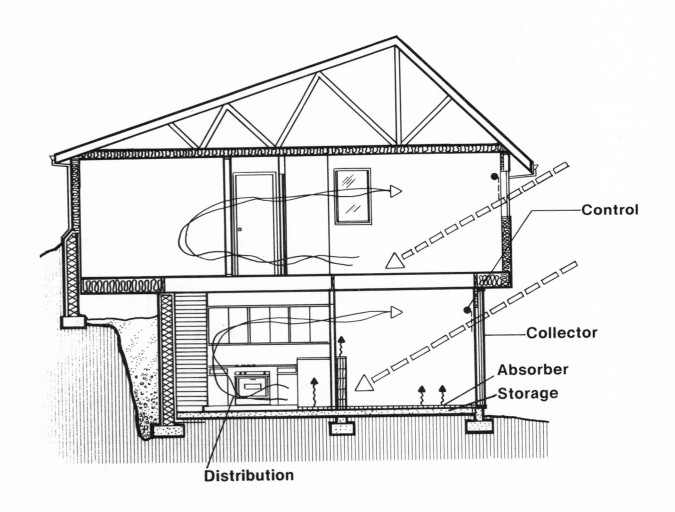

Control

Collector

Absorber

Storage

Distribution

A-A

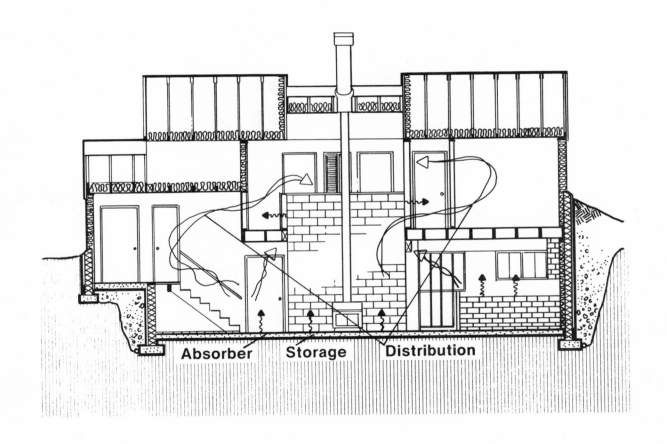

Absorber   Storage   Distribution

B-B

Davis, CA

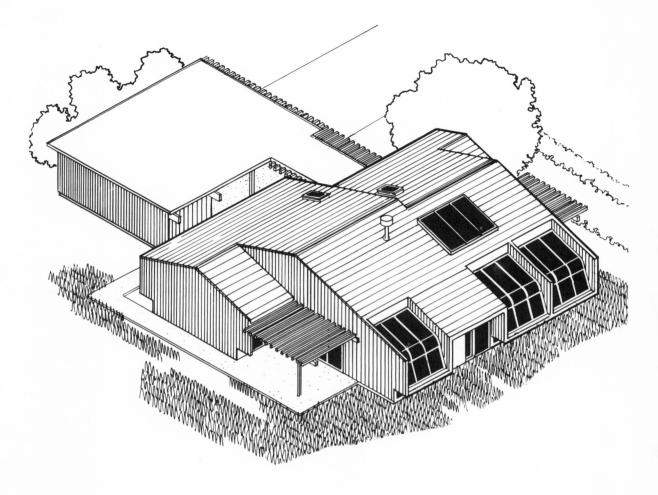

Builder: Hornbeek Construction Company, Davis, CA

Designer: Hornbeek Construction Company

Solar Designer: Hornbeek Construction Company

Price: $90,000

Net Heated Area: 1180 ft²

Heat Load: 40.7 x 10⁶ BTU / yr

Degree Days: 2419

Solar Fraction: 75%

Auxiliary Heat: 3.49 BTU / DD / ft²

Passive Heating System(s): Sun-tempering, direct gain, indirect gain, isolated gain

Recognition Factors: Collectors(s): Greenhouse glazing, sliding glass doors, 286 ft² **Absorber(s):** Greenhouse brick floor over concrete slab and sand, steel water tank surface **Storage:** Brick floor, concrete slab floor, water in steel tanks— **capacity:** 8906 BTU / °F **Distribution:** Radiation, natural ventilation **Controls:** Insulated curtain, greenhouse canvas shade, adjustable sunshade, tank insulating curtain, vents

Active Solar Heating: Active space heating back-up from DHW system

Back-up: Hot water is pumped through fan-coil units and baseboards

Domestic Hot Water: Active DHW system

Passive Cooling Type: Night-sky radiation, convection

All houses built in Davis, California, must conform to the city's energy-conservation ordinance. This traditional ranch house has been built almost to the book to meet these requirements.

Its compact form, with a heated area of 1180 square feet, avoids a box-like appearance by the use of protruding side wings for the two bedrooms, a gently sloping roof to deflect the north wind, and a separate car-port and shop wing attached by a breeze-way.

Windows on the east and west sides have been kept to a minimum; cross-ventilation has been emphasized to take advantage of the Sacramento delta winds; double glazing has been used throughout; and overhangs and trellises are included to protect the house from direct sun. The house is oriented 10 degrees east of true south.

Serving as **collectors** are three standard, double-glazed aluminum greenhouses incorporated into the south side of the house. Fin walls jutting out to the level of

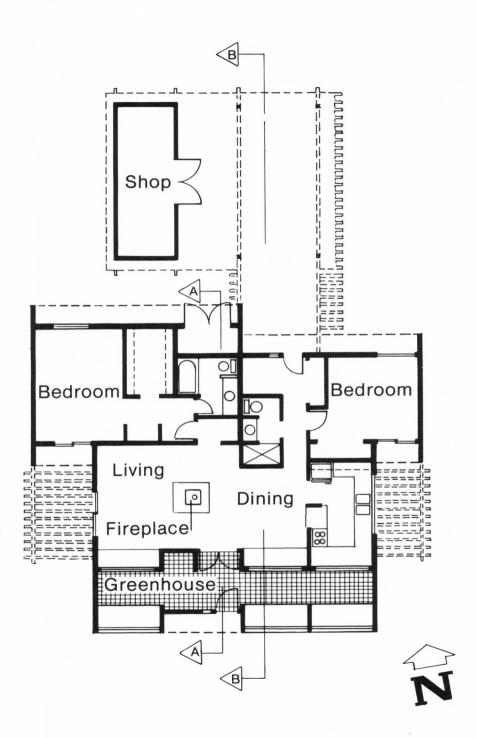

the entrance form "pockets" for the greenhouses. The center foyer opens on either side to the greenhouses.

On the east and west flanks of the house, two bedroom wings extend with sliding glass doors facing south to act as additional passive **collectors**. Opening onto trellis-covered patios, these allow some winter sun exposure for the bedrooms and excellent cross-ventilation in the summer.

Absorbing and **storing** solar radiation are brick floors in the greenhouses that are set in sand on 4-inch thick concrete slabs, and three black-painted steel water tanks, 2 feet high, dividing each greenhouse from the living room, dining room, and kitchen. The tanks are built in under functional counter tops with sliding glass windows closing off the greenhouses from the rest of the house.

On winter nights, stored heat is **distributed** by radiation from the tanks directly to the rooms and an insulating curtain is drawn to prevent back losses from the tanks to the greenhouses. A convective **distribution** is set up between the greenhouses and the remainder of the living area by opening the sliding glass windows over the three water tanks.

The amount of solar energy admitted to the house can be **controlled** by the raising or lowering by crank of three outside synthetic canvas (acrylic) blinds which are installed over the glass contours of the greenhouse.

A wood stove, centrally located in the living area, provides back-up heat.

On summer days, the adjustable sunshade is lowered, the tank insulating curtain is pulled down, the skylight shutters are closed, and the hatches to the attic and the vent-louvers to the garden are opened to allow cross-ventilation of the greenhouse. In the cool of the evening, moveable insulation is raised, and all hatches and vents opened to allow natural cooling. In the event that there are no breezes, an exhaust fan with a manually timed switch ventilates the house. The year-round climate in Davis is mild. Extreme summer heat can be taken care of by one air conditioning unit in the west wall of the living room.

An active solar domestic water heating system also provides an effective space heating back-up in winter. Hot water is pumped through fan-coil units and baseboards using, in the process, relatively little mechanical power.

The house could be considered a model for the energy-efficient requirements of the city of Davis. It has R-19 insulation in the walls and R-30 in the roof, double glazing, insulated and shuttered skylights, and windows and doors that are all caulked and weatherstripped. The R-6 perimeter insulation minimizes slab edge losses. The use of unnecessary glass has been avoided and windows facing east and west kept to a minimum to prevent summer overheating.

A storage room, a carport, and a shop form a separate wing of the house and are connected by a trellis-covered breezeway. This north-facing service area deflects north winds from bedrooms and bathrooms. The repetition of the trellis motif, along the south front and over the east and west south-facing patios, give the house an airy appearance and is another pleasing element of a house well designed in many ways.

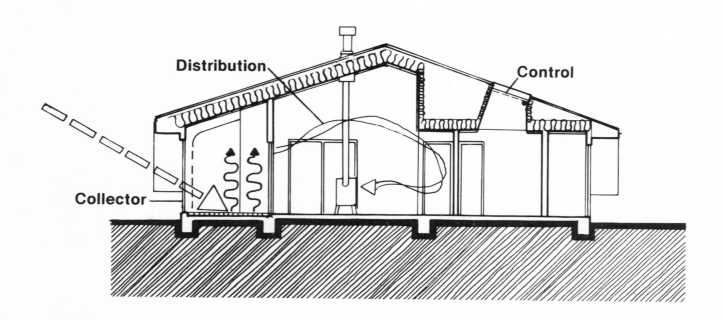

A-A

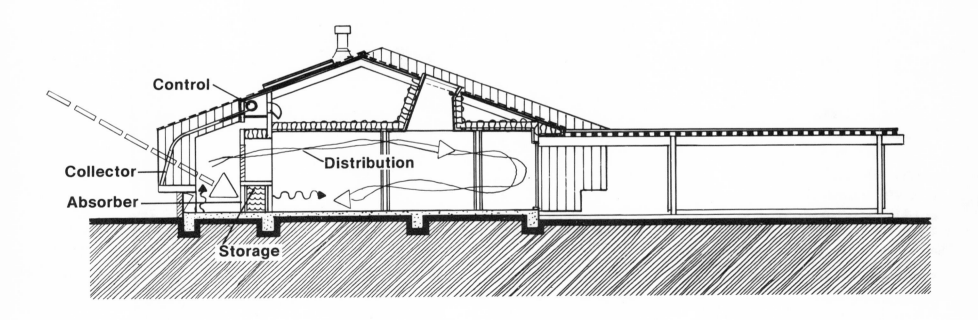

Control

Collector

Absorber

Storage

Distribution

B-B

Redwood City, CA

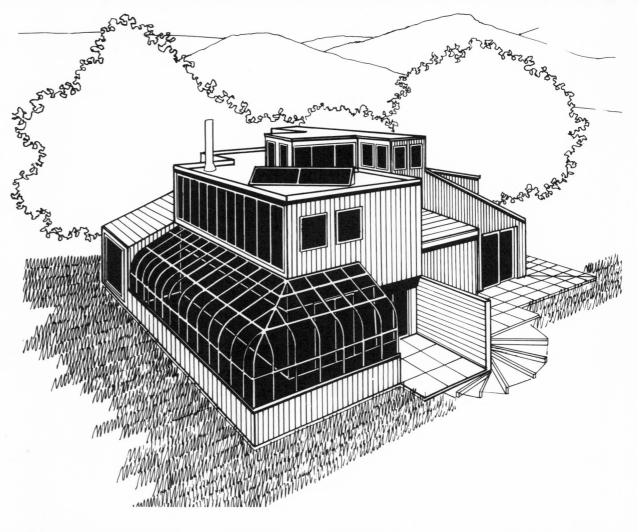

Builder: Redwood City Assoc./Baker Construction, Menlo Park, CA

Designer: VanderRyn, Calthorpe and Associates, Inverness, CA

Solar Designer: VanderRyn, Calthorpe and Associates

Price: $275,000

Net Heated Area: 2200 ft²

Heat Load: 85.4 x 10⁶ BTU/yr

Degree Days: 3042

Solar Fraction: 88%

Auxiliary Heat: 1.60 BTU/DD/ft²

Passive Heating System(s): Direct gain, indirect gain

Recognition Factors: Collector(s): South-facing double glazing, greenhouse glazing, 944 ft² **Absorber(s):** Tile-covered concrete floor, concrete block wall **Storage:** Concrete floor, concrete block wall—**capacity:** 14,210 BTU/°F **Distribution:** Radiation, natural convection **Controls:** Vents, shades, dampers, blinds, greenhouse roll-down shade

Back-up: Electric resistance heaters

Domestic Hot Water: Liquid flat-plate collectors (49 ft²)

This contemporary California split-level home is well suited to Cordilleras Heights, a luxury development in Redwood City, 20 miles north of San Francisco. The southeast and northeast sides of the lot have been banked to protect the house from prevailing winter winds. The design features an attached first-story greenhouse on the southeast and southwest sides, and a central belvedere with clerestory windows.

Greenhouse glazing **collects** solar heat, which is **absorbed** and **stored** in the bottom half of a 2-story high, 8-inch thick masonry Trombe wall. The wall is coated with a black selective surface to increase absorption. Additional **storage** is provided in the 4-inch thick exposed aggregate greenhouse floor. Solar heat is **distributed** by radiation and convection to the dining room and kitchen. Excess greenhouse heat is circulated to the interior of the house by a 500 cfm fan located in a joist space of the second floor.

Above the greenhouse on the southwest side, double-glazed fixed glass **collects** sunlight to be **absorbed** and **stored** by the upper half of the 2-story Trombe wall.

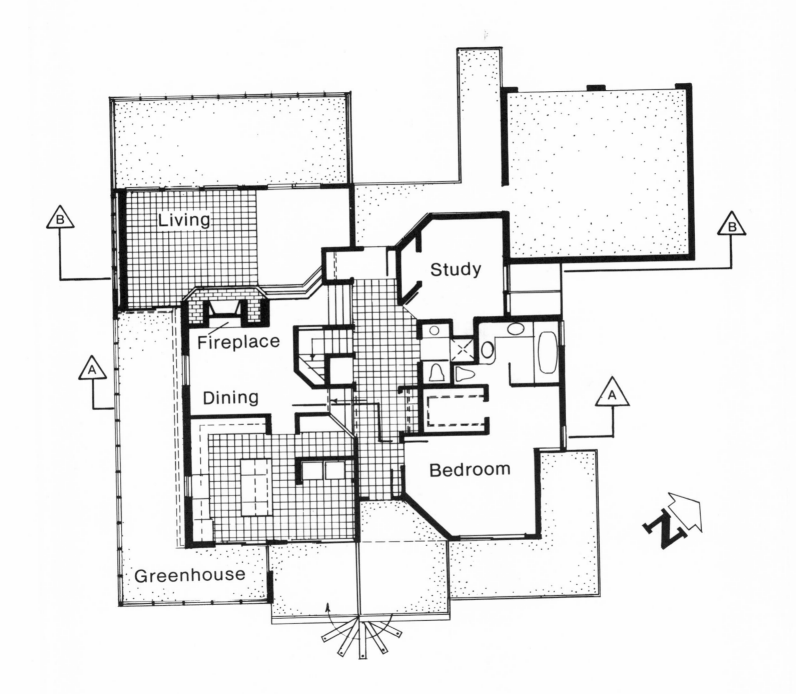

Living

B

Fireplace

A

Dining

Greenhouse

Study

B

A

Bedroom

N

Radiation and natural convection of heat stored in the wall provide nighttime heating for the second-story bathroom and bedrooms.

Afternoon sunlight **collected** through double glazing on the southwest side of the living room is **absorbed** and **stored** in an 8-inch thick, single-story masonry Trombe wall. Stored heat is radiated back into the living room at night.

During the day, direct solar radiation heats the first-story kitchen, breakfast room, master bedroom, and the second-story bedrooms. The clerestory windows of the belvedere **collect** direct solar heat for the 2-story stairwell and gallery that form the core of the house. None of these areas have significant storage mass. However, a destratification fan in the top of the belvedere redistributes solar heated air that has risen to the ceiling from other areas of the

house. A high transom and low vent in the study wall below the belvedere allow solar heat from the gallery to warm the study by natural convection.

The main effort to **control** heat in this house is directed toward limiting incoming solar radiation in the summer. Greenhouse and other south-facing glazing is equipped with roll-down shades to prevent sunlight from entering when heat is not needed. The

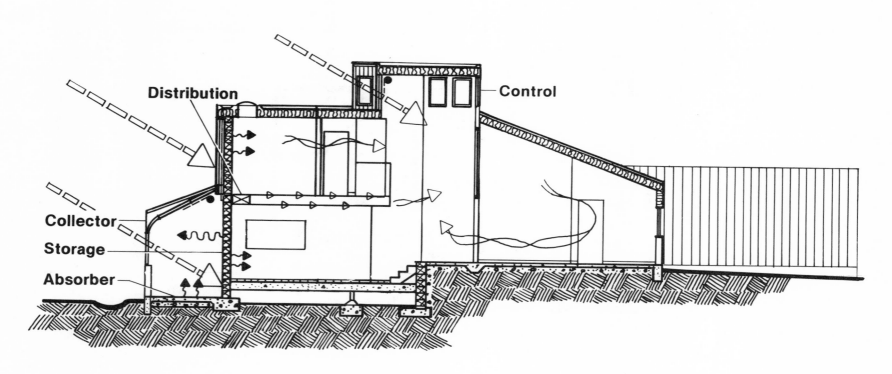

A-A

masonry walls act as convective drive for natural summer ventilation, taking full advantage of Redwood City's mild summers. Ventilation is induced by opening the windows at the top of south-facing glazing on both levels. Trombe wall vents with one-way dampers at floor level on both stories allow hot air to be pulled from the interior of the house into the stack between the masonry and glazing, and vented through the open windows. Opening upper-level bedroom windows, high belvedere windows, and vents in the study and master bedroom induces natural cross-ventilation.

The clerestory windows and southeast glass are shaded by narrow white venetian blinds.

An active solar collector for the domestic hot water system faces true south on the flat section of the roof.

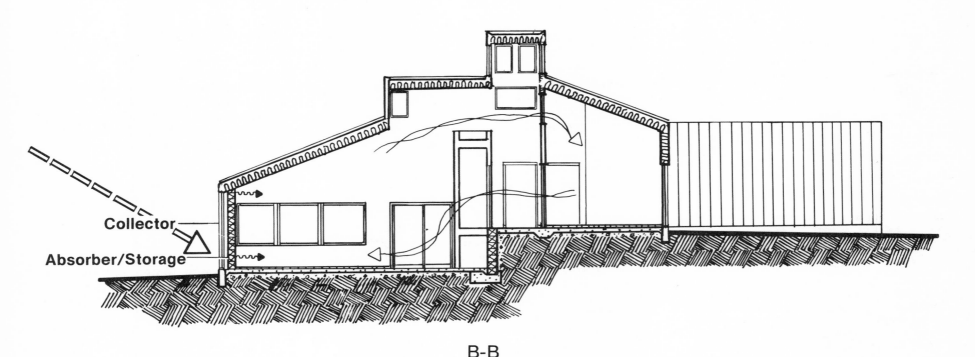

Collector

Absorber/Storage

B-B

Builder: Edeen Construction, Cheyenne, WY

Designer: Larry W. Rosentreter, Cheyenne, WY

Solar Designer: Larry Rosentreter

Price: $100,000 to $120,000

Net Heated Area: 3386 ft²

Heat Load: 143.9 x 10⁶ BTU / yr

Degree Days: 7381

Solar Fraction: 44%

Auxiliary Heat: 3.22 BTU / DD / ft²

Passive Heating System(s): Sun-tempering, direct gain, isolated gain

Recognition Factors: Collector(s): South-facing glazing, greenhouse glazing, skylights, 400 ft² **Absorber(s):** Brick pavers over concrete floor, brick walls **Storage:** Brick walls, concrete floor— **capacity:** 9723 BTU / °F **Distribution:** Radiation, natural and forced convection **Controls:** Solarium ducts, insulated window quilts, window shades

Back-up: Gas furnace (88,000 BTU / H) with electric-powered blower

This design for a 2-story, 3-bedroom home with stained board-and-bat exterior is a prototype for a moderately priced, conventional passive solar house in Wyoming, where the few existing solar homes are expensive custom designs. Energy-conserving features include R-19 fiberglass insulation in the walls and R-30 insulation in the roof, insulated windows with storm sashes and slim-shade shutters, and moveable insulation on all south-facing windows and skylights. Both exterior entries have airlock vestibules, and the garage is located on the west to protect against prevailing winter winds. Openings on non-south walls have been minimized as further protection against winter infiltration. The solar design incorporates a variety of passive systems including a greenhouse and three glazed masonry walls.

Solar heat is **collected** through the south-facing glazing of the greenhouse and then **absorbed** and **stored** in the masonry wall and floor. When the house thermostat calls

for heat, and, if air at the greenhouse ceiling is warm enough, a motorized damper automatically opens. The heated air is pulled into ceiling-level return grilles and then ducted into the blower unit of the back-up heating system for **distribution** throughout the house.

If the greenhouse ceiling temperature is not high enough when the house needs heat, a second motorized damper in the greenhouse by-pass duct closes, and only return air from the house is circulated. If the temperature of the return air is less than 70°F, and there is inadequate heat in the greenhouse, the standby gas-burning furnace is activated. At night, insulating window quilt shades are drawn in front of the greenhouse mass wall to **control** heat loss and the greenhouse itself becomes a buffer zone for the storage wall.

In another passive system, solar heat is **collected** through six double plexiglass skylights located along the east-west axis

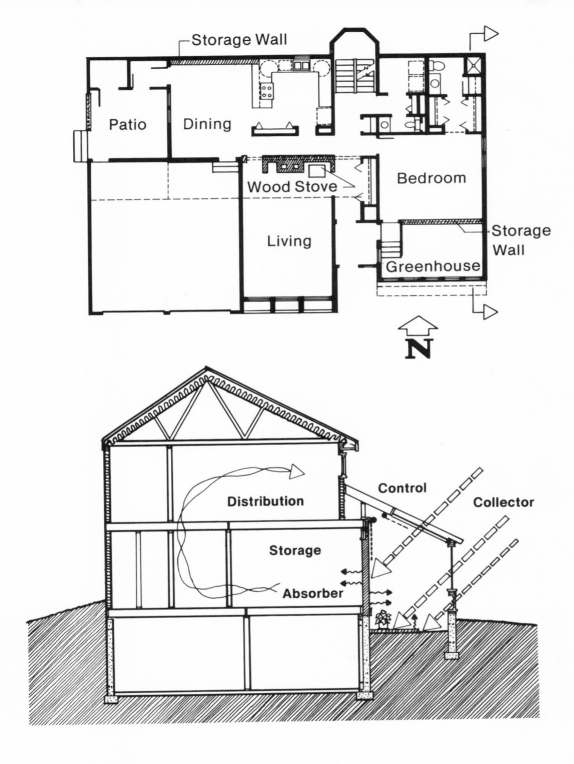

N

of the roof. The heat is **absorbed** and **stored** in the dining room masonry wall and floor, and in another masonry wall that separates the living room and kitchen on the first story, and a bedroom and balcony on the second story. This wall is also charged with heat from the living room wood stove. On fall and winter evenings, stored heat is **distributed** as it radiates into living and sleeping areas on both levels.

The second-story hallway and landing, the living room, and an unfinished basement room also receive direct sunlight, but there are no storage elements in these areas.

Summer cooling needs are minimal in the Wyoming climate. The collection and storage elements are protected from solar gain by roll-down and insulating shades and overhangs. During summer nights, shades are opened, allowing heat to escape to the outside. Windows are opened to permit cross-ventilation, and exhaust fans ventilate the greenhouse and dining room. A ''summer'' setting on the green-house motorized dampers allows them to be closed for the season, isolating the greenhouse from the forced-air distribution system. When the furnace blower is ac-tivated, cool night air is drawn in through a positive seal damper on the north wall, and is distributed throughout the house.

Builder: Energy Techniques, Colorado Springs, CO

Designer: Design Group Architects, Colorado Springs, CO

Solar Designer: Design Group Architects

Price: $85,000

Net Heated Area: 1558 ft²

Heat Load: 75.1 x 10⁶ BTU/yr

Degree Days: 6423

Solar Fraction: 48%

Auxiliary Heat: 3.93 BTU/DD/ft²

Passive Heating System(s): Direct gain, sun-tempering, isolated gain

Recognition Factors: Collector(s): Double-glazed windows and glass sliding doors, triple-glazed clerestory windows, 309 ft² **Absorber(s):** Brick pavers over concrete slab floor, concrete walls **Storage:** Concrete slab floor, concrete walls— **capacity:** 8804 BTU/°F **Distribution:** Natural and forced convection, radiation **Controls:** Thermostatically controlled fans, vents

Back-up: Natural gas forced-air furnace (39,500 BTU/H), airtight woodburning stove

This contemporary design is to be located in a large urban subdivision that includes other passive solar homes. The design specifies a highly insulated, high-mass structure for protection against the extremes of the Colorado climate. The low-profile house is bermed on the north, east, and west, and has air-lock entries that further reduce infiltration. The main living areas have been incorporated into an open "great room" that has access to an attached greenhouse.

On sunny winter days, solar heat is **collected** through greenhouse glazing and is **absorbed** and **stored** in the mass floor, a 4-inch concrete slab surfaced with brick pavers. **Stored** heat is later re-radiated to be **distributed** to the living area by opening the sliding glass doors that open to the great room. At night, greenhouse doors are closed to **control** heat loss from the living area.

A high clerestory allows solar heat to be **collected** through fixed, triple-glazed windows. Heat is **absorbed** and stored in the concrete mass walls and floors of the kitchen and utility room below, and is **distributed** radiantly at night when the house temperatures drop. Sunlight penetrates directly into the bedrooms and the dining room through south-facing sliding doors. Solar heat is **stored,** however, only in the dining room tile floor; the bedrooms have no storage mass. Winter **distribution** of solar heat can also take place through the air-handling system associated with the back-up gas-fired furnace. When the thermostat in the great room calls for heat, a fan in the furnace is automatically activated. If the temperature of solar-heated air accumulating at the top of the clerestory is above a predetermined point, the air is drawn down the return air duct, and is circulated to rooms through tubes embedded under and in the concrete slab floors. If the solar-heated air is not warm enough to contribute to house heating, the gas furnace is automatically activated.

During the summer, protection from unwanted heat gain through south-facing glazing is provided by overhangs. Opening windows and sliding doors throughout the house allows natural cross-ventilation, and thermostatically controlled fans can be activated to provide additional air movement.

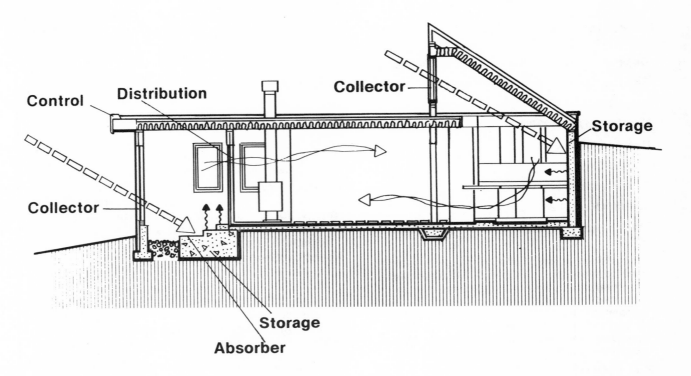

Builder: Holling & Associates, Inc., Grand Junction, CO

Designer: Crowther Architects Group, Denver, CO

Solar Designer: Crowther Architects Group

Price: $89,000

Net Heated Area: 2076 ft²

Heat Load: 81.9 x 10⁶ BTU/yr

Degree Days: 5605

Solar Fraction: 39%

Auxiliary Heat: 4.26 BTU/DD/ft²

Passive Heating System(s): Direct gain, indirect gain

Recognition Factors: Collector(s): South-facing glazing, clerestory windows, 170 ft² **Absorber(s):** Quarry tile floor, water tubes, concrete mass **Storage:** Water tubes, concrete and brick mass— **capacity:** 7980 BTU/°F **Distribution:** Radiation, forced and natural convection **Controls:** Thermostat, moveable insulating shutters and blinds, adjustable awnings, overhangs, and louvers

Back-up: Gas boiler (42,000 BTU/H)

Domestic Hot Water: 40,000 BTU/H DHW heater with 80-gallon storage

This tri-level, 3-bedroom western design features earth-bermed lower-story bedrooms and an upper-level family room with a clerestory. High R-value ceiling and wall insulation, coniferous trees on the north, and a sloped roof with a low north wall minimize winter wind infiltration. Additional protection is provided by an air-lock entry, foam caulking, and minimal north glazing. Low-activity areas form a buffer zone along the north wall; high-activity spaces are adjacent to south-facing glazing. The windows on the south are single glazed and are fitted with sliding insulation panels. All other windows are double glazed.

On the main-floor level, sunlight **collected** through south-facing windows is **absorbed** and **stored** by the quarry tile floor in the dining room, and by water-filled tubes

located directly behind the glazing in the living room. A 2-story masonry wall **absorbs** and **stores** direct radiation entering the upper-level family room through clerestory windows. The heat **stored** in the mass wall and floor is later re-radiated for **distribution** into the living, dining, family, and bedrooms. At night, sliding insulation panels on the living side of the main-level south windows are closed to **control** heat loss. The clerestory windows are protected by closing pulley-operated, insulating shutters.

In the family room, the 3-foot high south-facing divider wall is open to the kitchen below. Solar heat that has been **collected** and **stored** in the ground-level living spaces is carried by natural convection through this opening up to the peak of the family room, where air warmed by the clerestory windows also accumulates. An air intake grille located near the family room ridge admits the warm air to a duct that leads to a discharge grille located in the lower-level utility room wall. When the temperature at the ceiling peak reaches 85°F, a differential thermostat mounted near the intake grille activates the fan and heated air is pulled through the duct and into the utility room. When the lower-level doors are open, this solar-heated air warms the rooms. When the family room ceiling temperature drops to 72°F, the fan is automatically shut off, and distribution of solar air ceases.

During the summer, south-facing glass is shaded by fixed moveable overhangs, and by seasonally adjusted awnings. All windows are equipped with manually operated pull-down shades or blinds. The high space near the clerestory has a manually operated, dampered louver that is opened at sunset along with main- and lower-level windows to provide convective cooling of the house.

Cooling is provided by an evaporative cooler. The garage on the western side of the house has eliminated west-facing windows that would overheat the house on summer afternoons.

A domestic water preheat system uses collectors mounted on the south-facing garage roof, and a preheat tank with an immersed fin-tube heat exchanger in the utility room.

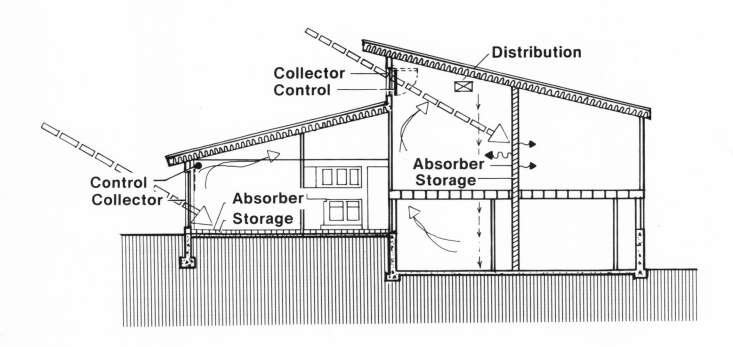

Walden, CO

Builder: Habitat Design and Construction Company, Walden, CO

Designer: Passive Solar Home Design Co., Denver, CO

Solar Designer: Passive Solar Home Design Co.

Price: $75,000

Net Heated Area: 1660 ft²

Heat Load: 168.3 x 10⁶ BTU / yr

Degree Days: 10,426

Solar Fraction: 36%

Auxiliary Heat: 6.20 BTU / DD / ft²

Passive Heating System(s): Direct gain, isolated gain, sun-tempering

Recognition Factors: Collector(s): Greenhouse glazing, south-facing glass doors, 295 ft² **Absorber(s):** Brick floor and wall, concrete wall, clay-tiled floor, water-filled benches **Storage:** Brick floor and wall, concrete wall, clay-tiled floor, water-filled benches—**capacity:**10,547 BTU / °F **Distribution:** Radiation, natural and forced convection **Controls:** Thermostat, ducts, vents, louvers, shades

Back-up: Gas boiler (100,000 BTU / H)

Domestic Hot Water: Liquid flat-plate collectors (70 ft²), 82-gallon storage

Passive Cooling Type: Convection

This 3-bedroom design has an attached greenhouse and a study loft opening onto a 2-story living room. The design includes extensive energy-conservation features dictated by the 10,000 degree day climate. The house is compact, with air-lock vestibules and closets along the north walls. Use of weatherstripping, high R-value insulation in walls and roof, and triple glazing on non-south windows reduces heat loss and infiltration. Double-glazed south windows are fitted with Window-Quilt™ insulating drapes.

Solar heat that is **collected** through greenhouse windows is **absorbed** and **stored** in the concrete wall separating the greenhouse and kitchen. Solar radiation passes through the greenhouse and then through the French doors into the dining room, where it strikes brick flooring that **absorbs**

and **stores** it for radiant **distribution** at night.

Greenhouse heat can be **distributed** to northern bedrooms with a fan assist. When the temperature in the greenhouse reaches a pre-set point, a sensor-**control** unit high on the wall activates a variable-speed fan that forces heated air to the north side of the house, through a duct in the loft floor joists. An attic duct then carries heat into the bedrooms and basement. Cool air is returned to the greenhouse through a basement vent. Nighttime heat losses in the greenhouse are **controlled** by the quilted insulating shades.

In the living room, solar heat **collected** through south-facing glass doors is **absorbed** and **stored** in the clay-tiled floor, the brick-faced walls, and two water-filled benches. At night, stored heat is **distributed** radiantly and accumulates near the ceiling of the loft. A thermostat **controls** a recirculating fan which pushes hot loft air back down to the living room floor.

During the summer days, the greenhouse is protected from overheating by a seasonally installed louver and by reflecting shades. Greenhouse ventilation is provided by turbine vent and a photovoltaic cell-**controlled** exhaust fan. The loft is vented directly through a roof turbine vent and an operable skylight. Natural cross-ventilation is adequate for cooling in this mountain climate where heat is often required in July.

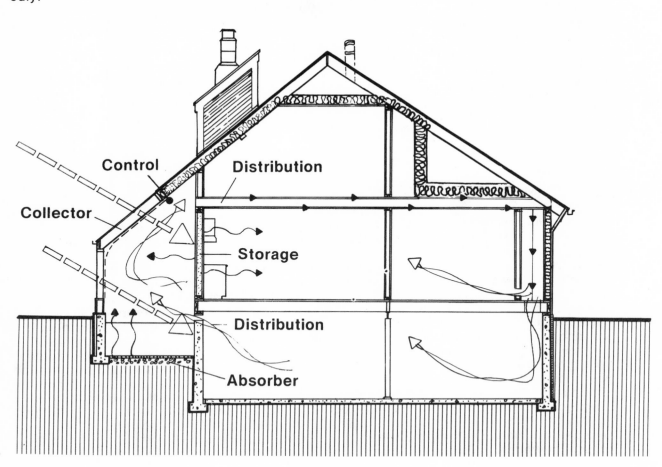

Boulder, CO

Builder: Ashcroft Constructors, Inc., Boulder, CO

Designer: Milburn-Sparn Energy Architects, Inc., Boulder, CO

Solar Designer: Milburn-Sparn Energy Architects Inc.

Price: $125,000

Net Heated Area: 1938 ft²

Heat Load: 107.6 x 10⁶ BTU/yr

Degree Days: 6500

Solar Fraction: 62%

Auxiliary Heat: 3.23 BTU/DD/ft²

Passive Heating System(s): Direct gain, isolated gain

Recognition Factors: Collector(s): South-facing glazing, greenhouse glazing, skylights, 343 ft² **Absorber(s):** Solarium floor, brick walls **Storage:** Solarium floor, brick walls, rock-bed storage—**capacity:** 17,460 BTU/°F **Distribution:** Radiation, natural and forced convection **Controls:** Dampers, fans, moveable insulation

Back-up: Electrically ignited gas furnace (64,000 BTU/H), woodburning stove

Domestic Hot Water: Liquid flat-plate collectors (49 ft²), 82-gallon storage

Passive Cooling Type: Induced ventilation

This contemporary Victorian condominium design is part of a Planned Unit Development that includes 28 passive solar residences. The steep north-sloping site was intentionally chosen to demonstrate the solar potential of a difficult location. The 3-bedroom, split-level unit has a cathedral ceiling living room with a balcony that opens to a greenhouse. Two skylights with louvered shades are located at the ceiling ridge. The building form is compact, with a long east-west axis to maximize solar penetration. Because of the difficult siting, the primary energy-conservation measures specify caulking, vapor barriers, and high R-value insulation in exterior walls to reduce infiltration.

Solar heat is **collected** primarily through south-facing greenhouse glazing and the skylights at the peak of the cathedral ceiling above the greenhouse. Heat is **absorbed** and **stored** in the greenhouse concrete floor and brick mass wall, and later is radiantly **distributed** into living spaces. In addition, solar heat is **stored** in a remote rock bin located in the basement beneath the greenhouse. The rock storage bed is connected with the back-up gas-fired furnace and air-handling system. During the heating season, a manually operated damper in the central return duct is left permanently in the open position. In the daytime heat storage mode, the fan in the air-handling system runs continuously, and an automatic reversing damper permits solar-heated greenhouse air to be pulled through the rock bed, charging it with heat. Air is then returned to the greenhouse at floor level. At night, when the house thermostat calls for heat, the position of the automatic damper is reversed, which reverses the direction of the air flow through the rock bin. Solar-heated air is then extracted from the bin and **distributed** to the house through supply ducts and floor registers. When solar heat from rock bed storage is insufficient to maintain indoor temperatures at the desired level, the furnace turns on.

During winter nights, heat loss is **controlled** by manually closing the skylids™ on the liv-

ing side of the skylights, pulling roller-type insulation shades down over windows in primary living spaces, and closing the moveable insulation under the greenhouse roof glazing.

Summer cooling in this sunny climate requires reducing heat gain during the day. This is accomplished by closing the skylight louvers and closing the sunscreen in the greenhouse each day. Permanent southern overhangs provide further shading. Forced ventilation of the house is accomplished by activating the fan and manually closing the summer damper in the return duct which prevents hot air from being circulated from the greenhouse to the

rock bed during the cooling season. When a north basement window and the skylights are opened and the basement stairway door is closed, the forced-air system can draw cool air into the rock storage bin and vent hot air through the skylight. The same effect can be created by natural circulation if the fan is shut off, but the circulation of air will be slower.

The design includes an active solar domestic water heating system that is used throughout the year. The system uses two flat-plate collectors, an antifreeze solution as the heat transfer medium, and a fiberglass insulated tank with 82 gallons of storage volume.

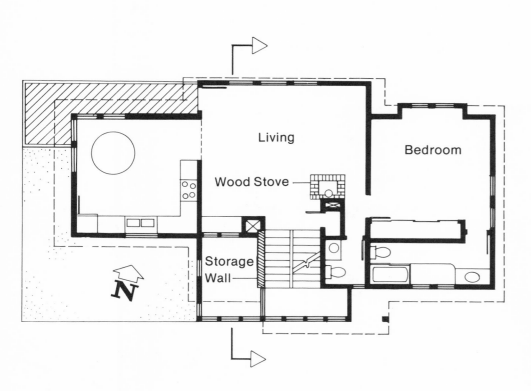

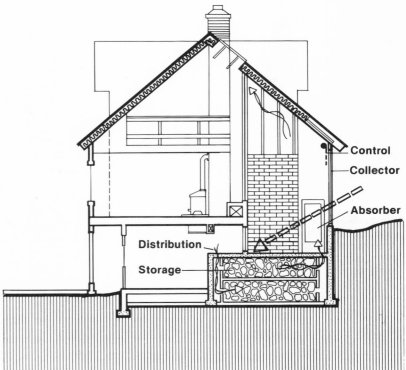

Colorado Springs, CO

Builder: Colorado Homes, Inc., Colorado Springs, CO

Designer: Colorado Homes, Inc.

Solar Designer: Rick A. Cowlishaw

Price: $85,000

Net Heated Area: 1840 ft²

Heat Load: 37.9 x 10⁶ BTU / yr

Degree Days: 6432

Solar Fraction: 82%

Auxiliary Heat: 0.58 BTU / DD / ft²

Passive Heating System(s): Direct gain, isolated gain

Recognition Factors: Collector(s): Greenhouse glazing, south-facing windows, 658 ft² **Absorber(s):** Brick pavers over concrete floor, surface of concrete walls, hot tub **Storage:** Concrete floor and walls, hot tub—**capacity:** 96,000 BTU / °F **Distribution:** Radiation, natural and forced convection **Controls:** Vents, blinds, overhangs

Back-up: Electric resistance baseboard heaters

Domestic Hot Water: Passive "bread-box" preheat, 40-gallon storage

This "Colorado Rustic" design with earth tone colors and cedar shake shingles features a 2-story greenhouse as part of a passive solar heating system based on the "envelope" concept. The house consists of two shells, one within the other. The living and sleeping spaces are located in the inner shell; the surrounding shell, or envelope, consists of the greenhouse, attic, north wall plenum, and crawl space. The envelope construction protects the living space from winter infiltration, and both shells are, in addition, well-insulated. Total insulation R-value is 38 in the east and west walls and the roof, and 40 in the north and south walls. An air-lock entry, a north wall buffer zone, and a limited number of non-south windows are additional energy-conserving features.

After solar heat is **collected** by the greenhouse windows, it is **absorbed** and **stored** in the concrete and brick paved floor and in

a 415-gallon hot tub. The concrete foundation walls also serve as remote **storage** elements. During the day, solar-heated air rises to the top of the greenhouse and is circulated through the envelope space by a ceiling fan. This circulation heats the foundation wall and the earth fill beneath the crawl space. At night, air temperature at the uninsulated greenhouse glazing is lower than in the north plenum. The heat that is radiated from the storage elements creates a reverse thermosiphon-flow in the envelope. The air flow carries the heat that is radiated back into the envelope from the storage elements. Because the living space within the inner shell is surrounded by the solar-heated "atmosphere" of the outer shell, the demand on the back-up electric resistance heating system is reduced. Greenhouse heat is **distributed** directly to the living space by a manually activated reversible fan in the interior wall between the living room and the greenhouse.

During the summer, opening the lower greenhouse windows, attic vent, and north windows induces ventilation of the envelope. Blinds (levelors) on the sloping greenhouse glass are closed during the day to **control** heat gain. They are opened at night to allow heat to radiate back to the outside.

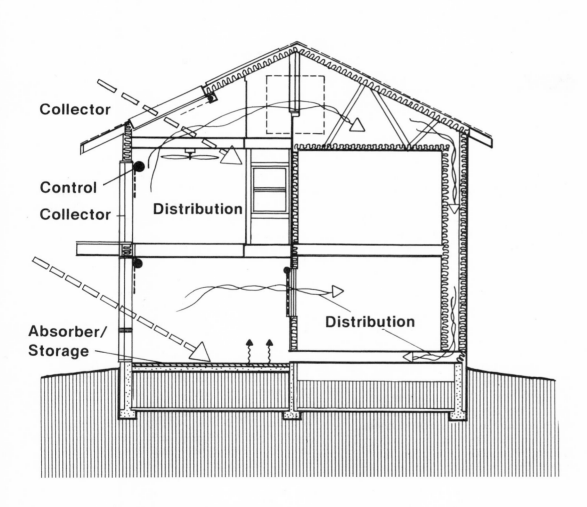

Collector

Control

Collector

Distribution

Distribution

Absorber/
Storage

Santa Fe, NM

Builder: Stanley Associates, Sante Fe, NM

Designer: Francis E. Stanley

Solar Designer: Francis E. Stanley

Price: $85,000

Net Heated Area: 1583 ft²

Heat Load: 90 x 10⁶ BTU/yr

Degree Days: 6007

Solar Fraction: 83%

Auxiliary Heat: 1.65 BTU/DD/ft²

Passive Heating System(s): Direct gain, indirect gain, sun-tempering

Recognition Factors: Collector(s): Double-glazed panels, sliding glass doors, 133 ft² **Absorber(s):** Concrete block Trombe wall, brick floor **Storage:** Concrete block Trombe wall, brick floor— **capacity:** 3247 BTU/°F **Distribution:** Radiation, natural convection **Controls:** Operable drapes, fixed overhang

Active Solar Heating: Air flat-plate collectors

Back-up: Gas furnace (50,000 BTU/H)

Domestic Hot Water: Air flat-plate collectors

212

This adobe design in Santa Fe, New Mexico, combines passive and active solar heating systems in a marketable home package. Energy-conservation features for this cool, high-altitude climate include a buffer zone along part of the north wall, R-24 insulation in walls and R-33 in ceilings, and double glazing for all windows. In addition, the siting takes advantage of a south-facing slope and of the wind protection offered by pinion pine trees to the north.

Two passive solar systems are integrated in the design. In the south-facing bedrooms, sunlight is **collected** through double-glass panels and is **absorbed** and **stored** in a solid concrete block Trombe wall immediately behind. For **distribution**, heat from the wall is radiated into the bedrooms during winter nights, and manually drawn drapes **control** heat loss. The other bedrooms **collect** solar radiation but have no mass to store it.

In the living room, solar heat is **collected** through south-facing sliding glass doors

and a west window, and is then **absorbed** and **stored** in the brick floor to be radiantly **distributed** at night. Drapes **control** winter heat loss and summer gain through these windows. The glass doors are further protected by a fixed overhang. The carpeted dining room is also solar heated but without any heat storage. It also has a west-facing window with manually operated drapes for **control** of unwanted solar gain.

Summer cooling in this climate is easily accomplished by opening windows at night to induce natural cross-ventilation, and by drawing drapes or shades across direct gain windows during the day.

A Solaron™ active, air-type solar heating system with single-glazed, flat-plate collectors furnishes both space heat and domestic hot water. Space heat is **stored** in a below-grade rock bed and distributed through the perimeter radial duct system associated with the back-up, gas-fired, counter-flow furnace.

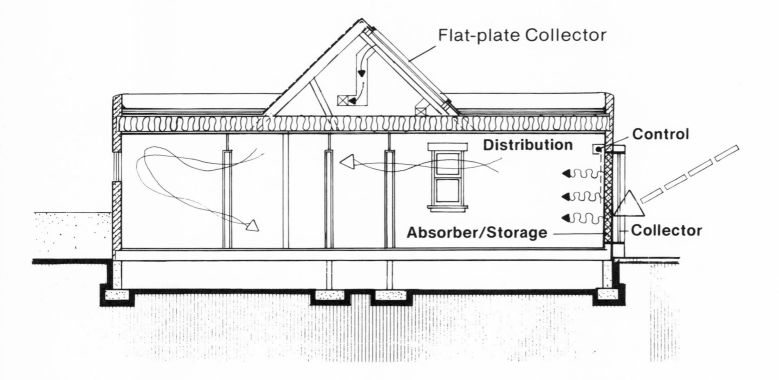

Flat-plate Collector

Control

Distribution

Absorber/Storage

Collector

Builder: Enecon, Inc., Sante Fe, NM

Designer: Clark-Germanas Architects, Sante Fe, NM

Solar Designer: Barkmann Engineering, Sante Fe, NM

Price: $75,000 to $80,000

Net Heated Area: 1500 ft²

Heat Load: 52.2 x 10⁶ BTU/yr

Degree Days: 5780

Solar Fraction: 75%

Auxiliary Heat: 1.55 BTU/DD/ft²

Passive Heating System(s): Direct gain, indirect gain

Recognition Factors: Collector(s): Double-glazed windows, double-glazed clerestory windows, 255 ft² **Absorber(s):** Water tubes, brick floor over concrete slab **Storage:** Water tubes, concrete slab—**capacity:** 13,917 BTU/°F **Distribution:** Radiation, natural convection **Controls:** Insulated venetian blinds, shutters and curtains, fixed overhangs and earth berming

Back-up: Woodburning stove, electric resistance mats

Domestic Hot Water: Active DHW collector

Passive Cooling Type: Natural ventilation

Part of a large development, this traditional pueblo house is consistent with the style of neighboring homes. Its exposed beams and plastered masonry walls help to keep this highly functional design aesthetically pleasing as well. Protection from prevailing winds is provided by pine trees to the northwest and partial earth-berming of the north wall. There is also a north retaining wall that extends beyond both ends of the house. Both of these extensions turn 90°F towards the front of the house to enclose terraces on the east and west sides and to provide wind protection.

Passive **collection** is accomplished at two south-facing sources: floor-to-ceiling windows for the lower level of the split-level plan, and clerestory windows for the rear raised level; all windows are double glazed. A roof-mounted active collector located above the utility room is used for preheating domestic hot water.

Sunlight entering the lower-level windows is **absorbed** and **stored** by a series of 19 darkened fiberglass water tubes. These are located directly inside the windows and are 8 feet high and 12 inches in diameter. The tops are left uncovered for humidification and easy refilling. The tubes are spaced

with 12-inch gaps that also allow direct radiation into the rooms to be **absorbed** and **stored** by brick flooring laid down over a 4-inch concrete slab. Sunlight **collected** through clerestory windows is absorbed by the darkened surface of a dense concrete masonry north wall with rigid exterior insulation.

Heat is **distributed** by radiation from the storage masses and by natural convection. Convective loops are set up within each room, using the shaded center wall to cool heated air that moves toward it. Some convection occurs between the living room and study through shuttered apertures.

Night heat loss through lower-level windows is **controlled** by insulated venetian blinds on vertical tracks. Manually operated polystyrene insulating shutters serve the same purpose on clerestory windows. The R-30 insulation in the roof and R-20 in the walls are also instrumental in creating a strong energy-conserving envelope.

In extreme cold, radiation from storage masses is supplemented by thermostatically controlled electric resistance mats embedded in all floor slabs. The mats are designed to turn on automatically when the

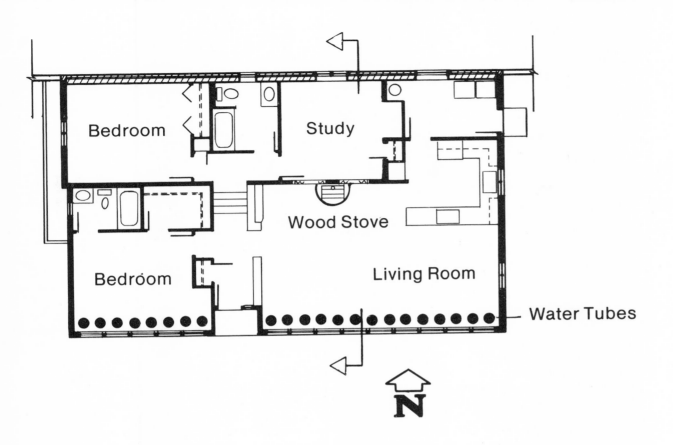

Bedroom

Study

Bedroom

Wood Stove

Living Room

Water Tubes

N

heat from these storage masses has been discharged. The rate of this discharge can be reduced by using the woodburning stove located on the north wall of the living room. Wall vents distribute some stove heat to rear-level rooms where the concrete floors have only minimal exposure to direct radiation.

During summer days, overhangs shade both collectors from direct radiation. Blinds and shutters are used as needed for additional control of solar energy. Daytime cooling is augmented if, during the night, windows are kept open so that night air can cool storage masses. If the main-level windows are closed during the day, heat rises and escapes through open clerestory windows.

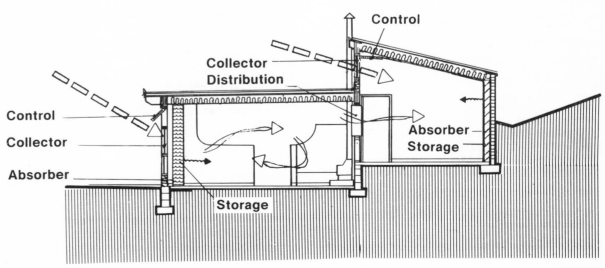

Control

Collector
Distribution

Control

Collector

Absorber

Absorber
Storage

Storage

Tucson, AZ

Builder: William L. Pritchett & Son, Inc., Tucson, AZ

Designer: William Lester Pritchett & Son, Inc.

Solar Designer: William Lester Pritchett & Son, Inc.

Price: $167,000

Net Heated Area: 2632 ft²

Heat Load: 71.4 x 10⁶ BTU/yr

Degree Days: 1800

Solar Fraction: 70%

Auxiliary Heat: 4.49 BTU/DD/ft²

Passive Heating System(s): Direct gain

Recognition Factors: Collector(s): South-facing sliding glass doors, skylights, 324 ft² **Absorber(s):** Ceramic tile-covered concrete slab floor, rock chimney wall, masonry wall **Storage:** Concrete slab floor, rock chimney wall, masonry wall— **capacity:** 32,000 BTU/°F **Distribution:** Radiation, natural and forced convection **Controls:** Venetian blinds, skylight shutters, fixed overhangs

Back-up: Electric resistance heaters

Domestic Hot Water: Ground-level flat-plate collectors (26 ft²)

Passive Cooling Type: Natural and induced ventilation

This contemporary 3-bedroom home uses nine sets of sliding glass doors to **collect** solar radiation on its south face. Six of these, located along the bedroom corridor, are sandwiched sets of single-glazed units with venetian blinds in the air space. The other sets—one on the southeast wall of the dining room and two in the living room—are all double glazed with venetian blinds and drapes on the interior side of the units. Three skylights in the roof above the main living area also act as passive **collectors.** Active **collection** for domestic water heating is achieved by a pair of ground-mounted flat-plate collectors.

Absorption and **storage** of solar heat in the living and dining room are by a ceramic tile-covered 5-inch thick concrete slab floor, and by the rock chimney wall at the center of the octagonally shaped main living area. A tiled slab floor is also used for **absorption** and **storage** along the entire length of the corridor; there is also a 16-inch masonry thermal **storage** wall opposite the collectors.

Heat that is re-radiated from the storage elements into this closed corridor is **distributed** either by natural convection— by opening sliding glass bedroom doors or the end door to the living area—or by being drawn into a ceiling plenum by the furnace blower, then ducted throughout the house. During the night, heat will radiate naturally from the masonry wall into the bedrooms. Radiation from storage masses and natural convection are used to **distribute** heat to the octagonal living areas. Back-up heat is available from the fireplace and from electric resistance elements in the furnace.

Cooling in summer is by ventilation and ceiling exhaust fans (two in the living room). For peak summer cooling there are two evaporative coolers that use the furnace duct system for **distribution.** Heat gain is **controlled** by venetian blinds on all glass, skylight shutters, and fixed overhangs.

The energy-conservation aspects of this home include a recessed north entry (away from prevailing southwest winds); use of

216

the garage as a winter wind buffer, and insulation values of R-30 for the roof and R-20 in the walls. Extensive caulking and weather-stripping are used throughout.

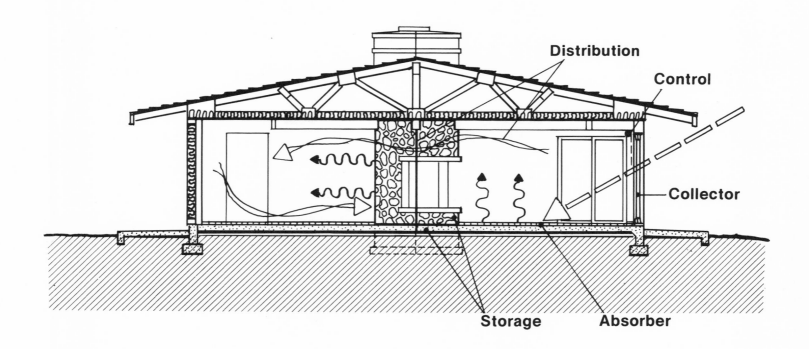

Distribution

Control

Collector

Storage

Absorber

Riverton, UT

Builder: Prowswood, Inc., Salt Lake City, UT

Designer: Kurt Brandle, Architect, Robert Boehm, Practical Engineer, Salt Lake City, UT

Solar Designer: Kurt Brandle, Robert Boehm

Price: $65,000

Net Heated Area: 1161 ft²

Heat Load: 41.3 x 10⁶ BTU/yr

Degree Days: 6052

Solar Fraction: 39%

Auxiliary Heat: 4.02 BTU/DD/ft²

Passive Heating System(s): Direct gain

Recognition Factors: Collector(s): Triple-glazed south-facing windows, 114 ft² **Absorber(s):** Black chromium venetian blinds **Storage:** Masonry walls —**capacity:** 1541 BTU/°F **Distribution:** Natural and forced convection **Controls:** Blinds, dampers, overhangs, floor registers

Back-up: Two kW inline duct heaters

Domestic Hot Water: Active DHW system

Solar **collection** in this single-floor structure occurs at the four large windows of the south wall: two in the living room and one in each bedroom. These windows are triple glazed and include integrated venetian blinds.

The heating system works as follows: light strikes the black venetian blinds and is **absorbed**, causing them to heat the air cavity around the blinds. Hot air within the cavity rises through vents into a header located above the venetian blind unit; cooler air is drawn into the cavity from the south rooms through vents at the bottom of each unit. On cold sunny days a ceiling duct system using inline blowers draws heat from the window headers and **distributes** it to each room of the house. When too much heat is supplied to any one room, a motorized damper automatically adjusts the amount of air flow to that room. When overheating occurs, warm air is ducted to north-side masonry **storage** walls in the kitchen and master bedroom. The air

is forced through ducts within these 8-inch masonry walls and discharged at floor registers. It is expected that, on sunny days, the **storage** masses will absorb enough excess heat to radiate at night so that the kitchen and master bedroom will be kept warm. For colder weather there are two kW inline duct heaters to further warm the air.

These heaters are also within the system of floor ducts and registers used to supplement room heat and provide heat to the bathroom.

For summer cooling, a roof-mounted evaporative cooler is incorporated into the duct system. Ventilation occurs if the front pane of the solar windows is opened and allowed to cool the blinds before they can heat the air. Also, overhangs on all south glass help to keep the blinds cool.

Roof insulation is R-38, with R-19 in the walls.

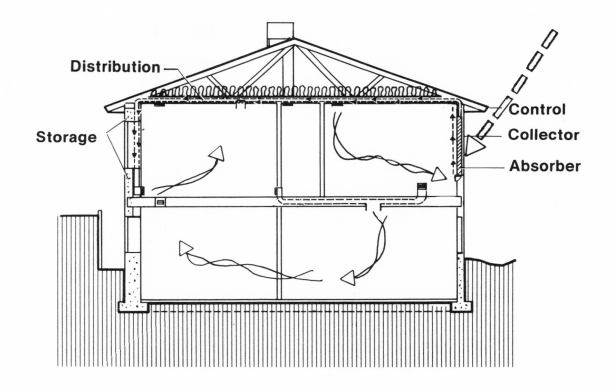

Distribution

Storage

Control

Collector

Absorber

Pocatello, ID

Builder: Larry D. Ratliff Construction, Pocatello, ID

Designer: Paul W. Jensen, Pocatello, ID

Solar Designer: Paul Jensen Architect, Inc.

Price: $92,000

Net Heated Area: 2662 ft²

Heat Load: 106.6 x 10⁶ BTU/yr

Degree Days: 6991

Solar Fraction: 77%

Auxiliary Heat: 1.35 BTU/DD/ft²

Passive Heating System(s): Direct gain, indirect gain, isolated gain

Recognition Factors: Collector(s): South-facing glazing, 494 ft² **Absorber(s):** Concrete floor and wall, water tubes, brick floor **Storage:** Concrete floor and wall, water tubes, brick floor—**capacity:** 23,942 BTU/°F **Distribution:** Radiation, natural and forced convection **Controls:** Moveable insulation, shade, damper, thermostat

Back-up: Electric resistance heater (75,000 BTU/H)

Domestic Hot Water: Liquid flat-plate collectors (58 ft²), 120-gallon storage

This modern 3-bedroom house has been recessed into the east slope of a mountain. A slight rise in grade directly south of the site, while not significantly reducing exposure of the solar collection area to the sun, provides a natural wind buffer. Earth berms, ranging from 4 to 9 feet, are also used to help stabilize the indoor temperature.

The primary **collector** in this solar design is a 1½-story greenhouse that dominates the south side of the building. Solar radiation passes through the structure's two layers of acrylic glazing and strikes a brick floor (an effective **absorber** and **storage** mass); at the rear of the greenhouse radiation passes through a wall of single-glazed windows that separates the greenhouse from the upper and lower living areas. Access to the greenhouse is possible from both floors. To the west of the greenhouse a Trombe wall with Kalwall Sunlight™ glazing **collects** heat for the master bedroom. This bedroom and the open area below it also receive direct sun from a stacked pair of

double-glazed windows located between the Trombe wall and the greenhouse. There are active solar collectors for preheating domestic water on the roof above the master bedroom.

On the lower level of the living areas, just on the interior side of the single-glazed windows that face the inside of the greenhouse, there is a series of 14 Kalwall Sunlite™ floor-to-ceiling water tubes that **absorb** and **store** heat. The tubes are each 12 inches in diameter and spaced apart so that direct radiation can pass between them and be **absorbed** by the tile flooring of the family room. This ceramic tile covers a 4-inch concrete slab that provides more thermal **storage**. There are water tubes directly overhead on the upper level, too, but these are only 30 inches tall to allow for view and direct solar heat gain. **Absorbing** and **storing** heat in the master bedroom is the 29-inch high concrete wall. Additional **storage** mass is supplied by a pair of 2-story concrete block walls located at the north end of the family room and utility room, and the bedrooms above them, but these do not receive direct solar radiation.

Heat is **distributed** throughout the house by a combination of natural and forced convection as well as radiation from the thermal mass. In the winter mode, the manual damper connecting the greenhouse to the attic is kept closed. Trapped heat can then pass into the second story through an opened glass door in the loft area. This door leads out onto the greenhouse bridge, and to the sundeck outside. At night when the greenhouse becomes cool, this door is closed and window quilts on the greenhouse side of the single-glazed glass wall are lowered to **control** heat loss to the greenhouse; radiation from interior storage masses then becomes the main source of heat. On the lower level the water tubes and floor slab heat the air which then rises. A 5-foot square opening in the loft floor allows the heat to convect up to the second floor. The heated air will then either cool and pass back down the north staircase as it loses buoyancy and falls, or collect at the ceiling from where it is redistributed by being drawn through the return air duct into an electric furnace and air handler, and blown back out through floor registers in all lower-level rooms including the slightly raised living room in the northeast corner. During winter months the air handler is left on low at all times to keep the warm air in circulation. In extreme cold the 5.5 kW electric coils within the furnace will turn on as the house demands more heat. When this happens, the high-speed fan comes on automatically. To reduce dependency on the electric coils there is a woodburning stove in the family room located directly beneath the opening in the loft to facilitate heat flow to the upper-level ceiling plenum.

For the master bedroom, which has the benefit of neither greenhouse heat nor a direct connection to the furnace duct system, there is radiation from its own Trombe wall as well as floor dampers that allow lower-level heat to rise directly into the room. If the day has been particularly sunny, there should have been enough surplus heat taken in so that the concrete block wall will also be capable of radiating heat during the night.

Cooling is not considered a problem in this northern climate, and for that reason is accomplished mainly by natural convection and ventilation. To prevent overheating of the greenhouse there is, however, a unique and rather elaborate shade cloth that is pulled down and supported by a series of eight cables extending from the roof to concrete footings 26 feet out from the base of the greenhouse. The canopy is all-weather and is designed to be operated seasonally.

Within the greenhouse there are further measures that can be taken to prevent overheating of this area. In the summer mode, the vent at the top of the greenhouse is left open so that rising heat will escape through it and exhaust at fixed open louvers in the roof located directly above the greenhouse. Windows on the east, west, and north sides are small, but large enough to allow ventilation if left open.

All entrances to the house are through unheated spaces or rooms, with the main entrance on the north side away from southwestern prevailing winds. Wind infiltration is further reduced with the extensive use of caulking and weatherstripping. In addition, there are vapor barriers in all exterior walls and ceilings. Insulation values are: R-38 for the attic and roof; R-19 in the walls, and R-10 at the foundation. Moveable night insulation for the single-glazed glass wall is rated at R-3.4.

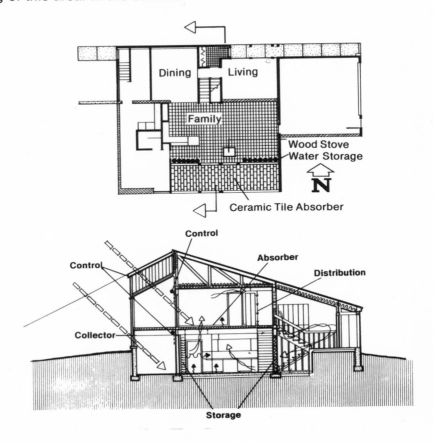

221

Bozeman, MT

Builder: Mountain Home Builders, Gallatin Gateway, MT

Designer: Solar Design and Consulting, Eugene, OR

Solar Designer: Robert M. Lorenzen

Price: $69,000

Net Heated Area: 1240 ft²

Heat Load: 96.9 x 10⁶ BTU/yr

Degree Days: 8126

Solar Fraction: 64%

Auxiliary Heat: 6.53 BTU/DD/ft²

Passive Heating System(s): Isolated gain, direct gain

Recognition Factors: Collector(s): Greenhouse glazing, skylights, 279 ft² **Absorber(s):** Mass wall and slab floor, tile floor **Storage:** Slab floors, mass walls—**capacity:** 13,888 BTU/°F **Distribution:** Natural and forced convection, radiation **Controls:** Fixed overhangs, earth berms, shades

Back-up: Woodburning stove and electric baseboard heaters

Domestic Hot Water: Single-tank thermosiphon system, 82-gallon storage

This ranch-style house is built into a south slope with half of its 2-story north wall earth-bermed for protection against the severe Montana winters. To protect the home from strong prevailing southwest winter winds, the south roof has been steeply pitched both to offer deflection and to reduce the amount of exposed wall area. A 2-car garage on the north wall acts as a buffer zone for the upper-floor entryway. R-38 insulation in the roof and R-19 in exposed walls together with extensive caulking around doors and windows ensure a tight, energy-conserving building.

Sunlight is **collected** along the south wall and roof by means of a combination of floor-to-ceiling windows and skylights that form a greenhouse; and windows, skylights and sliding glass doors that admit direct radiation to the living room and dining area. All windows are double glazed. An array of active flat-plate solar collectors for domestic water heating is offered to buyers as an option.

Sunlight collected in the greenhouse is **absorbed** and **stored** by a 4-inch concrete floor slab and a 12-inch, 2-story concrete wall that separates the greenhouse from the first- and second-floor bedrooms. In the living room, an 8-inch concrete wall **absorbs** and **stores** heat, and both the living room and dining area have a tile-covered, 4-inch concrete floor slab.

Distribution of heat is accomplished by radiation from storage masses as well as by natural convection which moves warm air to areas not receiving direct sunlight, such as the east bedroom, the bathrooms, and the utility room. Warm air from the greenhouse, as it rises, enters the second-story master bedroom through opened windows. Open doors and north wall vents allow this air to pass to the lower level as it cools and falls. The air is then drawn back into the greenhouse through open first-story bedroom windows for reheating.

The living room is two stories high with an open hallway on the second floor. Warm air from the living room storage masses rises and passes over this hallway, eventually circulating down the rear stairwell as it reaches the cooler north wall areas. Once downstairs, the air is drawn back into the living room for reheating.

At night windows and doors to the greenhouse are closed to **control** heat loss from the house through its glass. The house's back-up electric baseboard heaters and woodburning stove will supplement the solar heat except during moderate weather. The stove has been placed against the north wall of the living room and, like heat from the baseboard heaters, relies on direct radiation and natural convection for distribution.

Protection from overheating in the summer was a minor consideration due to the cool climate. However, shades are placed on the three living room skylights, and a roof overhang protects the south wall windows from the high summer sun.

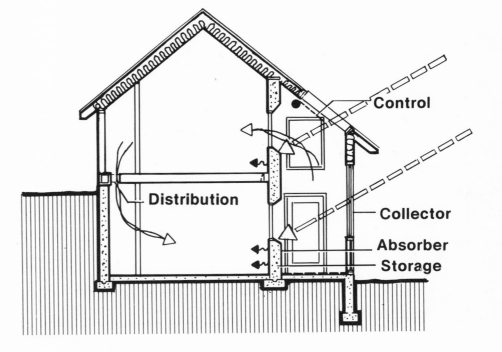

Port Townsend, WA

Builder: Burnham Construction, Port Townsend, WA

Designer: Burnham Construction

Solar Designer: Burnham Construction

Price: $92,000

Net Heated Area: 1596 ft²

Heat Load: 62.8 x 10⁶ BTU/yr

Degree Days: 5330

Solar Fraction: 65%

Auxiliary Heat: 2.52 BTU/DD/ft²

Passive Heating System(s): Direct gain, indirect (Trombe wall) gain, isolated gain

Recognition Factors: Collector(s): Trombe wall glazing, greenhouse, skylight, glass doors, 278 ft² **Absorber(s):** Surface of Trombe wall, mass walls and floors **Storage:** Trombe wall, greenhouse wall, living room wall, concrete slab floors— **capacity:** 9885 BTU/°F **Distribution:** Radiation, natural and forced convection **Controls:** Fixed overhangs, moveable shade, louvers on greenhouse, earth berming

Back-up: Woodburning stove, electric baseboard heaters

Domestic Hot Water: Active DHW flat-plate collectors (55 ft²)

This home was designed for 2-person occupancy in a neighborhood made up predominantly of retired couples. An additional bedroom/bathroom guest unit is expected to have only occasional use and can be shut off completely; there are electric baseboard heaters in all rooms, but only in this extra bedroom does the heater carry the total heating load. Styling is northwest rustic traditional and is typical of other homes in the area.

There are a variety of **collection** modes: a series of four sliding glass doors and skylight in the living room; a greenhouse with a connecting door to the living room and windows to the dining room; and a wall of glass (sections of which constitute a Trombe wall) for the den and master bedroom. All these apertures face south and are double glazed. For domestic water heating there are roof-mounted flat-plate collectors.

Direct radiation to the living room is **absorbed** and **stored** by a ceramic tile-covered 4-inch concrete floor slab and a 4-inch brick wall located behind the wood-burning stove in the northeast corner.

The den and master bedroom have as their south wall a 12-inch brick Trombe wall for **absorption** and **storage**. The brick wall in the dining room has as its **collector** the greenhouse, projecting 7 feet from the wall. Also, **absorbing** and **storing** heat in the greenhouse and dining room are 4-inch concrete floor slabs, each having exposure to direct radiation.

Distribution in the den and master bedroom is by natural convection and radiation from the Trombe wall. In the dining room, which is separated from the living room by a 42-inch high brick wall, warm air is drawn in from the greenhouse through opened windows, circulated by natural convection and returned, through cold air vents in the floor, to the greenhouse for reheating. There is also radiation from the brick wall at night, when the greenhouse loses its effectiveness. Radiation and natural convection from floors **distribute** warm air in the living room.

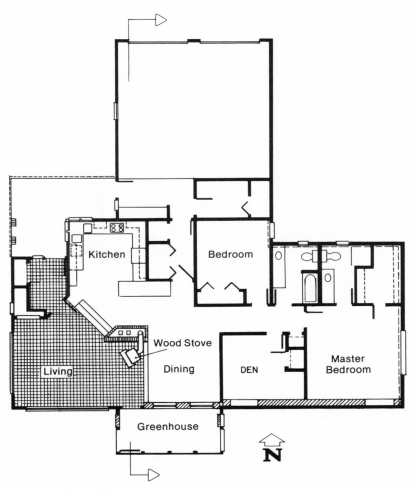

Kitchen

Bedroom

Wood Stove

Living

Dining

DEN

Master
Bedroom

Greenhouse

N

In colder weather, hot air that accumulates at the cathedral ceiling is drawn down the brick chimney enclosure by a small fan and vented onto the kitchen floor. This air is heated further when the stove is being used because the sealed flue within the chimney heats room air.

During summer months this system is sealed off and another fan at the top of the chimney exhausts hot air trapped at the ridge. Also used to **control** heat gain are overhangs on all south glass, moveable insulation on all windows, natural ventilation and wooden and fiber slats in the skylight and at the top of the greenhouse. These slats are adjusted manually. Because of strong summer sea breezes and good ventilation, there is no additional cooling system to backup the exhaust fan.

This design takes advantage of the gradual slope of the site through partial berming on the north, east, and west walls. The 2-car attached garage and air-lock entryway serve as buffer zones for winter entry. R-32 insulation is used in the roof and R-19 in all exposed walls.

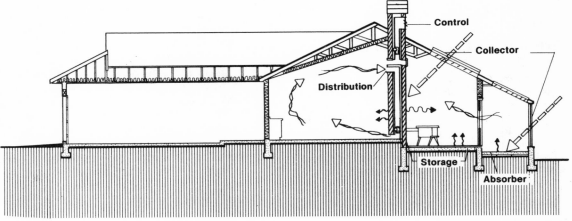

Control

Collector

Distribution

Storage

Absorber

Eugene, OR

Builder: Trans Western Investors, Inc., Eugene, OR

Designer: Trans Western Investors, Inc.

Solar Designer: Trans Western Investors, Inc.

Price: $86,000

Net Heated Area: 1498 ft²

Heat Load: 46.5 x 10⁶ BTU/yr

Degree Days: 4726

Solar Fraction: 57%

Auxiliary Heat: 2.83 BTU/DD/ft²

Passive Heating System(s): Direct gain, isolated gain, sun-tempering

Recognition Factors: Collector(s): South-facing glazing, skylight, 265 ft² **Absorber(s):** Concrete and tile floor, block mass wall, water wall surface, brick hearth, concrete wall **Storage:** Concrete and tile floor, block mass wall, water wall, brick hearth, concrete wall—**capacity:** 13,500 BTU/°F **Distribution:** Radiation, natural and forced convection **Controls:** Registers, shutters, awning, dampers

Back-up: Air-to-air heat pump, wood stove

Domestic Hot Water: Passive 40-gallon preheat

This compact, 2-story home in Eugene, Oregon includes a combination of passive solar space and water heating systems in a design that has demonstrated market acceptance. Energy-conservation features include landscaping that protects the house from winter winds, closets located along the north wall to reduce heat loss, air-lock entries, and insulated glass windows.

In one passive heating system, an insulated solar heat storage room is located in the rear of the garage. Heat is **collected** through the south-facing glass wall of this narrow room; the rear wall is surfaced with reflective Mylar™ to enhance collection. Solar heat is **absorbed** and **stored** in a 2-tiered bank of water-filled 55-gallon drums which then **distribute** heat to the room by radiation. If temperatures in the storage room are high enough and the house needs heat, a differential thermostat in the storage room opens a motorized damper, and heated air rises to the upper level of the house through an insulated duct. When the

fan in the air-handling unit for the back-up heat pump station is operating, solar heat from the storage room is **distributed** throughout the house via the heat pump ductwork. Cool air is returned to the heat storage room through a low register in the living room wall.

In the other passive heating system, solar heat is **collected** through south-facing windows and a skylight in the 2-story living room, and through south and west windows in a greenhouse. Masonry walls and tile floors **absorb** and **store** solar radiation. In the evening as the house gets cooler, the storage walls and floor **distribute** solar heat into the greenhouse, the living room, the adjacent stairwell, and the dining room by radiant flow. Heat accumulating near the greenhouse ceiling passes through a grille into the master bedroom right above. High and low supply registers in the masonry walls allow air to flow between the living room and greenhouse, and between the living room and stairwell.

226

Heat from the living room and greenhouse can also be returned to the air-handler and distribution system through a return duct in the upper-level powder room. A destratification duct conveys heated air accumulating near the second-story ceiling back to the first story.

All three bedrooms receive limited amounts of direct sunlight, but none of them have storage mass.

The south-facing collection area is shuttered at night to **control** heat loss: Pease ™ roll shutters are manually closed over windows in the living room and master bedroom; the heat storage room and greenhouse each have an automatic exterior shutter with reflective surfaces that, when the shutter is open, enhance solar collection. These shutters are **controlled** by adjustable photocells and operated by electric garage door openers.

In the summer, south-facing glazing in the heat storage room, greenhouse, and master bedroom can be shuttered during the day to reduce solar gain and the fold-down shutter on the greenhouse is converted to an awning. Cooling the house is accomplished by opening the skylight and the windows, which induces cross-ventilation. In the cooling season, the heat storage room is isolated from the house by closing the damper in the supply vent; this room can be ventilated by opening the east-facing door.

A preheat tank and the upper tier of water-filled drums in the heat storage room constitute a passive preheat system for domestic water. City water pressure forces water through the preheat components and into the domestic water heater.

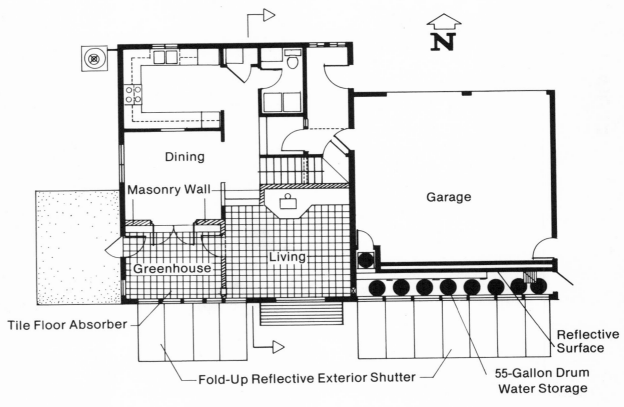

Dining

Masonry Wall

Greenhouse

Living

Garage

Tile Floor Absorber

Fold-Up Reflective Exterior Shutter

55-Gallon Drum Water Storage

Reflective Surface

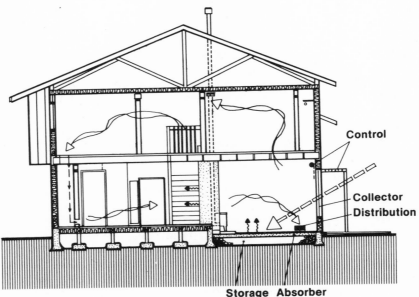

Control

Collector

Distribution

Storage Absorber

Builder: Turtle Island Building & Design, Coburg, OR

Designer: Turtle Island

Solar Designer: Turtle Island

Price: $85,000 to $90,000

Net Heated Area: 1597 ft²

Heat Load: 76.8 x 10⁶ BTU/yr

Degree Days: 4726

Solar Fraction: 34%

Auxiliary Heat: 6.70 BTU/DD/ft²

Passive Heating System(s): Direct gain

Recognition Factors: Collector(s): Clerestory windows, sliding glass doors, 254 ft² **Absorber(s):** Mass walls, tile floors **Storage:** Mass walls and slab floor—**capacity:** 6699 BTU/°F **Distribution:** Radiation and natural convection **Controls:** Clerestory shutters, fixed overhangs

Back-up: Woodburning stove and electric furnace with air-handler

Domestic Hot Water: Liquid flat-plate collectors (62 ft²)

Solar **collection** for the kitchen and living room occurs through two separate clerestories—one for each room. Sunlight is also **collected** through a pair of sliding glass doors in the dining room and a clerestory above the master bedroom. A pair of flat-plate collectors on the south edge of the garage is used for preheating domestic hot water.

Absorbing and **storing** heat from the kitchen clerestory is a masonry wall on the north side. As a common wall of the kitchen and living room, it radiates heat to both. At the north side of the living room is another masonry wall that also **absorbs** and **stores** heat. This wall is common with and supplies radiant heat to the upper-level loft behind it.

In the dining room, a ceramic tile floor **absorbs** heat for the concrete **storage** slab beneath.

Distribution is by natural convection and radiation from the storage masses. Winter back-up heat is available from either the woodburning stove located at the north wall of the living room, or by an electric furnace with wall registers in all rooms. (The master bedroom, because it lacks storage mass, relies almost entirely on heat from the back-up furnace).

Solar input through the clerestories is **controlled** in two ways: manually operated exterior roll-down shutters, and interior insulating shutters that, when lowered, completely shut off the clerestory spaces, thereby lessening the volume of space to be heated. There are also exterior shutters on the dining room glass doors, and fixed overhangs and wing walls on all south-facing glass. The front entrance, to reduce wind infiltration, is an air-lock vestibule located on the east wall away from prevailing winds. R-30 insulation in the roofs and R-19 in the walls helps to ensure a tight energy envelope.

Cooling is by natural convective flow out the clerestory and cross-ventilation.

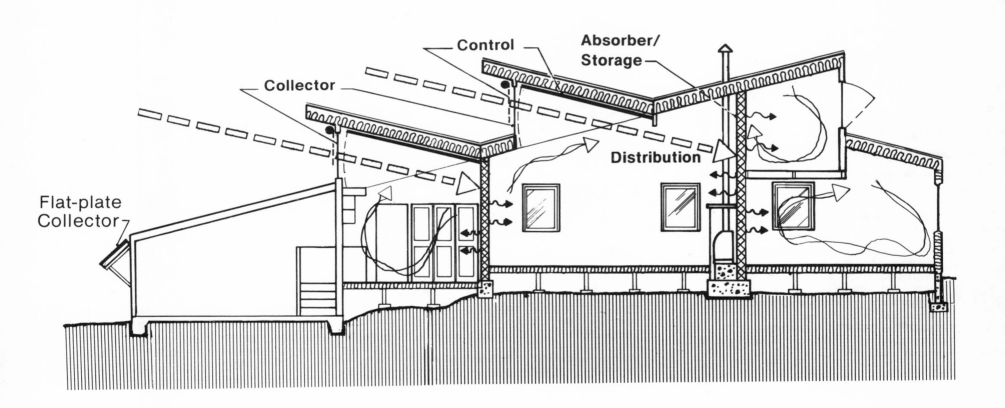

Springfield, OR

Builder: Paz Peterson McRae, Inc., Eugene, OR

Designer: Artemio Paz, Jr., Springfield, OR

Solar Designer: Artemio Paz, Jr.

Price: $100,000

Net Heated Area: 1719 ft²

Heat Load: 64.8 x 10⁶ BTU / yr

Degree Days: 4739

Solar Fraction: 60%

Auxiliary Heat: 3.23 BTU / DD / ft²

Passive Heating System(s): Direct gain, indirect gain, isolated gain

Recognition Factors: Collector(s): Skylight, Trombe wall glazing, greenhouse glazing, 320 ft² **Absorbers:** Concrete block wall, concrete block Trombe wall, greenhouse concrete slab floor **Storage:** Concrete block wall, concrete block Trombe wall, greenhouse concrete slab floor— **capacity:** 14,612 BTU / °F **Distribution:** Radiation, natural convection **Controls:** Moveable shading devices

Back-up: Electric resistance wall units, wood stove

Domestic Hot Water: "Breadbox" DHW collector, 60-gallon tank

Passive Cooling Type: Natural cross-ventilation, convection

This ranch house is sited on a south-facing slope overlooking Oregon's McKenzie Valley. Much of the slope is covered with Douglas fir and maple trees. Located 500 feet above the valley, the home is usually free from the region's morning fog. The garage/carport protects the living spaces from the southwest winter winds. North-facing window area has been kept to a minimum. The north wall and the ceiling are heavily insulated. The floor is insulated to R-19.

Solar energy is used by this home in three ways. The first system uses a skylight over the living room to **collect** sunlight, much of which strikes a solid grouted concrete block wall where it is **absorbed** and **stored**.

When the house temperature falls below the temperature of the wall, heat radiates from the wall and is **distributed** into the living space. Double glazing **controls** excessive heat loss through the skylight on winter nights, and shutters may also be installed to close the skylight completely.

The second solar energy system uses a glazed concrete block wall (Trombe wall) that collects sunlight that strikes the dark-colored wall where it is **absorbed**, and turns into heat. The heat slowly passes through the mass of the storage wall. Hours later, when the heat is needed, it is distributed by radiation from the interior side of the wall into the living space.

The third passive system is a greenhouse. Sunshine is **collected** by the greenhouse through south-facing windows and skylights. It is **absorbed** and **stored** by the concrete slab floor and by the concrete block wall that divides the greenhouse from the living room. Some of the sun's heat immediately enters the living space through vents that connect the greenhouse and the living room. Moveable shading devices on the greenhouse roof **control** overheating.

Heat stored in the greenhouse floor and some of the heat stored in the concrete block wall keep the greenhouse warm at night. The rest of the heat stored in the

230

concrete block wall passes through the wall and into the living room.

Back-up heating in the large common rooms is provided by a wood stove, and in the bedrooms and bathrooms by electric resistance wall units.

A "bread box" collector provides much of the home's domestic hot water: a black painted 60-gallon water tank is enclosed in a double-glazed space on the home's south-facing roof. Water flows into the tank to be heated by the sun, and is then drawn into a standard domestic water heater. Protection against freezing is provided by two shutters that are insulated to R-16. These shutters cover the glazing at night and on extremely cold days.

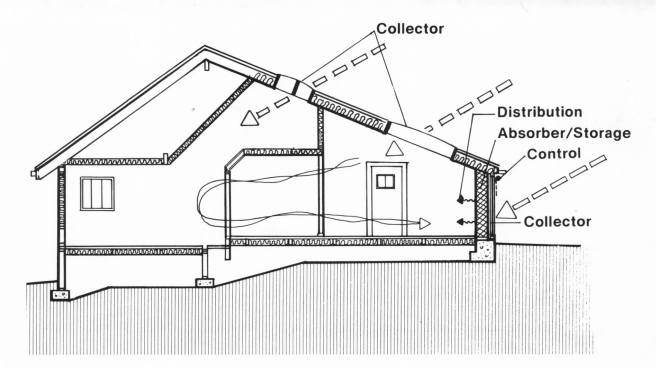

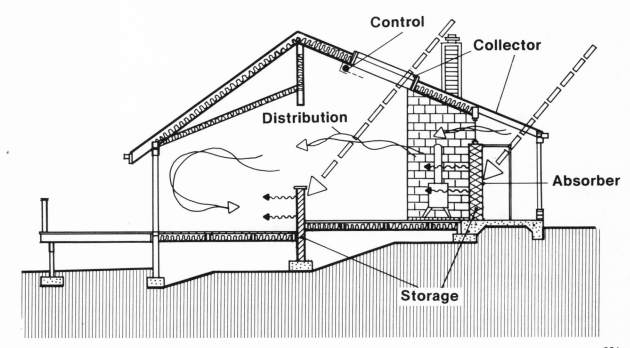

Truckee, CA

Builder: Mosedale Construction, Tahoe City, CA

Designer: Aeronautical Solar Architecture, Tahoe City, CA

Solar Designer: Pacific Sun, Inc., Menlo Park, CA

Price: $140,000

Net Heated Area: 1650 ft²

Heat Load: 63.2 x 10⁶ BTU / yr

Degree Days: 8438

Solar Fraction: 86%

Auxiliary Heat: 0.67 BTU / DD / ft²

Passive Heating System(s): Direct gain, isolated gain

Recognition Factors: Collector(s): South-facing windows, greenhouse glazing, 294 ft² **Absorber(s):** Tile-covered concrete floor, surface of water-filled tubes **Storage:** Tile-covered concrete floor, water-filled tubes—**capacity:** 9786 BTU/°F **Distribution:** Radiation, natural convection **Controls:** Insulating shades, vents

Back-up: Electric resistance heater (25,000 BTU/H), woodburning stove

Domestic Hot Water: Liquid flat-plate collectors (94 ft²)

Passive Cooling Type: Earth sheltering, convection, stack effect, evaporative cooling

232

This home is located near the mouth of a deep canyon that connects with the Truckee River Canyon. It is earth-sheltered so it can take advantage of seasonally constant earth temperatures to moderate the inside temperature. The home's unconventional octagonal shape reduces exterior wall area, and thus cuts down on heat loss.

Located in a climate with very cold winters and snow cover, the home is designed to collect snow on its flat roof. The snow acts as additional insulation.

The sun heats this home in two ways. Sunlight is **collected** through south-facing windows into the living space. It strikes the surface of the dark tile floor, where it is **absorbed**. The sun's heat passes into the tile and concrete floor where it is **stored**.

When interior temperatures drop, this heat is **distributed** to the living space by radiant heat. "Window quilt™" roll-up insulating shades are used to cover the windows to **control** excessive heating during summer days, or excessive heat loss during winter nights.

The home is also heated by an attached greenhouse where sunlight is **collected** by south-facing glazing. There it strikes the tile floor and water-filled Kalwall™ tubes. These surfaces **absorb** the solar radiation and turn it into heat. The heat is **stored** in the tile floor and by water inside the tubes.

When heat is needed in the living space, a vent between the living space and the water storage area of the greenhouse is opened, allowing heat stored in the greenhouse to be **distributed** to the living space by convection. Heat flow from the greenhouse is **controlled** by opening and closing the vent between the sunspace and the living area.

Back-up heat is provided by electric resistance baseboard heaters and by a wood stove. The home also features an active solar domestic water heating system that uses a hot tub for heat storage.

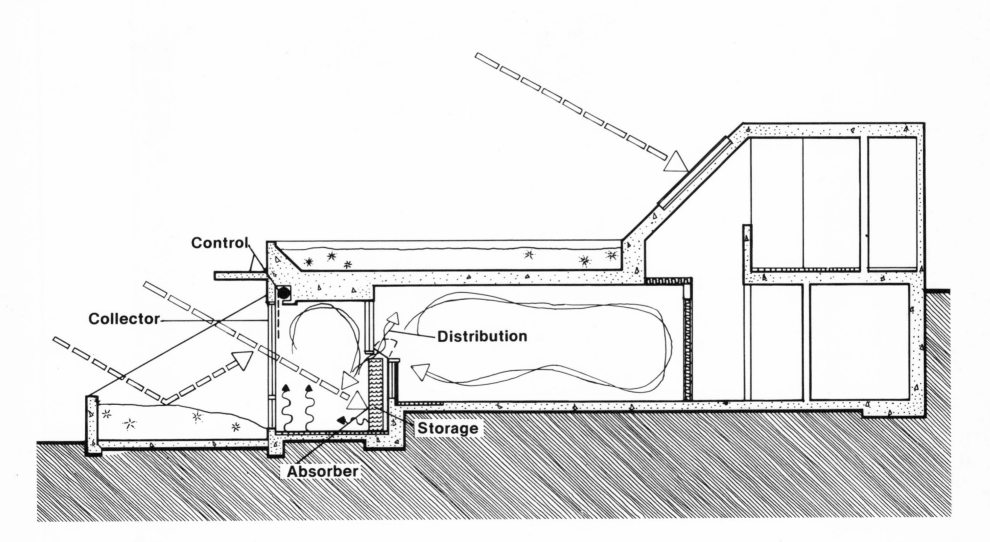

Elk Grove, CA

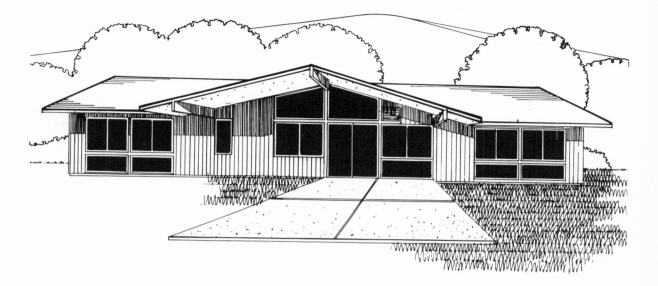

Builder: Streng Brothers Homes, Inc., Davis, CA

Designer: Carter Sparks, James Plumb, Sacramento, CA

Solar Designer: James Plumb

Price: $83,000

Net Heated Area: 1886 ft²

Heat Load: 46.5 x 10⁶ BTU/yr

Degree Days: 2499

Solar Fraction: 64%

Auxiliary Heat: 3.56 BTU/DD/ft²

Passive Heating System(s): Direct gain, indirect gain

Recognition Factors: Collector(s): South-facing windows, 288 ft² **Absorber(s):** Steel tank surface, concrete slab floor **Storage:** Water-filled steel tanks, concrete slab floors—**capacity:** 13,122 BTU/°F **Distribution:** Radiation, natural and forced convection **Controls:** Insulating drapes, thermostat

Back-up: Gas furnace (36,000 BTU/H)

Passive Cooling Type: Natural and induced ventilation

234

This passively solar-heated, contemporary home fits in nicely with its non-solar neighbors in the Sacramento, California, area. The nearly square shape of the home minimizes exterior wall area, thereby reducing the heat load.

The home uses the sun in two ways. The first is an attractive adaptation of the water wall concept. Sunlight is **collected** by south-facing windows. It is **absorbed** by the dark-painted surface of custom-designed steel tanks that stand behind the glazing. These tanks are capped with attractive wooden covers, and water inside them **stores** the sun's heat until it is **distributed** to the living space by convection and radiation. Insulating drapes can be drawn between the windows and tanks to **control** nighttime heat loss or to prevent summer overheating.

The second passive system uses direct radiation into the living spaces. Solar energy is **collected** through south-facing windows and **absorbed** and **stored** by the concrete slab floors. Heat is **distributed** by convection and radiation. Heat loss at night or excessive heat gain is **controlled** by insulating drapes that can cover the windows.

When the temperature in the south-facing living room reaches 79°F, a thermostat turns on a low-horsepower blower that carries some of the warmer air to the northern rooms. A setback thermostat in the north side of the home turns on the back-up gas furnace if the temperature drops to 68°F.

The home is equipped with appliances designed to reduce the use of electricity.

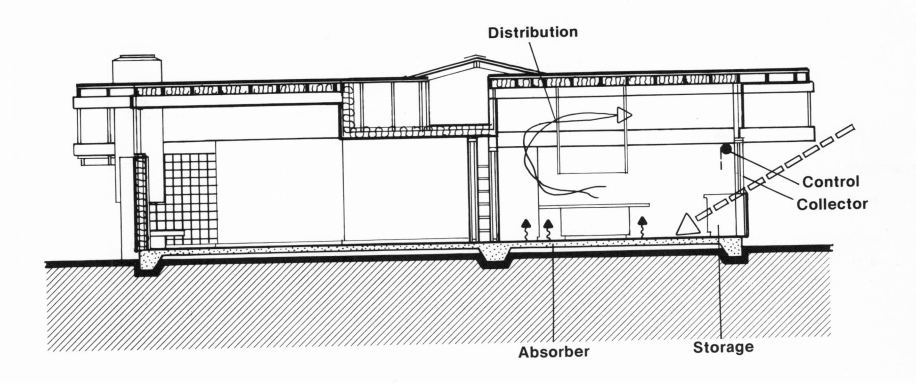

Distribution

Control

Collector

Absorber

Storage

Davis, CA

Builder: Walker, Donat & Co/Lien, Stonegate Co., Inc., Sacramento, CA

Designer: Charles Eley Associates, San Francisco, CA

Solar Designer: Charles Eley Associates

Price: $50,000

Net Heated Area: 1273 ft²

Heat Load: 39.6 x 10⁶ BTU/yr

Degree Days: 2819

Solar Fraction: 70%

Auxiliary Heat: 3.34 BTU/DD/ft²

Passive Heating System(s): Direct gain

Recognition Factors: Collector(s): Double-glazed windows, skylight, clerestory windows, 282 ft² **Absorber(s):** Concrete floor, water column surface **Storage:** Concrete floor, water column—**capacity:** 13,122 BTU/°F **Distribution:** Radiation, natural and forced convection **Controls:** Overhang, ducts, vents, draperies, sunscreens

Back-up: Gas furnace (36,000 BTU/H)

Domestic Hot Water: Active, liquid flat-plate collectors (42 ft²), 82-gallon storage

This duplex in energy-conscious Davis, California, is one of 15 similar units built by a large-volume builder in the Stonegate subdivision of a 300-acre development. The house is well insulated for its climate zone. The walls are R-11, the roof R-19 or better, and windows are double glazed.

Collectors for the passive heating system are the double-glazed doors and windows on the south side of the house, a south-facing sloped skylight over a small atrium entry, and the fixed glass in a belvedere above the entry. The glass along the south side of the house, where living rooms are located, is divided by wing walls into three areas: two fixed sections with awning windows at the bottom are on either side of a center sliding glass door. Above these three areas of glass are three pairs of clerestory panels, each divided into a fixed pane and a slider. A redwood overhang above the clerestory and a redwood trellis over the lower glazing provide summer shading for the collector. Solar heat is **absorbed** and **stored** in exposed aggregate concrete floors in the atrium and in the living and dining rooms. Four floor-to-ceiling water columns on the north side of the atrium entry provide thermal **storage** for energy collected through the atrium skylight and belvedere panels.

Distribution is by natural convection and radiation. Stored solar heat radiates into the living space from the mass floors. Jalousies opening into the north bedroom adjacent to the greenhouse allow heat radiating from the water columns to penetrate into the room. As a supplement to this simple mechanical system, an exhaust fan forces solar-heated air from the atrium ceiling through an attic duct and into the bedrooms via ceiling registers.

In the summer, the mild climate and prevailing winds promote cooling of the house by natural means. At night the north louvers of the belvedere and sliders and hatches on the south side of the house are opened to allow heat to escape and cool air to enter. Reversing the winter forced-distribution mode permits the exhaust fan system to expel heat from the back bedrooms through the atrium and belvedere.

The owner participation in the **control** of the passive heating and cooling systems includes a few important steps: the south wall draperies must be closed on winter nights and summer days; the hinged wooden louvers over the skylight must be opened in winter and closed in summer; sunscreens must be put in place on the east or west windows for the summer. A glass hatch between the atrium and belvedere should be opened in warm weather and closed when it is cold.

An active solar system on the roof heats domestic water; the storage tanks are on the north side of the house in the carport.

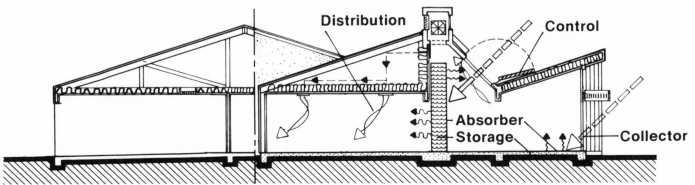

Lockford, CA

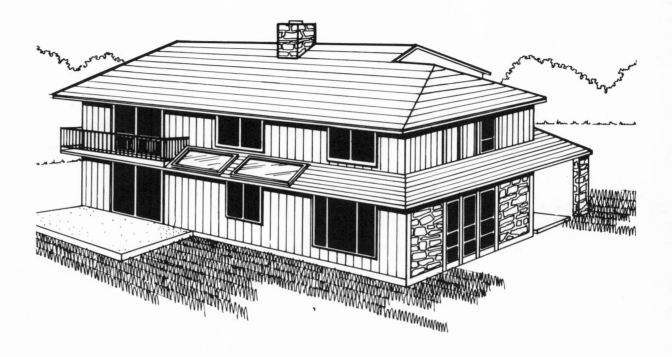

Builder: Jim F. Wadlow General Contractor, Lockford, CA

Designer: Sierra Engineering, Lodi, CA

Solar Designer: Tom Carver

Price: $95,000

Net Heated Area: 1705 ft²

Heat Load: 31.2 x 10⁶ BTU/yr

Degree Days: 2419

Solar Fraction: 61%

Auxiliary Heat: 2.89 BTU/DD/ft²

Passive Heating System(s): Indirect gain, sun-tempering

Recognition Factors: Collector(s): Double-glazed windows, Trombe wall glazing, 343 ft²
Absorber(s): Concrete Trombe wall, brick fireplace **Storage:** Concrete Trombe wall, brick fireplace—**capacity:** 9300 BTU/°F **Distribution:** Radiation, natural and forced convection **Controls:** Vents, overhangs, curtains over Trombe wall

Back-up: Electric heat pump, fireplace

Domestic Hot Water: Active solar DHW system, with two tanks

Passive Cooling Type: Natural ventilation, solar chimney

This solar-heated, 2-story ranch home is sited among large valley oak trees. It is extensively insulated, and all windows are double glazed. The attached garage is located on the north side to block winter winds. All exterior doorways face away from prevailing winds.

The home is designed to use passive solar energy in three ways. Much of the south-facing first floor wall is solid concrete, which is painted black on the exterior surface. Double glazing is positioned in front face. Double glazing is positioned in front

of this wall. Solar energy is **collected** through the glazing, and then strikes the surface of the concrete wall, where it is **absorbed**. The heat is **stored** within the wall until room temperatures drop below the temperature of the wall. At that time, it is **distributed** throughout the living space by convection and radiation. Vents at the top and bottom of the wall are opened during the day to allow the hot air between the wall and the glazing to be **distributed** for daytime heating.

Some of the solar energy that directly enters the living space strikes the brick fireplace and chimney where it is **absorbed** and **stored**. When the room becomes cool, the heat is **distributed** by convection and radiation.

In the summer, heat gain is **controlled** by roof overhangs that shade the glazed collection areas. The home also uses an active solar energy system to provide domestic hot water.

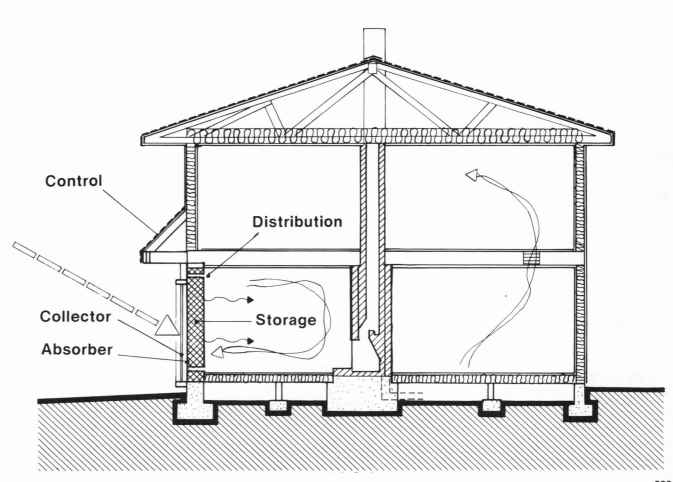

Control

Distribution

Collector

Absorber

Storage

Santa Rosa, CA

Builder: Solera Builders, Sonoma, CA

Designer: Cal-West, Inc., Santa Rosa, CA

Solar Designer: Cal-West, Inc.

Price: $169,000

Net Heated Area: 1815 ft²

Heat Load: 30.1 x 10⁶ BTU/yr

Degree Days: 3065

Solar Fraction: 80%

Auxiliary Heat: 1.20 BTU/DD/ft²

Passive Heating System(s): Isolated gain

Recognition Factors: Collector(s): Greenhouse glazing, 405 ft² **Absorber(s):** Greenhouse floors and walls **Storage:** Greenhouse floors and walls—**capacity:** 17,108 BTU/°F **Distribution:** Radiation, natural and forced convection **Controls:** Greenhouse door

Back-up: Electric resistance heaters (22,000 BTU/H), wood stove

Domestic Hot Water: Liquid flat-plate collectors (120 ft²), 175-gallon storage

What sets this home apart from surrounding homes is its use of solar energy and its innovative double-envelope design. This is literally a house within a house.

On the north and south sides, two sets of walls, located more than a foot apart, are each insulated to R-11. The two roofs are both insulated to R-19.

Sunlight is **collected** by a greenhouse, and is partially **absorbed** by its floors and walls. Convection and radiation **distribute** this heat throughout the living areas when the connecting doors are open.

Some of the solar heat is **stored** in the walls and floors. In addition, some of the collected heat will travel by natural convection to the attic, drop down through the hollow north wall and flow across the crawl space where some of the heat will be **absorbed** by its earth floor, for later re-radiation. The loop is completed when this cooled air returns through the floor of the greenhouse where the cycle begins again. Distribution will take place by **radiation** through the floor and by convection through the floor and the space between the double shells and the home.

For those times when the stored solar is not adequate, electric baseboard heaters provide back-up. Two fireplaces supplied with outside air for combustion may also be used.

The home is also equipped with an active solar domestic water heating system. Potable water is circulated from the storage tank to the solar collectors on the roof. The water is drained down from the collectors when it is in danger of freezing.

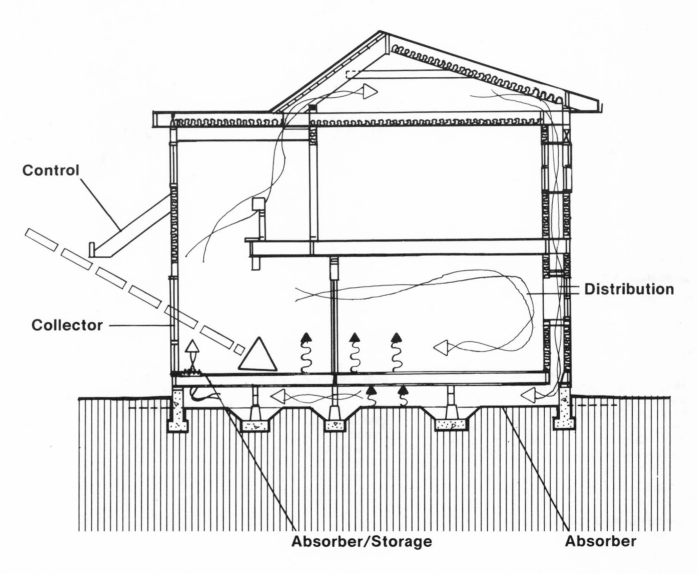

Control

Distribution

Collector

Absorber/Storage

Absorber

Davis, CA

Builder: Concept Interior Designs, Inc., Construction Division, Davis, CA

Designer: Design Associates, Davis, CA

Solar Designer: Design Associates

Price: $100,000

Net Heated Area: 2059 ft²

Heat Load: 30.7 x 10⁶ BTU/yr

Degree Days: 2499

Solar Fraction: 71%

Auxiliary Heat: 1.74 BTU/DD/ft²

Passive Heating System(s): Direct gain, isolated gain

Recognition Factors: Collector(s): South-facing windows, greenhouse glazing, 413 ft² **Absorber(s):** Concrete floor, steel, water-filled tank surface **Storage:** concrete floor, water-filled steel tanks—**capacity:** 21,740 BTU/°F **Distribution:** Radiation, natural and forced convection **Controls:** Moveable curtains and insulation, vents, overhang

Back-up: Gas heater (wall type), electric resistance heaters, woodburning stove

Domestic Hot Water: Thermosiphon DHW, 82-gallon storage

Passive Cooling Type: Natural ventilation, convection

Davis, California, has become the solar showplace of America. This home provides the town with another example of passive solar heating.

The sun is used in two ways to heat this home. With the direct system, sunlight is **collected** through windows on the south side. It strikes the concrete interior surfaces of the home, where much of it is **absorbed** and **stored**. Stored heat is **distributed** as radiant heat into the living space. Insulating curtains are used to cover the windows to **control** excessive heat loss during winter nights. Low-horsepower blowers can also be used to **distribute** and **control** the stored solar energy.

The home is also heated by an attached greenhouse. Sunlight is **controlled** through the glazing and strikes the concrete floor and water-filled steel tanks where it is **absorbed** and **stored**. Heat from the greenhouse is **distributed** to the living space by natural convective flow through connecting vents. These vents are opened and closed to **control** heat flow.

The back of the greenhouse's water tanks extend into the living space. When the living space cools, heat is **distributed** by radiation from the surface of these tanks. On winter nights, insulated panels are attached onto the greenhouse side of the tanks to **control** heat loss to the outside. In the summer, these panels are attached during the day to **control** excessive heat gain. An overhang awning also helps to **control** excessive summertime heat gain. And cooling is further assisted by small exhaust fans and by natural convection. A partial double-envelope roof design maximizes this convection.

All walls are insulated to R-19, and the roof is insulated to R-30.

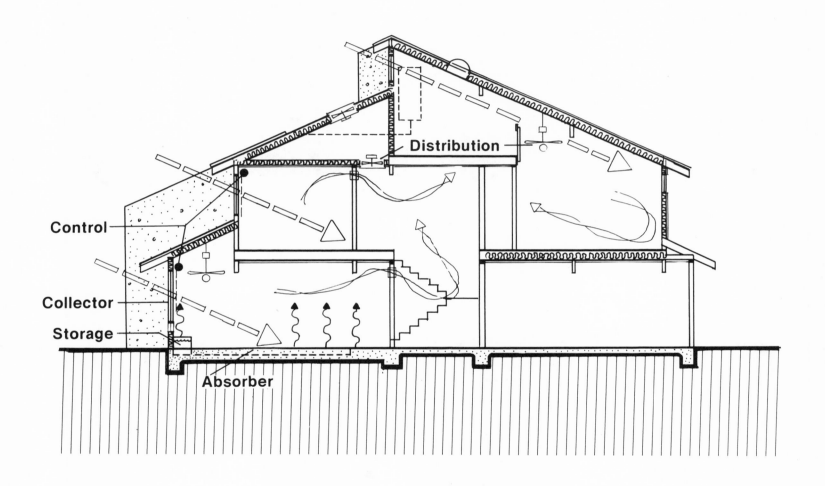

Distribution

Control

Collector

Storage

Absorber

Mat-Su Borough, AK

Builder: Solarctic Construction Co., Anchorage, AK

Designer: Ronald J. Bissett, Anchorage, AK

Solar Designer: Ronald J. Bissett

Price: $85,000

Net Heated Area: 1466 ft²

Heat Load: 57.9 x 10⁶ BTU/yr

Degree Days: 10,667

Solar Fraction: 62%

Auxiliary Heat: 1.40 BTU/DD/ft²

Passive Heating System(s): Direct gain, indirect gain (Trombe wall), isolated gain

Recognition Factors: Collector(s): Single-glazed Trombe wall glass, double-glazed greenhouse glass, triple-glazed glass, 565 ft² **Absorber(s):** Tile pavers, greenhouse floor, concrete block Trombe wall **Storage:** Concrete slab floor, Trombe wall, greenhouse floor—**capacity:** 19,264 BTU/°F **Distribution:** Radiation, natural convection **Controls:** Retractable shades, Trombe wall registers, floor vents, fans, moveable insulation

Back-up: Woodburning stove (50,000 BTU/H), electric resistance heaters (25,000 BTU/H)

Domestic Hot Water: Liquid flat-plate collectors (129 ft²), 120-gallon storage

In an effort to combat a winter outdoor design temperature of −20° F, conservation has been stressed in the design of this home. Situated on a hill overlooking a lake, this 2-story, compact form has plentiful trees and natural foliage on all sides (except south) acting as a buffer against prevailing north winds. Northern exposure has been minimized with partial earth berming, and further buffered with the location of utility areas (pantry, mudroom, etc.) along that wall; all entry to the house is through these unheated spaces on the first floor.

Ceiling insulation is a remarkable R-78, with all walls but the south masonry wall at R-40; moveable insulation on the south wall is rated at R-10, but the greenhouse there acts as a buffer zone.

The predominant **collection** device for this 2-bedroom house is the 2-story greenhouse on the south wall. This double-glazed structure admits solar radiation to its own 6-inch concrete slab floor, as well as to the **collectors** at its back wall; these **collectors** take the form of triple-glazed windows for direct solar gain into the living spaces, and single-glazed with Trombe walls. In addition to the greenhouse collectors, there are triple-glazed windows on the southeast and southwest sides that also collect heat.

Absorption and **storage** of heat occurs at the greenhouse floor and the solid block of the Trombe wall. This 16-foot high wall is continuous, but is divided into upper and lower sections by a retractable sun-shading device. **Absorbing** heat on the lower level of the living areas are tile pavers atop a 6-

inch concrete storage floor. The pavers extend back to the north wall of the house, though the slab floor is only 3 inches thick beyond the front rooms.

Distribution is entirely by natural convection and radiation. During cold winter days, air in the space between the glazing and the darkened surface of the Trombe wall heats up and flows into the living area through wall registers at the ceiling. Cooler air is drawn into the heating space through wall registers at the floor. This process takes place at both levels of the Trombe wall. At night, moveable insulation is lowered to control loss of heat stored in the mass wall. Wall registers are closed, and the mass can then radiate its stored heat. Convective flows are set up between floors by open floor vents and the north stairwell. Back-up heating is by a woodburning stove that is centrally located on the lower level, drawing its combustion air from the outside. As further back-up, there are electric baseboard heaters in all rooms except the pantry and mudroom.

For preheating domestic water there are six roof-mounted flat-plate collectors.

Cooling is not considered a problem in this region and for that reason is accomplished by ventilation alone. There are single ventilation windows on the north, east, and west walls. All windows have built-in adjustable reflective shades to control sun gain. Windows on the southeast and southwest sides can be opened. To prevent overheating of the mass wall there is the fixed overhang formed by the roof over the greenhouse, and a retractable canvas overhang between floors that extend almost 4 feet into the greenhouse. To vent heat that does build up in the greenhouse there is a fan on the east side and a vent on the west.

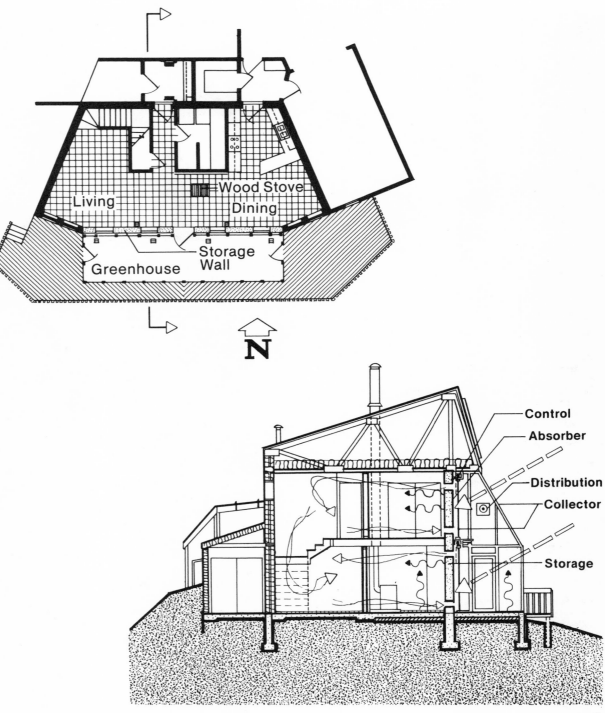

245

Eagle River, AK

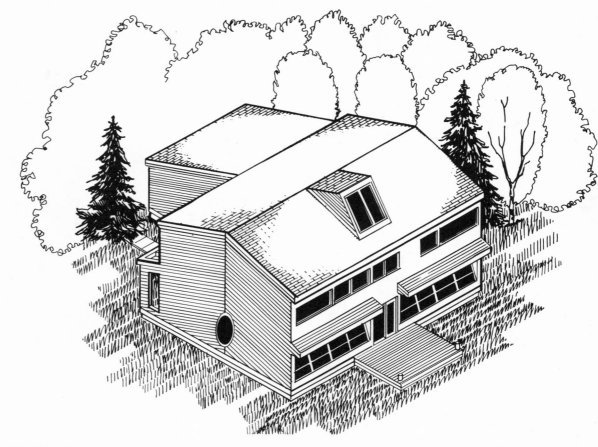

Builder: Land Trust Realty/Development Conservation Enterprises, Eagle River, AK

Designer: Architecture/Environmental Design, Anchorage, AK

Solar Designer: Jimmy Anderson

Price: $122,000

Net Heated Area: 2218 ft²

Heat Load: 102.36 x 10⁶ BTU/yr

Degree Days: 10,850

Solar Fraction: 42%

Auxiliary Heat: 2.48 BTU/DD/ft²

Passive Heating System(s): Sun-tempering, direct gain

Recognition Factors: Collector(s): South-facing glazing, 313 ft² **Absorber(s):** Living room, dining room, bedrooms **Storage:** Same as absorber—**capacity:** 3997 BTU/°F **Distribution:** Radiation **Controls:** Exterior shutters, overhang, moveable insulation

Back-up: Gas furnace (32,000 BTU/H), wood stove

Domestic Hot Water: Passive DHW preheat (36 ft²)

This compact 2-story, 3-bedroom design near Anchorage, Alaska, combines contemporary styling with an emphasis on passive solar heating and energy-conservation features. The garage and other low-use areas including closets, stairs, and baths are located on the north side of the house to provide protection from the extreme winter climate; an "arctic" vestibule entry is included in the design. All windows are triple glazed, shim spaces are caulked, and all south glazing has automatic moveable insulation. The house is heavily insulated, with R-40 urethane in the walls and R-62 in the roof.

Because of the expense and difficulties of poured concrete construction and the

danger of frost damage to the foundation in Alaska, the design specifies wood frame construction over a masonry foundation and crawl space. This construction intentionally allows a substantial amount of heat to be transferred from the house to the ground below to protect the footings from frost damage.

In this design, solar heat is **collected** through south-facing windows on both levels; direct radiation penetrates the living room, dining room, and the three upstairs bedrooms. There is little storage of the solar heat in the house, but with a long heating season, low solar availability, and high heating loads, overheating is unlikely and radiant solar heat is immediately used whenever it is available. Nighttime heat losses are **controlled** by the closing of motorized insulating exterior shutters on all south glazing. There are no east windows, and only one window each on the north and west sides.

In the summer, lower-level windows are shaded by an overhang, and upper-level windows by an overhang and by "Slim-shades™". Cooling needs are minimal, and are easily met by opening windows to induce cross-ventilation.

The design includes a passive "bread box" domestic water preheating system. Three black tanks are located behind tempered glass in the attic. The system is pressurized by the cold water supply, which forces solar-heated water through the conventional hot water heater. The system is drained down in the winter, when water is circulated through a preheat tank located in the combustion chamber of the woodburning stove.

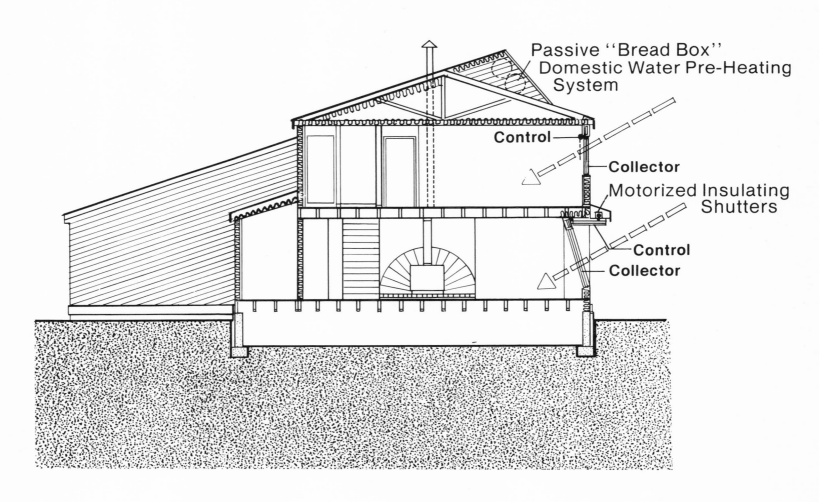

Passive "Bread Box" Domestic Water Pre-Heating System

Control

Collector

Motorized Insulating Shutters

Control

Collector

Passive Solar: How To Do It

The design and the construction of passive solar and energy-conserving homes involve a number of practices that are not yet standard within the home building industry. Fortunately, these modifications of approach make good sense and if sensibly applied will lead to a better, more attractive, and more marketable product.

Environment and Site

Climate

In the age of energy-conscious building, climate is the context in which all solar/conservation strategies are rooted. A house built in Green Bay, Wisconsin is not going to follow the same approach as one built in Roanoke, Virginia. This is because the heating demand in Green Bay is so much greater. It averages over 8,000 heating degree days per year, whereas Roanoke averages just over 4,100 per year. The need for the house in Green Bay will be primarily to make it comfortable in a long cold winter. In Roanoke, the need will be to balance the cooling for the summer months with the heating required for the relatively mild winters.

The amount of available sunlight, the number and sequence of cloudy days, the direction and average speed of the prevailing winter wind, the average daily temperatures and their average daily ''swing,'' and the average relative humidity are the major factors that provide a common base for all homes built within a climatic region. These data are found in the climate information sources listed in Appendix II, the Bibliography. Tempering these conditions is a matter of working carefully with the building site.

Degree days are accumulated daily throughout a heating season by subtracting the average outdoor temperature from a base of 65°F — the temperature at which heat is presumed to be needed.

250

South-facing slope is a good location for a passive solar home.

The Building Site

The major purpose for careful use of the building site is to "level off" the extremes of the local climate. The site includes a number of factors that affect the passive solar house. These factors include topography ("the lay of the land"), soil, drainage, and vegetation. (The most important concern "solar access" is described in the next subsection.)

An ideal location for a passive, energy-conserving house is a south-facing slope with evergreen trees to the north of the building site. This type of site can provide clear (or clearable) access to sunlight as well as an opportunity to build the house into the slope to protect its north wall against the prevailing winter winds. If the house is left completely exposed to these winds, increased heat loss will occur. On a flat site, wind protection can be achieved by the use of "earth berming" which is a continuous mound of dirt built up along the north and sometimes east and west walls of the house. This will also protect the house against air infiltration and temperature extremes.

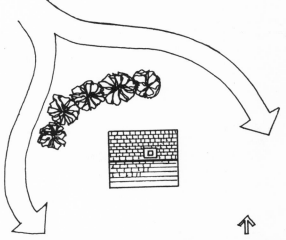

Trees can be used as windbreakers to reduce heat loss.

Earth-berming, a mound of dirt built up around the perimeter of a house, reduces exposure to cold and wind.

Protected on the north by trees, the southern side of the house remains open for summer breezes.

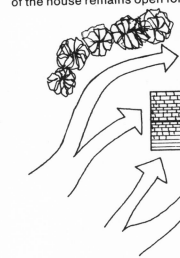

The size, location, and number of existing trees is also important. A healthy stand of evergreens to the north, northeast, and northwest will provide a superb windbreak for a house. On the other hand, if there are trees to the south that are tall enough and close enough to shade the solar collection area, they will have to be removed. In the absence of beneficial trees, the builder can landscape to deflect the path of winter winds. Thick hedgerows, for example, can be effective windbreaks and will grow rapidly.

If possible, build where the water table is low and where there is good drainage. Besides causing damp basements and floor slabs, wet soil will conduct heat away from the house at a much higher rate than dry soil. Soil is a moderately effective insulator when it is dry. When it is wet, however, soil is a heat sponge.

The house should also be sited with consideration for summer cooling needs. Just as it is protected from winter north winds, the house can be open to summer breezes, which usually blow from a southerly direction. And particular attention should be paid to shading west-facing windows. These will be hit by the hot afternoon sun as it sinks down to the western horizon. Trees can effectively shade the house from this low sun, which can otherwise add a great deal to the house's cooling load.

The well-planned use of a building site will give a house a distinct advantage against the whims of climate. On the other hand, the combined effects of ill-considered siting may result in drastically reduced performance for a passive solar house, especially during extreme weather conditions. A broader discussion of design strategies for various types of climates can be found in *Regional Guidelines For Building Passive Energy Conserving Homes*, which is listed in Appendix II, the Bibliography.

Solar Access

A passive solar house has at least one prerequisite: a building site with adequate access to sunlight. This is not generally a difficult problem for single-family houses, but the builder of a solar house must be sure that access can be established before beginning a project.

Ideally, a solar house should face within 30 degrees of true south. On December 21, the shortest day of the year, the sun has reached its lowest point in the sky, and shadows are their longest. The passive solar house should receive all sunlight between 9 a.m. and 3 p.m. on that day. The solar collection area should not be shaded by trees, land forms, or other buildings during these hours, which constitutes the peak period for collecting solar heat. Sunlight collected before 9 a.m. and after 3 p.m. is also of value, and access to it will determine whether or not some east- or west-facing windows are used to collect it. One advantage of early morning sunlight is that it can provide quick warmth to an east-facing breakfast area.

The essential geometry of solar access is known as the "solar window." Figure 1 shows how all of the dimensions of the solar window are determined, using the times 9 a.m. and 3 p.m. for the left and right boundaries, and the paths of the sun on December 21 and June 21 as the upper and lower limits.

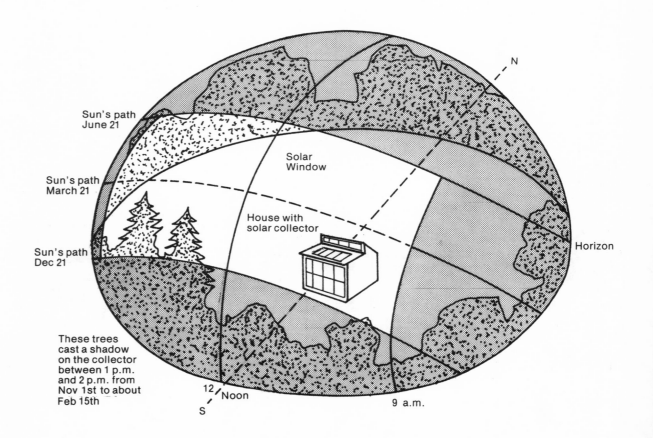

Sun's path June 21

Sun's path March 21

Sun's path Dec 21

Solar Window

House with solar collector

N

Horizon

These trees cast a shadow on the collector between 1 p.m. and 2 p.m. from Nov 1st to about Feb 15th

12 Noon

S

9 a.m.

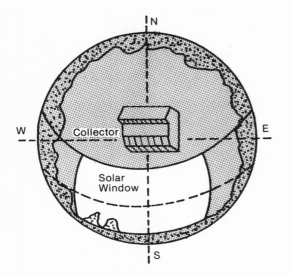

For Planned Unit Developments, where higher densities can raise the risk of solar obstruction, careful planning for solar access is especially important. An extensive, in-depth treatment of solar access and its related issues can be found in *Site Planning for Solar Access: A Guidebook for Residential Developers and Site Planners*, available from the National Solar Heating and Cooling Information Center, Box 1607, Rockville, MD 20850.

Energy Conservation

The basic issues in energy conservation for a passive solar house are the shape and orientation of the building, and the layout of interior spaces. The shape of a building affects its rate of heat loss and solar gain, and the goal here is to maintain a low ratio of exterior surface area to interior volume by building a compact house that does not sprawl all over its site.

The orientation of the building, obviously, must be set to collect solar radiation, which means it should face within 30 degrees of true — not magnetic — south. The long axis of the house should run east to west, allow-

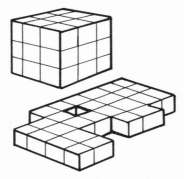

A more compact form leaves less exterior area of a building exposed to the elements.

ing for a south-facing solar collection area that is large enough to share with all or most of the major living spaces.

The layout of living spaces should, while taking direct advantage of solar heat gains and natural circulation patterns enhance the energy-conserving function of the building. An important goal in the floor plan is to place all low-use and unheated spaces along the north wall where they can serve as a buffer zone between that wall and the major living spaces. These spaces include storage areas, pantries, closets, vestibules, and utility rooms. Where a garage is planned, it should also be positioned to serve as a buffer.

The next issue of energy conservation is the insulation and sealing of the building envelope. Many of the methods discussed below are already standard practice throughout much of the building industry because of the dramatic escalation in fuel costs.

A major factor in heat loss is air leakage through cracks around doors and windows and through the numerous joints in the building walls and roof. These leaks can be minimized through the use of weatherstripping around doors and windows and by the caulking of construction joints. Vapor barriers between the interior wall finish and

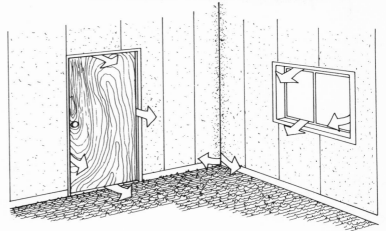

Infiltration of cold air into a building occurs through the building joints, under doors, and around windows.

wall insulation will also help curb infiltration. A house can, however, be made too tight, which will result in condensation and air stagnation. Therefore, a rate of 0.5 air changes per hour of the total volume of house air is recommended.

Another source of heat loss is by conduction through windows. This problem can be solved by a combination of tactics, the first of which is to reduce or eliminate window areas on the north-facing wall and, particularly in northern climates, to limit window area on the east and west walls. The next step is to double glaze all windows (triple glaze in harsh climates). Windows that traditionally would have been allocated to the north, east, and west walls can be concentrated on the south, where they can serve as solar collectors. Oversizing south windows can cause a problem in more moderate climates by adding to the summer cooling load.

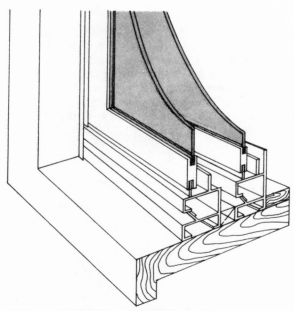

Heat lost by conduction through windows can be reduced through the use of double glazing.

The walls, ceilings, and floors of a building lose heat by conduction through their materials. Reducing this loss calls for adequate and properly installed insulation in the walls, floors, crawl space, roofs, and at the foundation. It is important, when using energy conservation techniques, to exercise tight quality control during installation. For instance, batt and blanket insulation should fit snugly in wall and ceiling spaces because heat will quickly move through gaps and be lost to the outside. Loose fill insulation (e.g., cellulose) must not be packed down or it will lose much of its potential R-value. Vapor barriers should be tight to curb infiltration and keep moisture from reaching insulation. Careful attention should be paid to caulking building joints, window frames, and door perimeters.

The opening and closing of outside doors, especially where people are coming and going with great regularity, is yet another source of heat loss. Every time an entryway is opened directly into the living space, a large volume of cold air from outside is exchanged for an equal amount of heated indoor air. This can be countered by sheltering the entryways within an "air-lock," an unheated vestibule that creates a two-door entry, whereby only the cool air inside the air-lock has the potential for exchange with the warmed house air. This reduces the losses that occur each time the door is opened.

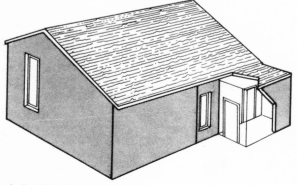

A double entry way

With the heating requirement of the house reduced through the use of these energy-conserving measures, the foundation has been laid for passive solar heating systems.

Passive Solar Building Details

The specification and construction of building components meant to serve as passive solar elements is a new experience for most builders. The materials involved, however, are generally familiar items among the building trades. The "newness" is mainly a function of how these materials are used.

The five major components of any passive solar system (collector, absorber, storage, distribution, and control) must all be designed and built to work with one another. The advantage of the passive solar house is that these components are integral to the building's structure rather than added on.

The passive building details that follow are intended to give a general but thorough illustration of materials and typical specifications for the standard passive approaches that are found throughout the projects described in this report. It should be noted that moveable insulation, examples of which are shown in these details, is crucial to passive system performance. It must, however, be kept simple and inexpensive if it is to remain cost effective.

DIRECT GAIN

1. **Collector:** glazing in multiple layers, as appropriate to climate.

2. **Absorber:** dark colored surface (tile, brick, or concrete) exposed to direct sunlight with minimal coverage by carpet or furniture.

3. **Storage:** concrete slab in direct contact with absorber surface; insulation below.

4. **Distribution:** re-radiation of heat stored in concrete floor.

5. **Control:** overhang sized to provide full shading of collector glass at summer solstice (June 21).

6. **Control:** automatic or manual roll-down insulation.

7. **Control:** High and low vents for summer ventilation, protection against over-heating.

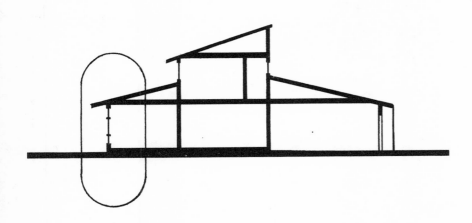

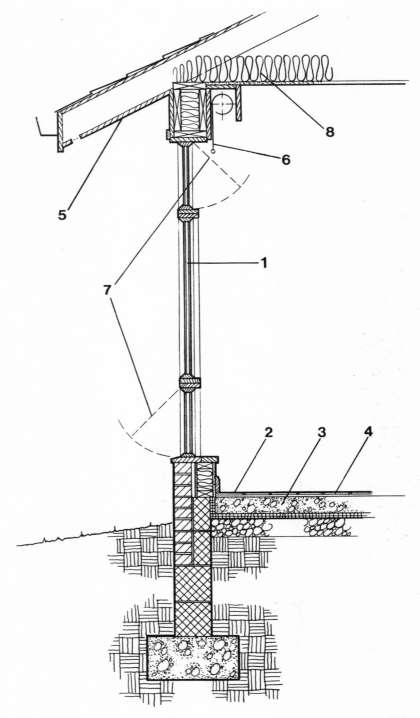

CLERESTORY AND SKYLIGHT INSULATION

1. **Collector:** (glass, acrylic, fiberglass, etc.) in multiple layers (as appropriate to climate) mounted to be air- and water-tight and accessible for maintenance.

2. **Control:** shading device to block all sun at summer solstice (June 21).

3. **Conservation:** compression-type weatherstripping around full perimeter minimizes losses of stratified warm air.

4. **Control:** hinged insulating panel swings down during daytime, admitting light and warmth, and upward during night to conserve heat in rooms below.

5. **Distribution:** opening from clerestory ridge to outside allows hot stratified air to be vented during summer months; opening to be sealed tightly with insulating panel during winter months.

6. **Control:** pulley and cord mechanism permits control of insulating panel from below.

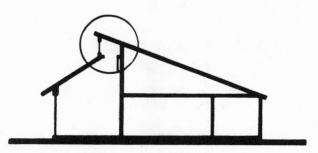

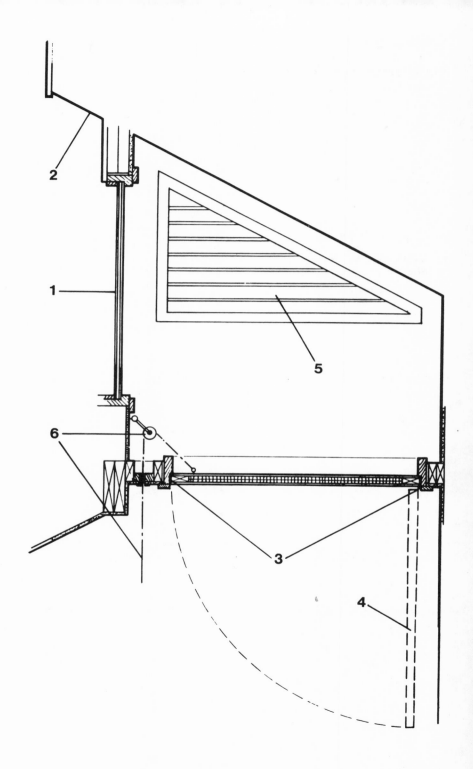

DOMESTIC WATER PREHEAT

1. **Storage:** fluid (antifreeze solution or water) to preheat domestic hot water. If water is used, freeze protection such as a draindown system for the winter. If antifreeze solution is used, a double-walled heat exchanger must separate the fluid from the potable water supply.

2. **Absorber:** dark surface of tank converts radiation to heat.

3. **Collector:** glazing (glass, acrylic, fiberglass, etc.) in multiple layers (as appropriate to climate) mounted to be air- and water-tight and removable for cleaning and repair.

4. **Construction:** waterproof shield drains to adjacent roof top, prevents damage from potential condensation.

5. **Collector:** reflective surface on roof in front of glazing increases heat gain potential of collector.

6. **Control:** insulation and air tight construction minimizes heat loss and increases system efficiency.

7. **Reflectors inside:** increase efficiency of system.

8. **Pressure and Temperature:** relief valve to protect from overheating.

9. **Extra weight:** on rafters requires structural planning.

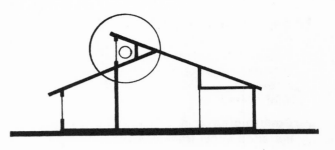

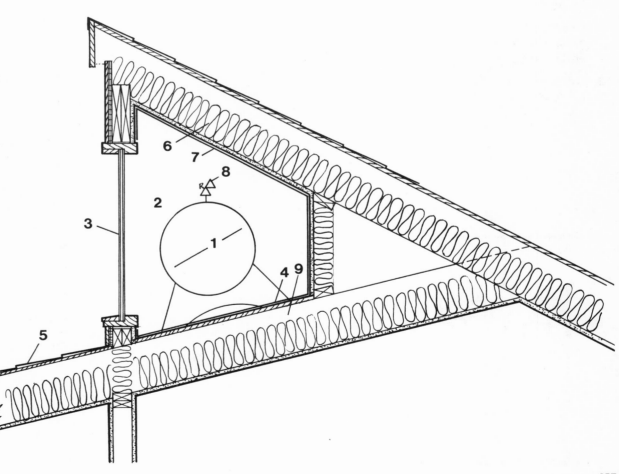

BI-FOLDING MOVEABLE INSULATION

1. **Conservation:** compression-type weatherstripping at jamb, sill, head, and where two sections of bi-fold panel meet minimizes infiltration.

2. **Construction:** piano hinges securely fastened allow trackless panel hanging and result in panel storage flush to adjacent wall; track-mounted systems open 90° only.

3. **Conservation:** sliding bolt type latches at floor and head; panels lock in sealing configuration minimizing perimeter infiltration.

4. **Control:** moveable insulating panels over glass reduce both winter night heat loss and summer day heat gain.

5. **Control:** space between glazing and moveable insulation should be vented to exterior side by a top opening to avoid potential summer overheat.

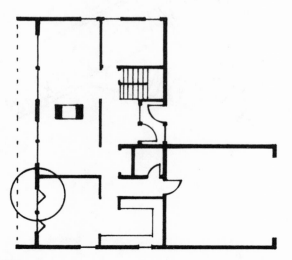

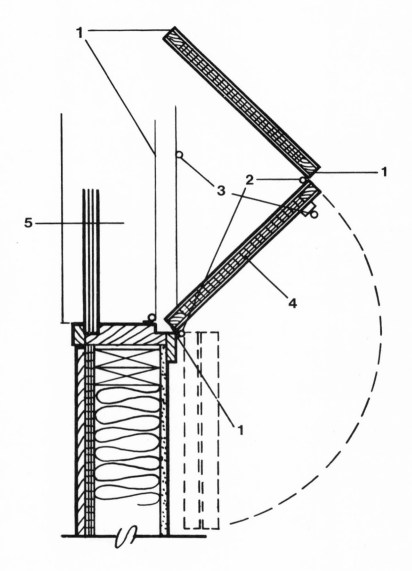

RADIANT TROMBE WALL AND SUMMER SHADING DEVICES

1. **Control:** wood or metal louvers sized and tilted to provide full shading at summer solstice (June 21) and minimal shading at winter solstice (Dec. 21).

2. **Collector:** glazing (glass, acrylic, fiberglass, etc.) in multiple layers (as appropriate to climate) mounted to be air- and water-tight but removable for cleaning; sliding glass doors are shown.

3. **Absorber:** dark surface color to promote absorption. Use a product capable of withstanding 150°.

4. **Storage:** solid high density material (concrete, fully grouted brick or block, 8 to 12 inches thick).

5. **Distribution:** interior finish material applied directly to storage mass with no airspace or furring; minimal book shelving and artwork covering will allow effective radiant distribution of heat to adjacent room.

6. **Control:** moveable insulating drape permits adjustment of radiant distribution to the room.

7. **Control:** space between collector glazing and absorber surface should be vented to outside during summer months by use of top and bottom vents or by use of operable glazing frames.

8. **Conservation:** thermal break at top of wall minimizes loss from storage to unheated spaces.

9. **Conservation:** insulation on both interior and exterior of storage wall minimizes conductive heat loss to adjacent earth.

10. **Conservation:** masonry not behind glazing may be filled with insulation, if structurally feasible, to minimize stored heat losses downward.

11. **Control:** fabric awning sized to provide full shading at summer solstice and removable during heating season.

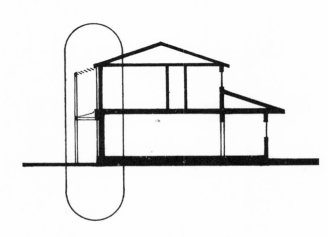

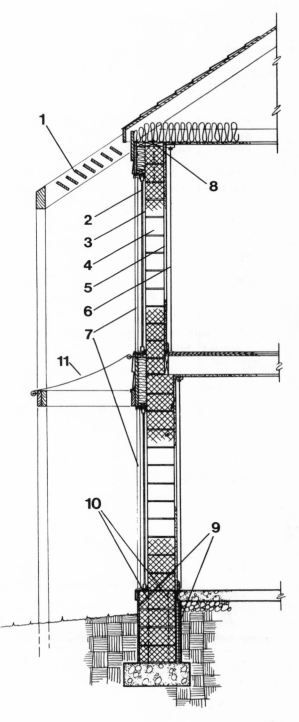

GREENHOUSE AND WATER TANK STORAGE

1. **Collector:** glazing (glass, acrylic, fiberglass, etc.) in multiple layers (as appropriate to climate) mounted to be air- and water-tight.

2. **Absorber:** dark surface color to promote absorption. Use a product capable of withstanding 150°F.

3. **Storage:** water with rust inhibitor in welded metal tank.

4. **Distribution:** face of metal tank exposed directly to adjacent room for radiant distribution, vents in countertop aide convective distribution.

5. **Control:** roll-down insulation shade reduces heat losses from storage to greenhouse.

6. **Absorber:** dark surface color and minimal shading by plants and furniture.

6a. **Storage:** concrete or other high density material with insulation below.

7. **Distribution:** operable glass that allows surplus hot air from greenhouse to circulate to adjacent room.

8. **Control:** exterior shade to block summer sun.

9. **Control:** insulation shade required in colder climates to maintain temperatures above freezing if greenhouse is to be used for plants.

10. **Control:** insulated ridge vent with tight compression seal. Open in summer to allow hot air to escape.

11. **Control:** insulated low wall vent with tight compression seal opens in summer for ventilation.

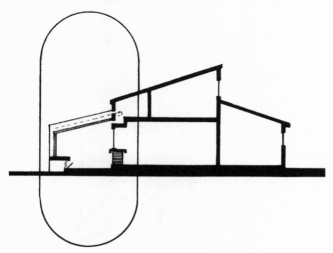

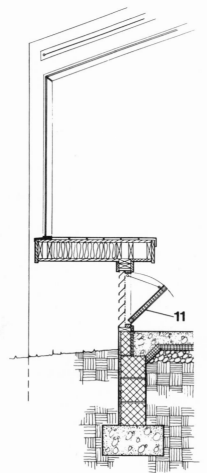

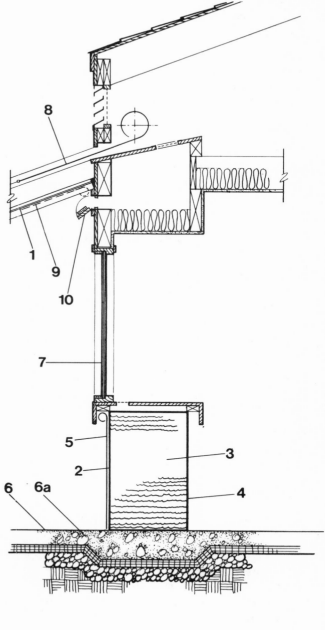

THERMOSIPHONING TROMBE WALL

1. **Control:** overhang sized to provide full shading of collector glass at summer solstice (June 21).

2. **Conservation:** attic vents and clear space between top of insulation and bottom of roof sheathing promotes attic ventilation.

3. **Control:** automatic or manual roll-down insulation.

4. **Maintenance:** provide panels to roll insulation.

5. **Control:** sweep minimizes heated air lost to unheated space.

6. **Conservation:** thermal break at top of wall minimizes loss from storage to unheated space.

7. **Distribution:** outlet area should equal approximately half the cross sectional area of the air space.

8. **Control:** register closed during summer to minimize circulation of warm air to interior of house.

9. **Collector:** glazing (glass, acrylic, fiberglass, etc.) in multiple layers (as appropriate to climate) mounted to be air- and water-tight and removable for cleaning and repair.

10. **Absorber:** dark colored surface promotes absorption; use product capable of withstanding 150°F.

11. **Storage:** solid high density material (concrete, fully grouted brick, or block 8 to 12 inches thick).

12. **Distribution:** interior finish material applied directly to storage mass with no airspace or furring; minimal bookshelf and artwork wall covering will allow effective radiant distribution of heat to adjacent room.

13. **Control:** flexible backdraft damper automatically prevents cool exterior air from settling into the room during winter nights.

14. **Conservation:** insulation on both interior and exterior of storage wall minimizes conductive heat loss to adjacent earth.

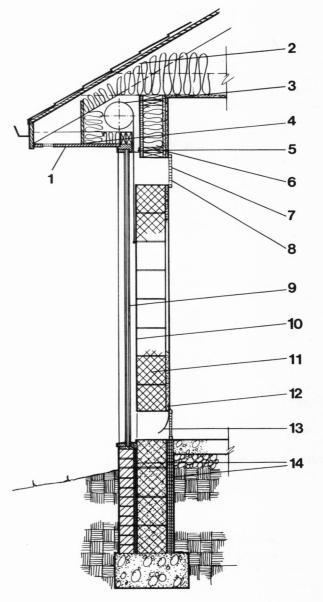

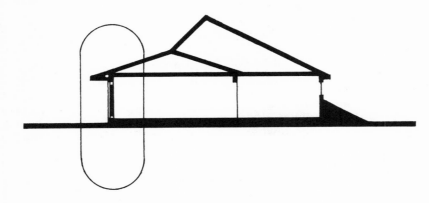

Market Issues

Passive solar heating already has a potential market. It consists of tens of thousands of *home buyers* who are looking for an answer to a big question: How do I stay warm in my new home without going broke?

Those buyers who can afford to remain unconcerned about home energy costs are a vanishing species. A passive solar home in the hands of a smart builder who knows his or her market should sell more rapidly than a conventional home. And, as the upward trend in energy costs continues, the passive solar home will claim a dominant share of the new housing market sometime during the 1980s.

Although passive solar is going to have strong market appeal, it is only part of the entire home package. If, for instance, the builder does not include a family room when building for a market that expects one, then a passive solar system is not likely to make the buyer forget what he or she wants in the way of living space. The builder should make sure when showing any passive house that the buyer knows that all of the other expected amenities are present and accounted for.

After properly considering the needs and tastes of his or her market, the builder's first step toward successfully including passive solar is a careful selection of passive design elements. There are a number of options to choose from, and the right combination is as important to market strategy as it is to the system's performance. The way that these elements are worked into a design will determine the project's marketability.

As an example, either a solar greenhouse or an atrium, properly and tastefully integrated into a design, will be a strong selling point because each is an attractive amenity, a luxury that is also very practical.

The builder must keep in mind, however, that passive solar, whatever else it might be, is a heating system and heating systems are meant to provide comfort, not compromise it. For instance, the use of a concrete floor as a storage element could meet buyer resistance. Floors cannot be carpeted if they are to be effective absorber and storage elements. This effect can be softened by covering them with attractive ceramic tiles and by locating them where they will not interfere with comfort: in the greenhouse or the family room. But the builder may decide not to use storage floors at all. There are other choices. Masonry walls or room dividers, which are more easily lived with, can also be effective storage elements, and remote rock storage bins can be used in some types of homes. The use of enough mass to absorb and store the solar heat collected by the house is crucial to nighttime heating and to the prevention of daytime overheating of the living spaces.

That leads to another important point. Passive homes are often designed so that they undergo daily temperature swings that will be greater than most people are used to. Buyers must be alerted to this. But they should also be reminded that before the temperature becomes uncomfortably low, a back-up system will supplement the solar heat.

As demonstrated by many of the 91 designs described and illustrated in this book, a house can be designed to use two or three different types of passive heating systems. These passive elements can be selected according to the needs of the home: a Trombe wall is a good way to heat a space where privacy is especially important, such as a ground level bedroom, and it is particularly well suited for delayed heating of rooms that will be used primarily at night. Direct gain is appropriate to rooms where immediate daytime heat is most welcome, such as a breakfast or dining room, a family room, or kitchen. Either greenhouses or atriums, on the other hand, create isolated spaces that lend themselves to different uses. Clerestories and skylights are a good way to get sunlight into rooms along the north wall where window area has been kept to the very minimum.

Designs in this book demonstrate that any traditional Cape Cod, ranch, salt-box, or colonial plan generally can be modified to tastefully include most passive solar elements. Certainly there will be differences that the buyer will notice and ask about, but with good location, the standard package of amenities, and a price in the market's current range, passive solar should provide a competitive edge over more conventional homes.

The Economic Advantage

The most tangible benefit of a passive energy-conserving home is economic. Because such a home is built to have far less of an energy requirement than a conventional home and because a good portion of the remaining demand can be met by natural means (i.e., the sun to warm, natural ventilation to cool), the owner is going to be on top of—rather than snowed under by—his home energy costs. All other market factors considered, the reduced energy demand of the passive solar house should enhance its rate of turnover.

The purchase price of a house that incorporates passive design features may be a bit higher than that of a conventional house. But the cost of ownership and operation will be less.

For those buyers who see only their monthly mortgage payment as the bottom line that dictates what they can afford, the seller of a passive solar home should be ready to explain how the added cost of the passive features is offset by fuel savings.

A passive solar house in New England, for instance, might cost an extra $5,000, which amounts to an increased monthly payment of $16.66 for a 25-year mortgage of 12 percent interest. But if the passive solar system saves $500 the first year in oil at $1/gallon (a price that will continue to rise), these savings would amount to $41.66 per month in 1980 dollars. Thus, the combined cost of ownership and operation for this passive solar house would be $25 per month ($300 per year) *less* than a comparable conventional home. This economic advantage is a powerful marketing tool. It would be wise for the seller to have on hand a very clear, concise economic fact sheet that spells out these advantages.

The marketing of a passive solar home will require that the seller educate the buyer in the operation of the house's thermal systems. This instruction should be clear, simple, and complete. The builder's market will affect the degree to which the house is designed to include owner participation in the operation of the passive solar system. Is the moveable night insulation operated automatically or manually? How much seasonal operation is there, and how much work does it require? There is a real challenge here to keep things simple and effective. And all of it should be easily explained by an owner's manual, something for the owner to refer to after he has been walked through the operation by the builder or the builder's well-informed sales representative.

Other Points to Consider

Solar energy is still news in many communities. The builder should contact the local newspaper and let them know about his new solar homes. But, a word of caution: it is wise to think twice before a model is opened up to a public stampede. It might be overrun by lookers who will scare the buyers away. If the response is overwhelming, the model should be shown by appointment only. The builder should avoid turning his homes into solar exhibits.

Passive solar may be unfamiliar to local lenders. It is a good idea for the builder to talk with a few mortgage officers. By explaining to them what he is doing, he can get informal commitments from them to provide mortgages. A strong commitment for rapid financing will ensure a quick turnover. Banks do not like surprises; they should be prepared well in advance.

The on-site sales effort should be well coordinated to present the passive solar features in the most effective way. Sales people should know what they are talking about, and brochures and other promotional materials should reflect the tastes of the market. Sell the house, not the solar system.

Passive solar homes offer a sure alternative to crippling oil bills. That's strong language in the marketplace. The buyer of a new home would like to look forward to being warm and snug, economically. The builder who can answer that need is one step ahead of the game.

Appendix I
Glossary

Absorber: The surface in a collector that absorbs solar radiation and converts it to heat energy.

Absorptivity: The ratio of the energy absorbed by a surface to the energy absorbed by a black body at the same temperature.

Active Solar Energy Systems: In contrast to passive solar energy approaches, an active solar energy system uses outside energy to operate the system and to transfer the collected solar energy from the collector to storage and distribute it throughout the living unit. Active systems can provide space heating and cooling and domestic hot water.

Air-lock Entry: A vestibule enclosed with two airtight doors; it reduces heat loss by limiting the movement of heated air.

Altitude: The angular distance from the horizon to the sun.

Ambient Temperature: The natural temperature surrounding an object; it usually refers to outdoor temperature.

Atrium: An interior court to which other rooms open; it is often used for passive solar collection.

Auxiliary Heating: (See Back-up Energy System.)

Azimuth: The angular distance between true south and the point on the horizon directly below the sun.

Back-up Energy System: A back-up energy system using conventional fuels should be capable of providing all of the energy demand during any period when the solar energy system is not operating.

BTU (British Thermal Unit): Basic heat measurement, equivalent to the amount of heat needed to raise one pound of water 1° Fahrenheit.

Building Envelope: The elements (walls, roof, floors) of a building which enclose conditioned spaces.

Charge: Putting heat into storage through radiant absorption or convective heat transfer (blown-in).

Clerestory: Vertical window placed high in wall near eaves, used for light, heat-gain, and ventilation.

Collection: The act of trapping solar radiation and converting it to heat.

Collector Aperture: The glazed opening being used for admitting solar radiation.

Comfort Zone: The range of temperature and humidity in which most people feel comfortable.

Conduction: The flow of heat between a hotter material and a colder material that are in direct physical contact.

Conductivity: The property of a material indicating the quantity of heat that will flow through one foot of a material for each degree of temperature difference.

Controls: The assembly of devices used to regulate the processes of collecting, transporting, storing, and utilizing solar energy.

Convection, Forced: Commonly, the transfer of heat by the forced flow of air or water.

Convection, Natural: The natural movement of heat that occurs when a warm fluid rises and a cool fluid sinks under the influence of gravity.

Cooling Pond: A large body of water that loses heat from its surface, largely by evaporation but also by convection and radiation.

Damper: A control which permits, prevents, or controls the passage of air through a duct.

Deciduous Trees: Trees which shed their leaves each winter at the end of the growing season.

Degree Day (DD): The degree day is a unit of heat measurement equal to one degree variation from a standard temperature in the average temperature of one day. If the standard is 65° and the average outside temperature is 50°for two days, then the number of degree days is 30.

Design Heating Load: The total heat loss from a building under the most severe winter conditions likely to occur.

Diffuse Radiation: Indirect scattered sunlight which casts no shadow.

Direct Radiation: Sunlight which casts shadows, also called beam radiation.

Direct Solar Gain: The most common type of passive solar heating system, in which solar radiation passes through the south-facing living space before being stored in the thermal mass for long-term heating.

Discharge: Removing heat from storage by radiation or convective heat transfer (blown out).

Distribution: The movement of collected heat throughout living areas from collectors or storage.

Diurnal Temperature Range: The variation in outdoor temperature between day and night.

Double-glazed: Covered by two layers of glazing material (commonly, glass or plastic).

Earth Berm: A mound of dirt that abuts a building wall to stabilize interior temperature or to deflect the wind.

Emittance: A measure of the propensity of a material to radiate energy to its surroundings.

Energy Audit: An accounting of the forms of energy used during a designated period, such as monthly.

Energy Budget: Energy budget refers to the non-renewable energy required by the back-up systems for heating, cooling, and domestic hot water. Heating is measured in terms of BTU/ft² of heated area/degree day. Cooling is measured in terms of BTU/ft² of cooled area/year. Domestic hot water is measured in terms of BTU/year.

Energy Conservation Features: Construction features such as insulation, storm windows designed to prevent heat loss, weatherstripping and caulking to minimize infiltration, and similar building elements that reduce the loss of energy in winter or the gain of energy in summer.

Evaporative Cooling: A method of space conditioning which requires the addition of bodies of water or moisture for cooling the living spaces.

Evergreen/Coniferous Trees: Trees which do not shed their leaves at the end of the growing season.

Fan Coil: A unit consisting of a fan and a heat exchanger which transfers heat from liquid to air (or vice versa); usually located in a duct.

Forced-air Heat: A conventional heating distribution system which uses a blower to circulate heated air.

Glazed Area (or Glazing): For solar collection, glazing refers to all materials which are translucent or transparent to short-wave solar radiation, including glass, plexiglass, Kalwall™, and the like.

Greenhouse: In passive solar design, an attached glazed area from which heat is withdrawn to the living space during the day.

Heat Capacity: A property of a material denoting its ability to absorb heat.

Heat Exchanger: A device which transfers heat from one fluid to another.

Heat Gain: As applied to heating or cooling load, that amount of heat gained by a space from all sources (including people, lights, machines, sunshine).

Heat Pump: An electrically operated machine for heating and cooling.

Heat Sink: A massive body which can serve to absorb and store solar heat.

Heat Storage: A device or medium that absorbs collected solar heat and stores it for use during periods of inclement or cold weather.

Heat Storage Capacity: The amount of heat which can be stored by a material.

Heat Transfer: Conduction, convection, or radiation, or a combination of these.

Heating Load: The rate of heat flow required to maintain indoor comfort; measured in BTU/hr.

Heating Season: The period from early fall to late spring (in the Northern Hemisphere) during which additional heat is needed to keep a house comfortable for its occupants.

Hybrid System: A hybrid system is one incorporating a major passive aspect, where at least one of the significant thermal energy flows is by natural means and at least one is by forced means.

Indirect Solar Gain: In these passive applications, the fabric of the house collects and stores solar energy, but the sun's rays do not travel through the living space to reach the storage mass; a storage mass collects and stores heat directly from the sun, and then transfers heat to the living space (e.g., Trombe wall, water wall, or roof pond).

Infiltration: The uncontrolled movement of outdoor air into a building through leaks, cracks, windows, and doors.

Insolation: The amount of solar radiation (direct, diffuse or reflected) striking a surface exposed to the sky; measured in BTU/ft²/hr.

Insulation: A material with high resistance (R-value) to heat flow.

Internal Mass: Massive materials with heat storage potential contained within the building as walls, floors, or free-standing elements.

Isogonic Chart: Shows magnetic compass deviations from true north.

Isolated Gain: A type of passive solar heating system in which heat is collected in one area to be used in another (e.g., greenhouse or attic collector).

Langley: A measure of solar radiation; equal to one calorie per square centimeter.

Life-cycle Cost Analysis: The accounting of capital, interest, and operating costs over the useful life of the solar system compared to those costs without the solar system.

Microclimate: The variation in regional climate at a specific site; caused by topography, vegetation, soil, water conditions, and construction.

Moveable Insulation: A device which reduces heat loss at night or during cloud periods and permits heat gain in sunny periods; it may also be used to reduce heat gains in summer.

Nocturnal Cooling: A method of cooling through radiation of heat from warm surfaces to a clear night sky.

Nonrenewable Energy Source: A mineral energy source which is in limited supply, such as fossil (gas, oil, and coal) and nuclear fuels.

Passive Solar Energy Systems and Concepts: Passive solar heating applications generally involve energy collection through south-facing glazed areas; energy storage in the building mass or in special storage elements; energy distribution by natural means such as convection, conduction, or radiation with only minimal use of low-power fans or pumps; and a method of controlling both high and low temperatures and energy flows. Passive cooling applications usually include methods of shading collector areas from exposure to the summer sun and provisions to induce ventilation to reduce internal temperatures and humidity.

Payback: The time needed to recover the investment in a solar energy system.

Peak Load: The maximum instantaneous demand for electrical power which determines the generating capacity required by a public utility.

Percent Possible Sunshine: The amount of radiation available compared to the amount which would be present if there were no cloud cover; usually measured on a monthly basis.

Plenum: A cavity of air space through which air is moved.

Preheat: The use of solar energy to partially heat a substance, such as domestic potable water, prior to heating it to a higher desired temperature with auxiliary fuel.

Radiation: The process by which energy flows from one body to another when the bodies are separated by a space, even when a vacuum exists between them.

Renewable Energy Source: Solar energy and certain forms derived from it, such as wind, biomass, and hydro.

Re-radiation: Radiation resulting from the emission of previously absorbed radiation.

Retrofit: To add a solar heating or cooling system to an existing home, previously conventionally heated and/or cooled.

Rock Bed (Remote): A heat storage container filled with rocks, pebbles, or crushed stone.

R-value (Resistance): Capability of a substance to impede the flow of heat. The term is used to describe insulative properties of construction materials.

Shading Coefficient: The ratio of the amount of sunlight transmitted through a window under specific conditions to the amount of sunlight transmitted through a single layer of common window glass under the same conditions.

Solar Access or Solar Rights: The ability to receive direct sunlight which has passed over land located to the south; the protection of solar access is a legal issue.

Solar Collector: A device which collects solar radiation and converts it to heat.

Solar Degradation: The process by which exposure to sunlight deteriorates the properties of materials and components.

Solar Fraction: The percentage of a building's net heating load met by solar gain.

Solar Gain: The absorption of heat from the sun. The amount of solar radiation (BTUs) received on an identified surface.

Solar Mass Wall: (See Trombe Wall.)

Solar Radiation: Energy radiated from the sun in the electromagnetic spectrum; visible light and infrared light are used by solar energy systems.

Solarium: A living space enclosed by glazing; a greenhouse.

Stack Effect: The rising of heated air over a dark surface by natural convection to create a draft; used to provide summer ventilation in some passive houses.

Stagnation: Trapped heat, no air movement.

Storage: The device or medium that absorbs collected solar heat and stores it for later use.

Storage Capacity: (See Heat Storage Capacity.)

Sunspace: A living space enclosed by glazing; a solarium or greenhouse.

Sun-Tempering: Sun-tempering is a method which involves a significant daytime solar gain and an effective distribution system, but generally lacks a storage system.

Supercharge: Process of heating a storage material or room air beyond its heat capacity. Used in solarium or isolated gain designs as a means of increasing storage temperature.

Thermal Capacitance: Heat storage potential of a substance.

Thermal Chimney: A vertical cavity through which heated air moves as a result of the stack effect. Used as a means of passive solar heat distribution or induced ventilation.

Thermal Energy: Heat possessed by a material resulting from the motion of molecules which can do work.

Thermal Envelope: The enclosure of a building which exhibits thermal resistance.

Thermal Lag: In an indirect gain system, the time delay for heat to move from the outer collecting surface to the inner radiating surface.

Thermal Mass: The heat capacity of a building material (brick, concrete, adobe, or water containers).

Thermal Radiation: Electromagnetic radiation emitted by a warm body.

Thermal Resistance: (See R-value.)

Thermosiphoning: Heat transfer through a fluid (such as air or liquid) by currents resulting from the natural fall of heavier, cool fluid and rise of lighter, warm fluid.

Time-lag Heating: A process of heating a building's interior by using the heat loss properties of massive materials to delay the movement of solar heat.

Trombe Wall: Masonry, typically 8 to 16 inches thick, blackened and exposed to the sun behind glazing; a passive solar heating system in which a masonry wall collects, stores, and distributes heat.

Trombe Wall Cavity: The space between a solar mass wall and its exterior glazing in which air is heated. This air will rise and may be vented into the building's interior for distribution.

Ultraviolet Radiation: Electromagnetic radiation with wavelengths slightly shorter than visible light.

U-value: The capability of a substance to transfer the flow of heat. Used to describe the conductance of a material or composite of materials used in construction.

Vapor Barrier: A waterproof liner used to prevent passage of moisture through the building structure. Vapor barriers in walls and ceilings should be located on the heated side of the building.

Ventilation, Induced: The thermally assisted movement of fresh air through a building.

Ventilation, Natural: The unassisted movement of fresh air through a building.

Water Storage Wall: See Trombe Wall.

Zoned Heating: The control of the temperature in a room or a group of rooms independently of other rooms.

Appendix II
Bibliography

Climatic Information

American Society of Heating, Refrigeration and Air Conditioning Engineers. ASHRAE Handbook Of Fundamentals. New York, NY: ASHRAE Publications, 1977, $40.00 plus $2.00 handling.

National Bureau of Standards. Hourly Solar Radiation Data For Vertical And Horizontal Surfaces On Average Days In The United States And Canada. Washington: Government Printing Office, 1977, GPO Stock No. 003-003-01698-5, $4.65.

National Climatic Center. Climatic Atlas Of The United States. Ashville, NC: National Climatic Center, 1968, $6.00.

U.S. Department of Housing And Urban Development. HUD Intermediate Minimun Property Standards Supplement: Solar Heating And Domestic Hot Water Systems. Washington: Government Printing Office, 1977, GPO Order No. 4930-2, $12.00.

Energy Conservations

American Institute of Architects Research Corporation. Regional Guidelines For Building Passive Energy Conserving Homes. Washington: Government Printing Office, 1978, GPO Stock No. 023-000-00481-0, $5.25.

American Society of Heating, Refrigeration and Air Conditioning Engineers. ASHRAE Standard 90-75. Energy Conservation In New Building Design. New York, NY: ASHRAE Publications, 1975, $5.00 members, $10.00 nonmembers.

U.S. Department of Housing and Urban Development. In The Bank . . . Or Up the Chimney. Washington: Government Printing Office, 1977, GPO Stock No. 023-000-00411-9, $1.70.

Solar Access

American Planning Association. Residential Solar Design Review — A Manual On Community Architectural Controls And Solar Energy Use. Washington: Government Printing Office, 1980, GPO Stock No. 023-000-00633-2, $4.00.

_____. Site Planning For Solar Access: A Guidebook For Residential Developers And Site Planners. Washington: Government Printing Office, 1979, GPO Stock No. 0-23-000-00545-0, $4.75.

Passive Solar

American Institute of Architects Research Corporation. A Survey Of Passive Solar Buildings. Washington: Government Printing Office, 1978, GPO Stock No. 023-000-00437-2, $3.75.

_____. A Survey Of Passive Solar Homes. Washington: Government Printing Office, 1980.

_____. Passive Solar Design: A Short Bibliography For Practitioners. Springfield, VA: National Technical Information Service, 1978, Report No. HCP/CS-4113, $6.00, available from NTIS.

_____. Passive Solar Design: An Extensive Bibliography. Springfield, VA: National Technical Information Service, 1978, Report No. HCP/CS-4113-3, $13.00, available from NTIS.

Balcomb, J.D. et al. Passive Solar Design Handbook, Volume Two: Passive Solar Design Analysis. Springfield, VA: National Technical Information Service, 1980, Report No. DOE/CS-0127/2, $22.00, available from NTIS.

Franta, G. (ed.). Proceedings Of The 4th National Passive Solar Conference. Killen, TX: International Solar Energy Society, American Section, 1979, $17.00 members, $65.00 non-members.

Haskins, D. and Stromberg, R.P. (eds.). Passive Solar Buildings. Springfield, VA: National Technical Information Service, 1979, Report No. SAND 79-0824, available from NTIS.

Mazria, E. The Passive Solar Energy Book. Emmaus, PA: Rodale Press, 1979, $10.95, $24.95 (professional ed.).

McCullough, J.C. (ed.). The Solar Greenhouse Book. Emmaus, PA: Rodale Press, 1978, $8.95.

National Solar Heating and Cooling Information Center. The First Passive Solar Home Awards. Washington: Government Printing Office, 1978, GPO Stock No. 023-000-00571-4, $5.50.

Prowler, D., Duncan, I., and Bennett, B. Passive Solar: State Of The Art, Vols. 1-3, Proceedings Of The Second National Passive Solar Conference. Killen, TX: International Solar Energy Society, American Section, 1978, $14.00 members, $50.00 nonmembers.

Total Environmental Action, Inc. Passive Solar Design Handbook, Volume One: Passive Solar Design Concepts. Springfield, VA: National Technical Information Service, 1980, Report No. DOF/CS-0127/1, available from NTIS.

Wright, D. Natural Solar Architecture: A Passive Primer. New York, NY: Van Nostrand Reinhold Co., 1978, $7.95.

Active Solar

Duffie, J.A. and Beckman, W.A. Solar Energy Thermal Processes. New York, NY: John Wiley and Sons, Inc., 1974, $18.00.

International Telephone and Telegraph Corporation. Solar Heating Systems Design Manual. Skokie, IL: 1976, $2.50.

Kreider, J.F. and Kreith, F. Solar Heating And Cooling: Engineering, Practical Design, And Economics. New York, NY: McGraw-Hill Book Co., 1975, $24.75.

National Solar Heating and Cooling Information Center. Hot Water From The Sun. Washington: Government Printing Office, 1980, GPO Stock No. 023-000-00620-1, $4.75.

_____. Installation Guidelines For Solar DHW Systems In One- And Two-Family Dwellings. Washington: Government Printing Office, 1980, GPO Stock No. 023-000-00520-4, $4.25.

General Solar

American Institute of Architects Research Corporation. Solar Dwelling Design Concepts. Washington: Government Printing Office, 1976, GPO Stock No. 023-000-00334-1, $2.30.

Anderson, B. and Riordan, M. The Solar Home Book. Andover, MA: Brick House Publishing Co., 1976, $9.50.

McPhillips, M. (ed.). The Solar Age Resource Book. New York, NY: Everest House, 1979, $9.95.

Real Estate Research Corporation. Selling The Solar Home '80: Market Findings For The Housing Industry. Washington: Government Printing Office, 1980, GPO Stock No. 023-000-00568-9, $3.00.

Sunset Books. Sunset's Homeowner's Guide To Solar Heating. Menlo Park, CA: Lane Publishing Co., 1978, $2.95.

Watson, P. Designing And Building A Solar House. Charlotte, VT: Gorden Way Publishing, 1977, $8.95.

Calculations

Egan, M.D. Concepts In Thermal Comfort. Englewood, NJ: Prentice-Hall, Inc., 1975, $13.95.

Solar Magazines

Solar Age. Harrisville, NH: Solar Vision, Inc., Monthly, $20.00/year.

Solar Engineering. Dallas, TX: Solar Engineering Publishers, Inc., Monthly, $15.00/year.

Source List

GPO
Superintendent of Documents
Government Printing Office
Washington, DC 20402

NTIS
National Technical Information Service
5285 Port Royal Road
Springfield, VA 22161

Appendix III
Calculations

All solar buildings, either active or passive, must be energy conserving to realize a worthwhile contribution of solar energy. Many calculation techniques are available to analyze the energy requirements of buildings. The application form for the Cycle 5 Grant Program included a step-by-step procedure for determining a building's energy requirements and estimating the solar energy contribution a particular passive system would provide. The following example illustrates the calculation technique for one of the award-winning buildings.

The building under consideration is described on pages 230-231. It is a ranch house, located in Springfield, Oregon, that incorporates several energy conserving and passive solar techniques. The three passive sub-systems include direct gain skylights for the living room, an indirect gain Trombe wall, and a greenhouse (isolated gain).

In order to compute the energy savings resulting from the passive solar energy system, it is necessary first to calculate the heating load. This may be done by following the simplified whole house calculation method outlined in Figure 1.

Figure 1 — A Simplified Whole House Calculation Method

Calculate monthly heating loads and list in Table 1, Col. 3; include heating load calculations as Appendix (3). The calculations as a minimum* must include:

1. Wall/Roof Heat Loss to Air = Σ UAΔT in BTU/mo

Detail No.	U Value (BTUH/ft²/°)		A Area (ft²)		UA (BTUH/°F)
_____	_____	×	_____	=	_____
_____	_____	×	_____	=	_____
_____	_____	×	_____	=	_____

Winter Σ UA (Total) = _____

$$\Sigma \text{ UA} \times (T_{INDES} - T_{OUTDES}^{**})\ 24\ \frac{\text{hrs}}{\text{day}} \times \frac{\text{days}}{\text{mo}} = \text{BTU/mo}$$

or Σ UA × DD***/mo × 24 hrs/day = BTU/mo

2. Perimeter Heat Loss to Air = FPΔT in BTU/mo

Factor F (BTUH/ft/°F) × Perimeter ft × $(T_{INDES} - T_{OUTDES})$°F × 24 hrs/day × days/mo = BTU/mo

With a factor F of .81 with no insulation, .55 with insulation and a ΔT as above.

3. For Heat Loss to Ground for slabs and subgrade walls, follow 1977 ASHRAE FUNDAMENTALS, Chapter 24. Rough approximations are given by

K Conductance BTUH/ft² × Area ft² × 24 hrs/day × days/mo = BTU/mo

Where K = .1 BTUH/ft² basement floor, .2 BTUH/ft² basement walls.

4. Infiltration Loss = .018 BTU/ft³/°F × House Volume ft³ × Air Changes/hr × $(T_{INDES} - T_{OUTDES})$°F × 24 hrs/day × days/mo = BTU/mo

With a minimum air change of 1/2 allowable only if the building is well sheltered from the winter winds, very tightly constructed, and without extensive operable window area causing natural air crossing channels.

5. Total Heat Loss

Monthly heat loss = 1 + 2 + 3 + 4. Repeat for each month and total for seasonal heat loss from house.

*As a maximum, heat loss calculations would be room by room and hour by hour. No contributions may be taken for internal gains in winter.

**T = T indoor Design – T outdoor Design with an indoor design temperature of 68°F and a monthly outdoor mean design temperature from Col. 1, Table 1.

***Degree Days from Col. 2, Table 1.

There are four main components of the heating load:

(1) Wall/roof heat loss to air — Represents the typical conduction losses of walls, roof, windows, and doors.

(2) Perimeter heat loss to air — Includes losses from slab edges, for example.

(3) Heat loss to ground for slab and subgrade walls — Applies only to slab on grade and to heated basements.

(4) Infiltration loss — Estimates the losses due to exchanges of heated and outside air through cracks and other leaks. An appropriate value for the number of air changes in a well-insulated building is 0.5-0.75 air changes/hour.

These contributions are calculated on a monthly basis and the monthly total heat loss is computed from

$$\text{Monthly heat loss} = (1) + (2) + (3) + (4)$$

The total seasonal (annual) heat loss is also computed. These monthly and annual values are entered in Table 1, Col. (3).

This procedure has been followed for the sample building and the final results are tabulated in Table 1.

Table 1 — Building Heat Loads

	(1) Outside Mean Daily Temperature °F Ref. MOAA Table II.C	(2) Reference Heating Degree Day Ref. IMPS (Solar) Table A-3	(3) Calculated Building Heating Load (10^6 BTU)
JAN	39	794	10.4
FEB	44	602	8.1
MAR	46	592	7.9
APR	50	441	5.9
MAY	56	289	4.1
JUN	61	133	2.2
JUL	67	41	1.0
AUG	66	51	1.1
SEP	62	119	2.1
OCT	53	366	5.2
NOV	46	582	7.6
DEC	41	729	9.3
TOTAL	—	4739	64.8

Figure 2

The next stage in the calculation is to estimate the ability of the passive solar energy system to meet these monthly loads. The procedure is outlined in Figure 2 and used to complete Table 2. When the building contains more than one passive subsystem, it is necessary to complete some additional calculations as shown on the Multi-system Worksheet. This procedure is explained in some detail below.

Simple case (one passive system only). Table 2 is completed by following the outline in Figure 2. The procedure involves estimating, for each month, the solar energy transmitted through the passive aperture (Col. (3)), computing the ratio of the solar energy absorbed to the heat load (solar load ratio, SLR) (Col. (4)), determining the solar heating fraction from the appropriate curve (Col. (5)), and estimating the gross (Col. (6)) and net (Col. (8)) passive solar contributions by predicting the operating energy (Col. (7)). Note that sometimes slightly different steps are required for different types of passive systems (indicated by A, B, C, and D). By following this procedure, the passive performance of any of the four system types may be estimated.

Multi-system case. This situation, which applies to many of the buildings described in this book, is more involved since it is necessary to apportion the contributions of each of the passive subsystems toward meeting the total heat load of the building. This is accomplished by filling out a separate copy of Table 2 for each subsystem, and by using the (Mixed) Multi-system Worksheet (Table 3) at several points in the computation (see Figure 5).

The Multi-system Worksheet links the total load to the solar contributions of the individual apertures. Col. (i) on the worksheet represents the total solar energy absorbed from all passive apertures. Col. (j) is the solar load ratio for the entire system. Using col. (i), the relative contribution or weighting factor of each subsystem is determined (cols. (b), (d), etc.).

Finally, using identical solar load ratios for each subsystem, the general procedure for completing each Table 2 yields the monthly and annual passive solar contribution for the individual subsystems. These separate contributions may be summed to get the total passive contribution. This procedure has been carried out for the sample building (see Tables 2 and 3).

The final step in the energy calculation is the completion of the Tally Sheet (see Figure 6). Here values for the total annual heating load and for the total annual passive contribution are used to compute the total auxiliary requirement. The auxiliary energy is next divided by both the annual degree days and by the heated floor area of the building to give a single figure, which can be used to compare projects in different parts of the country. For many passive buildings this number is about equal to 5 BTU/DD/ft². Values appropriate to the sample building are shown on the Tally Sheet.

*A = Sun-tempering
B = Direct Gain
C = Indirect Gain
D = Isolated Gain

Col. (1) for A,B,C, or D: List the Gross Building Heating Load (10^6 BTU) for each month in Col. (1) of Table 2. This load must include the heat loss through the solar aperture.

Col. (2) for A,B,C, or D: List the Average Daily Horizontal Incident — Radiation (BTU/ft²) for each month in Col. (2) for reference. Source of data see IMPS (Solar). See Appendix II (Bibliography).

Col. (3) for A,B, or C: Obtain the Daily Normal Incident Radiation (BTU/ft²) either from NBS Hourly Radiation Data or determined by multiplying the values in Col. (2) by the appropriate correction factors for orientation and tilt for each aperture surface. Multiply the Daily Normal Incident Radiation (BTU/ft²) on each aperture surface by its respective net glazed aperture area (ft²) and add all of the partial products. Multiply this total by the number of days for each month, by the percent of the aperture unshaded by building overhangs, louvers, adjacent trees, etc., and by the total transmittance of the glazing. List this result as the Monthly Radiation Transmitted (10^6 BTU) in Col. (3).

for D: Obtain the Daily Normal Incident Radiation (BTU/ft²) either from NBS Hourly Radiation Data or determined by multiplying the values in Col. (2) by the appropriate correction factors for orientation and tilt for each aperture surface. Multiply the Daily Normal Incident Radiation (BTU/ft²) by the common wall area (ft²) between the sunspace/greenhouse and the house. Multiply this total by the number of days for each month, by the percent of the aperture unshaded by building overhangs, louvers, adjacent trees, etc., and by the total transmittance of the glazing. List this result as the Monthly Radiation Transmitted (10^6 BTU) in Col. (3).

Col. (4) for A or B: Divide the Monthly Radiation Transmitted from Col. (3) by the Monthly Building Load, Col. (1) to obtain the Monthly Solar Load Ratio (SLR). List the Solar Load Ratio for each month in Col. (4).

for C or D: Multiply the Monthly Radiation Transmitted from Col. (3) by the predicted wall absorptance and divide by the Monthly Building Load, Col. (1) to obtain the Monthly Solar Load Ratio (SLR). List the Solar Load Ratio for each month in Col. (4).

NOTE: Wall absorptance typically ranges from 65%-70% for medium colored walls and from 90%-95% for dark colored walls.

Col. (5)   Using the Solar Load Ratio from Col. (4), determine the Monthly Solar Heating Fraction (SHF) by using the appropriate curve as indicated. Enter these values in Col. (5).

for A or B: See Figure 3.
for C or D: See Figure 4.

Col. (6) for A,B,C, or D: Multiply Col. (1) by Col. (5) and list the Gross Passive Solar Contribution (10^6 BTU) for each month in Col. (6).

Col. (7) for A: Not applicable.

for B,C, or D: Predict the Operating Energy (10^6 BTU) used by solar equipment (i.e., fans) for each month when applicable and list in Col. (7). This is determined by the following equation:

Operating Energy (10^6 BTU) = Predicted Operation (hrs/mo) × Equipment Power (hp) × 0.002547 (10^6 BTU)/hp.hr.

Col. (8) for A: Multiply the Gross Passive Solar Contribution in Col. (6) by an Exposed Capacity Coefficient to obtain the Net Sun-tempering Contribution. List the Net Sun-tempering Contribution in Col. (8).

NOTE: The Exposed Capacity Coefficient used to account for the effects of solar radiation absorbed by low mass objects within the space may not exceed 0.41.

for B,C, or D: Subtract the Operating Energy Use in Col. (7) from the Gross Passive Solar Heating Contribution in Col. (6) to obtain the Net Passive Solar Heating Contribution. List the Net Passive Solar Heating Contribution for each month in Col. (8).

Figure 3

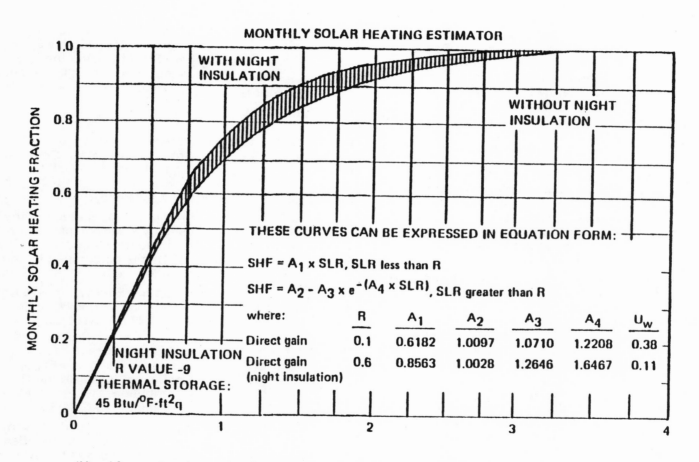

MONTHLY SOLAR HEATING ESTIMATOR

(chart: MONTHLY SOLAR HEATING FRACTION vs. horizontal axis 0 to 4)

WITH NIGHT INSULATION

WITHOUT NIGHT INSULATION

THESE CURVES CAN BE EXPRESSED IN EQUATION FORM:

$SHF = A_1 \times SLR$, SLR less than R

$SHF = A_2 - A_3 \times e^{-(A_4 \times SLR)}$, SLR greater than R

where:	R	A_1	A_2	A_3	A_4	U_w
Direct gain	0.1	0.6182	1.0097	1.0710	1.2208	0.38
Direct gain (night insulation)	0.6	0.8563	1.0028	1.2646	1.6467	0.11

NIGHT INSULATION R VALUE -9
THERMAL STORAGE: 45 Btu/°F·ft²q

(Used for system types A = Sun-tempering and B = Direct Gain)

$$\text{MONTHLY SOLAR LOAD RATIO (SLR)} = \frac{\text{MONTHLY SOLAR ENERGY ABSORBED}}{\text{NET MONTHLY THERMAL LOAD}}$$
(including the static conduction through the solar wall, $A_w \times U_w \times DD$)

276

Figure 4

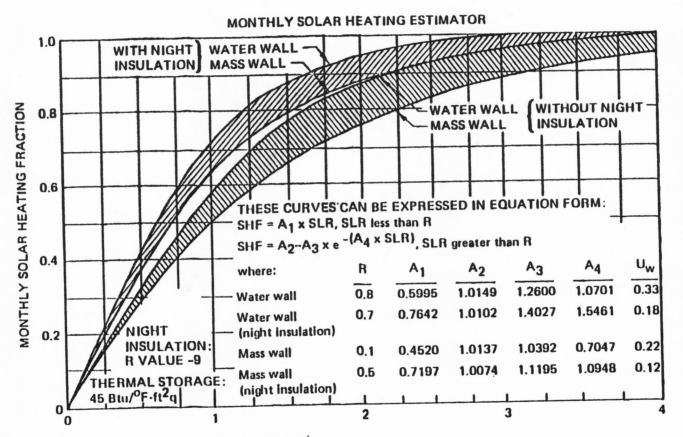

MONTHLY SOLAR HEATING ESTIMATOR

WITH NIGHT INSULATION } WATER WALL MASS WALL

WATER WALL MASS WALL { WITHOUT NIGHT INSULATION

NIGHT INSULATION: R VALUE -9

THERMAL STORAGE: 45 Btu/°F·ft²q

THESE CURVES CAN BE EXPRESSED IN EQUATION FORM:

$$SHF = A_1 \times SLR, \quad SLR \text{ less than } R$$

$$SHF = A_2 - A_3 \times e^{-(A_4 \times SLR)}, \quad SLR \text{ greater than } R$$

where:

	R	A_1	A_2	A_3	A_4	U_w
Water wall	0.8	0.5995	1.0149	1.2600	1.0701	0.33
Water wall (night insulation)	0.7	0.7642	1.0102	1.4027	1.5461	0.18
Mass wall	0.1	0.4520	1.0137	1.0392	0.7047	0.22
Mass wall (night insulation)	0.5	0.7197	1.0074	1.1195	1.0948	0.12

(y-axis) MONTHLY SOLAR HEATING FRACTION

Note: Use water wall curves for roof pond.
(Used for system types C = Indirect Gain and D = Isolated Gain)

MONTHLY SOLAR LOAD RATIO (SLR) = $\dfrac{\text{MONTHLY SOLAR ENERGY ABSORBED}}{\text{NET MONTHLY THERMAL LOAD}}$
(including the static conduction through the solar wall, $A_w \times U_w \times DD$)

Figure 5 — Multi-system Worksheet:

STEP 1 — Fill out Cols. (1), (2), and (3) on each Universal Table (one table for each system)

(Col. (1) is <u>total</u> Building Heat Load; it will be the same on all sheets)

STEP 2 — Copy Col. (3) from each table onto worksheet (for C,D: first multiply each Col. (3) value by the appropriate absorptance before entering it onto worksheet)

STEP 3 — Sum all Col. (3) values for each month into Col. (i) on worksheet

— Calculate Solar Load Ratio (SLR):

$$SLR = \frac{Col.\ (i)}{Col.\ (1)\ on\ any\ sheet}$$

— Put this SLR figure into Col. (j) on the worksheet

— Calculate: $\frac{(a)}{(i)}$ and put into Col. (b); $\frac{(c)}{(i)}$ and put into Col. (d); $\frac{(e)}{(i)}$ and put into Col. (f); $\frac{(g)}{(i)}$ and put into Col. (h)

STEP 4 — Copy (j) from worksheet into Col. (4) on each·table

STEP 5 — For each table use correct SLR curve to determine the Solar Heating Fraction (SHF) for each system (Col. (5))

STEP 6 — Gross Passive Heating Contribution =

Col. (1) × Col. (5) × Col. (b) for System 1;

Col. (1) × Col. (5) × Col. (d) for System 2;

Col. (1) × Col. (5) × Col. (f) for System 3; and

Col. (1) × Col. (5) × Col. (h) for System 4.

— Put this figure in Col. (6) on each table

STEP 7 — Calculate Operating Energy Use per instructions

STEP 8 — Calculate Net Passive Solar Heating Contributions per instructions

STEP 9 — Total Passive: Sum all Col. (8) values for each system to get total monthly and total annual passive contribution.

Table 2.1 Passive Solar Heating Systems

B = Direct Gain   (This form must be completed separately for each passive system in house.)

	(1) Calculated Building Heating Load from Col. (3) Table 1 (10^6 BTU)	(2) Daily Horizontal Incident Radiation Data Source (BTU/ft²/day)	(3) Monthly Radiation Transmitted (10^6 BTU) from A ⒷC D	(4) Solar Load Ratio (SLR) from A ⒷC D	(5) Solar Heating Fraction (SHF) from A ⒷC D	(6) Gross Passive Solar Heating Contribution (10^6 BTU)	(7) Operating Energy Use (10^6 BTU) from A ⒷC D	(8) Net Passive Solar Heating Contribution (10^6 BTU) from A ⒷC D
JAN	10.4	500	1.3	.59	.50	1.1	0	1.1
FEB	8.1	738	1.6	.83	.69	1.3	0	1.3
MAR	7.9	1027	1.9	.91	.73	1.5	0	1.5
APR	5.9	1398	2.1	1.19	.84	1.5	0	1.5
MAY	4.1	1671	2.2	1.67	.93	1.2	0	1.2
JUN	2.2	1836	2.1	2.95	.99	.7	0	.7
JUL	1.0	1770	1.9	6.07	1.0	.3	0	.3
AUG	1.1	1633	2.4	7.01	1.0	.3	0	.3
SEP	2.1	1311	2.2	3.82	1.0	.6	0	.6
OCT	5.2	989	2.2	1.70	.93	1.2	0	1.2
NOV	7.6	580	1.5	.87	.71	1.2	0	1.2
DEC	9.3	432	1.2	.61	.55	1.1	0	1.1
TOTAL	64.8	—	22.6	—	—	12.1	0	12.1

A = Sun-tempering   B = Direct Gain   C = Indirect Gain   D = Isolated Gain

Table 2.2 Passive Solar Heating Systems

C = Indirect Gain

(This form must be completed separately for each passive system in house.)

	(1) Calculated Building Heating Load from Col.(3) Table 1 (10⁶ BTU)	(2) Daily Horizontal Incident Radiation Data Source (BTU/ft²/day)	(3) Monthly Radiation Transmitted (10⁶ BTU) from A B ©C D	(4) Solar Load Ratio (SLR) from A B C D	(5) Solar Heating Fraction (SHF) from A B ©C D	(6) Gross Passive Solar Heating Contribution (10⁶ BTU)	(7) Operating Energy Use (10⁶ BTU) from A B ©C D	(8) Net Passive Solar Heating Contribution (10⁶ BTU) from A B ©C D
JAN	10.4	500	1.5	.59	.33	.8	0	.8
FEB	8.1	738	1.5	.83	.43	.8	0	.8
MAR	7.9	1027	1.4	.91	.47	.7	0	.7
APR	5.9	1398	1.1	1.19	.57	.5	0	.5
MAY	4.1	1671	.9	1.67	.69	.3	0	.3
JUN	2.2	1836	.7	2.95	.88	.2	0	.2
JUL	1.0	1770	.7	6.07	1.0	.1	0	.1
AUG	1.1	1633	1.1	7.01	1.0	.2	0	.2
SEP	2.1	1311	1.4	3.82	.94	.3	0	.3
OCT	5.2	989	1.9	1.70	.70	.8	0	.8
NOV	7.6	588	1.6	.87	.45	.8	0	.8
DEC	9.3	432	1.4	.61	.34	.8	0	.8
TOTAL	64.8	—	15.4	—	—	6.2	0	6.2

A = Sun-tempering   B = Direct Gain   C = Indirect Gain   D = Isolated Gain

Table 2.3 Passive Solar Heating Systems

D = Isolated Gair

(This form must be completed separately for each passive system in house.)

	(1) Calculated Building Heating Load from Col.(3) Table 1 (10⁶ BTU)	(2) Daily Horizontal Incident Radiation Data Source (BTU/ft²/day)	(3) Monthly Radiation Transmitted (10⁶ BTU) from A B C (D)	(4) Solar Load Ratio (SLR) from A (B) C D	(5) Solar Heating Fraction (SHF) from A B C (D)	(6) Gross Passive Solar Heating Contribution (10⁶ BTU)	(7) Operating Energy Use (10⁶ BTU) from A B C (D)	(8) Net Passive Solar Heating Contribution (10⁶ BTU) from A B C (D)
JAN	10.4	500	3.5	.59	.35	2.0	0	2.0
FEB	8.1	738	3.9	.83	.50	2.2	0	2.2
MAR	7.9	1027	4.1	.91	.54	2.3	0	2.3
APR	5.9	1398	4.1	1.19	.66	2.2	0	2.2
MAY	4.1	1671	4.0	1.67	.80	1.9	0	1.9
JUN	2.2	1836	3.9	2.95	.96	1.2	0	1.2
JUL	1.0	1770	3.6	6.07	1.0	.6	0	.6
AUG	1.1	1633	4.5	7.01	1.0	.6	0	.6
SEP	2.1	1311	4.7	3.82	.99	1.1	0	1.1
OCT	5.2	989	5.1	1.70	.81	2.3	0	2.3
NOV	7.6	588	3.8	.87	.52	2.1	0	2.1
DEC	9.3	432	3.2	.61	.37	1.8	0	1.8
TOTAL	64.8	—	48.5	—	—	20.4	0	20.4

A = Sun-tempering   B = Direct Gain   C = Indirect Gain   D = Isolated Gain

Table 3 (Mixed) Multisystem Worksheet

	System 1 From Col.(3) (a)	System 1 $\frac{(a)}{(i)}$ (b)	System 2 From Col.(3) (c)	System 2 $\frac{(c)}{(i)}$ (d)	System 3 From Col.(3) (e)	System 3 $\frac{(e)}{(i)}$ (f)	System 4 From Col.(3) (g)	System 4 $\frac{(g)}{(i)}$ (h)	Total System (a)+(c)+(e)+(g) (i)	Total System SLR = $\frac{(i)}{Col.(1)}$ (j)
JAN	1.3	.22	1.4	.24	3.3	.54			6.1	.59
FEB	1.6	.24	1.4	.21	3.7	.55			6.7	.83
MAR	1.9	.27	1.3	.18	3.9	.55			7.2	.91
APR	2.1	.30	1.1	.15	3.9	.55			7.1	1.19
MAY	2.2	.32	.8	.12	3.8	.56			6.8	1.67
JUN	2.1	.32	.7	.11	3.7	.57			6.5	2.95
JUL	1.9	.32	.7	.11	3.4	.57			6.1	6.07
AUG	2.4	.31	1.1	.14	4.3	.56			7.7	7.01
SEP	2.2	.28	1.4	.17	4.4	.55			8.0	3.82
OCT	2.2	.25	1.8	.21	4.8	.55			8.8	1.70
NOV	1.5	.22	1.5	.23	3.6	.54			6.6	.87
DEC	1.2	.21	1.4	.24	3.1	.54			5.7	.61

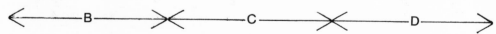

$$\text{Total Passive} = B + C + D$$
$$= 12.1 + 6.2 + 20.4$$
$$= 38.7 \times 10^6 \text{ BTU/yr}$$

$$\text{Solar Fraction} = \frac{38.7}{64.8} = 60\%$$

Tally Sheet

Heating Conditions

1. Annual Heating Loads:
   Load (reflects **All** energy conservation features)

   <u>64.8</u> (10^6 BTU/yr)
   (Col. 3, Table 1)

2. Annual Passive Heating Contributions:

   <u>38.7</u> (10^6 BTU/yr)

3. Net Total:
   Loads — Contributions =

   <u>26.1</u> (10^6 BTU/yr)

4. BTU/DD/ft²:
   (BTU/yr)/(Degree Day/yr)/(ft² Heated Area) =

   <u>3.2</u> (BTU/DD/ft²)

This report was prepared by the Franklin Research Center for the
Department of Housing and Urban Development.

Credits:

Editors:
  Martin McPhillips
  Peter C. Powell, AIA

Art Director:
  Marsha Biderman

Illustrations by:
  American Institute of Architects/Research Corporation
  Mark Beck Associates
  Franklin Research Center

Editorial Policy and Review:
  Members of the HUD Division of Energy, Building Technology
  and Standards, Office of Policy Development and Research
    Joseph Sherman
    David Moore
    William Freeborne
    Robert C. Jones
    David Engel
    Mr. Michael Lenzi

Writers:
  Sally Reynolds
  Tim Sosinski
  Robert Fritzche
  Marcia Johnson
  Eric Wright
  Jeremy Coleman
  Robert Schultz
  Caron Chess

Copy Editors:
  Richard Barrett
  Janet Francendese

Production and Graphics:
  Mary Ann Ostberg
  Miriam Seidel
  Vicki Fox
  Dava Jennings

Editorial Assistant:
  Patti O'Donnell

Proofreaders:
  Pam Ballinger
  Patti O'Donnell